INSIDE SOUTHEAST ASIA

Niels Mulder

INSIDE SOUTHEAST ASIA

Religon • Everyday Life • Cultural Change

THE PEPIN PRESS
Amsterdam • Kuala Lumpur

First published by The Pepin Press in 1996

Second revised and enlarged edition of *Inside Southeast Asia. Thai, Javanese and Filipino Interpretations of Everyday Life*, Editions Duang Kamol, Bangkok (1992).

© 1996, Niels Mulder
© for this edition, The Pepin Press BV

ISBN 90 5496 028 0

A CIP record for this edition is available from the publisher and from the Royal Dutch Library, The Hague.

This book is edited, designed and produced by The Pepin Press
Editor: Dorine van den Beukel
Cover photos: Photobank

The Pepin Press
POB 10349
1001 EH Amsterdam
TEL 31 20 4202021
FAX 31 20 4201152

Printed in Singapore

Contents

CONCLUSION

Preface

Studying at the University of Amsterdam in the 1950s, students of social science were inevitably confronted with teachers who had gained their experience in the colonies, and who thus taught about the wonders and thrills of Indonesia. Yet, for a young Dutchman, the late 1950s were not the best period to visit that country. Being denied a visa, I spent considerable time in Malaysia when the populace celebrated the first anniversary of their Independence. I also caught some glimpses of Southern Thailand, Saigon, and Manila, and I liked what I saw. Ever since that first visit in 1958, Southeast Asia has charmed me and the spell has never been broken.

In 1965, I got my first chance to look at Southeast Asia through the eyes of an academic. Still, Indonesia was not the place to go to and my professor advised me to go to "another Indianized country" of the region. According to him, nobody in any Dutch university knew anything about Thailand, so that country would be the opportune place to go. Supported by a Thai UNESCO grant and a moderate sum from the Netherlands' Ministry of Education, I began the work that I am still doing: trying to understand the ways people live in Southeast Asia.

Soon it became clear to me that the social scientific categories that I had studied at the university were a defective guide in trying to understand what I saw, heard, and experienced. What I needed to get a grasp on, if I wanted to understand anything at all, was the way people looked at life, their mentality and way of understanding. By this I do not mean to say that sociological system theory is useless, but that I use relatively little of it in my attempt to come to grips with the rationale of action of the people I study. I am primarily interested in their subjective point of view and historical experience.

The main stations on my path through Southeast Asia are Java, Thailand, and the Philippines. In 1969-70, I had my first opportunity to do research in Java, which was followed up with frequent visits during the early 1970s when I worked in Bangkok for the United Nations. In late 1973, I returned to Europe to write my dissertation about mysticism and everyday life in Java. The end of 1975 saw me back in Thailand;

when I left again in late 1978, I also left behind the manuscript about my interpretation of everyday life in Thai society. Around the turn of the 1980s, I had three opportunities to study cultural change in Java which stimulated my interest in cultural dynamics, as I have recorded elsewhere in my explorations of the relationship between individual and society in Java.

Having gained some expertise in two so-called "Indianized" countries of Southeast Asia — meaning that in the past both received important cultural inputs of Indian origin — I was now keen to do research in a very different cultural environment, for which the possible candidates would obviously be Vietnam and the Philippines if I wanted to stay in Southeast Asia. So, from 1983 onwards, I began field work in Manila and Lucena in the Tagalog region of Luzon. As my research advanced, I became more and more interested in the possibilities of comparing my Philippine material with what I thought I knew about Thai and Javanese culture and society. Apparently I was in the process of discovering Southeast Asia. In spite of the Indic symbols in Thailand, the merged Indian and Islamic heritage on Java, or the churches and neo-classical buildings of the Philippines, there appeared to be many things that were eminently comparable because they were so similar. This book, then, is about the similarities among three culturally and politically dominant peoples of Southeast Asia.

The insights that I have gained in the course of twenty-five years of professional life — roughly half of it in Southeast Asia — are due less to my merit than to my good fortune. I have had much good luck in meeting people, Thais, Javanese, and Filipinos, who explained, who were patient with me, interested and encouraging. More still, because of all those who have produced the huge fund of literature about the region, be it anthropological, social analytical, journalistic, historical and biographical, or in the form of novels and short stories. And even further luck in being associated with so many colleagues fascinated with that part of the world. With so many inputs, I often have the feeling that I am merely chewing the cud of others' ideas.

In this place it is not really possible to enumerate all the people I owe a debt of gratitude to. The most prominent among them have been acknowledged in my books about Java and Thailand. With my Philippine work still in progress, I received many comments from

Filipinos, such as Honey A.-Carandang, O.D. Corpuz, Prospero Covar, Doreen Fernandez, Angelita Gregorio-Medel, Bien Lumbera, Raul Pertierra, and Fernando Zialcita. For recent discussions about my work, I am especially indebted to Hans-Dieter Evers and other colleagues in the Sociology of Development Research Centre of the University of Bielefeld, Eldar Braaten, Han ten Brummelhuis, and Jürgen Rüland. I am confident that none of them will fully subscribe to what I have made of our discussions because, even while ruminating, I have left traces of my own. I do hope, however, that this presentation for which I am also indebted to my editor Geoffrey Walton, publisher Suk Soongswang, and typesetter Edward Stauffer — may be useful for further discussion and shed some light on how life is lived and changes in that fascinating part of the world that is Southeast Asia.

Niels Mulder
Amsterdam, September 1991

Preface to the second edition

The present edition is the fruit of the generosity of Khun Suk Soongswang, the chairman of Editions Duang Kamol, and the enthusiasm of Pepin van Roojen of The Pepin Press in Amsterdam. The venture of reissuing the book offered me the opportunity to make some revisions and to enlarge it with a chapter on the evolution of the western ideas of democracy and human rights, together with a conclusion that consolidates the basic ideas presented through the length of the text. By presenting a tentative model of the common cultural construction of social life of inner littoral Southeast Asia, the book should be more valuable still for introductory courses on the region. With this in mind, I have also revised and updated the bibliography.

Niels Mulder
Amsterdam, August 1995

Note on spelling of words and names

Generally, Thai words and names have been romanized in accordance with the international phonetic system, such as the one introduced for Thai by Mary Haas (1964), excepting, however, the diacritical tonal marks and some vowels: the vowel-sound **o** as in *lot* has been transcribed as **ǫ**, the dull **e** as **oe**, and the acute **e** as **ae**; vowel length has not been distinguished for **oe** and **ae**. In contrast to Tagalog/Filipino, Thai distinguishes long and short vowels, **o** being short, **oo** long. In Filipino **oo** means that the vowel is repeated, the word *loób*, for instance, being pronounced as *lo-ób*.

Javanese and Indonesian distinguish the consonants **j** and **ty**, and spell the sound **ty** as **c**, as is usual in many languages, and also in the phonetic system; consequential the **c** is also used that way for Thai. Since Thai has aspirated and explosive consonants, **t** and **th** have to be distinguished, the **th** sounding like the **t** in *time* and certainly not as the **th** in *thigh*; the **t** then stands for the plosive pronunciation of the French, such as in *Toulouse*.

In cases where I am familiar with the generally preferred romanizations of Thai names, I have written them accordingly; otherwise, I have transcribed them phonetically. Often Javanese and Indonesian names are still spelled according to Dutch conventions, whereas the modern spelling of these languages and of Tagalog/Filipino follows phonetical conventions rather closely. Where required, Thai words have been marked by Th, Indonesian by I, Javanese by J, and Tagalog/Filipino by TF.

Introduction

For many, the fascination of Southeast Asia is due to its abundance of elaborate and divergent cultural forms. As a cross-road between two major Asian civilizations, namely the Indian and the Chinese, it received influences from both. Also others travelled through it and exerted influence, whether they were Sri Lankan Buddhist monks, Chinese pilgrims, Muslim merchants, or western colonizers. All of them left traces. So, today, all the so-called great religions are represented: Hinduism flourishes in Bali, while most of the rest of Indonesia, together with Malaysia, and parts of Southern Thailand and the Philippines, profess Islam. Theravada Buddhism spread to most of mainland Southeast Asia, with the exception of Vietnam, which fell within the orbit of Chinese civilization. Chinese culture is also alive and well among many of the immigrant Chinese groups, for instance, in Singapore, Malaysia, and Southern Thailand, and leaves its marks wherever the far-flung Chinese in Southeast Asia still take pride in their origin. The same can be said of the Indian immigrants, mostly in Malaysia, who tenaciously stick to their customs. In the Philippines, Christianity and western ideas obtained their foothold.

This book is not written to provide insight into that treasure trove of cultural diversity, to which one could still add the many, more tribally organized, peoples of Southeast Asia who attract tourists and anthropologists alike. On the contrary, this book presents a preliminary attempt to identify the similarities between Thais, Javanese, and Filipinos, to pin-point the correspondences between their styles of everyday life, and the thinking that guides it.

At first sight, such an attempt may seem preposterous. Whereas a certain likeness between Javanese and Thai culture may derive from the shared heritage of Indic culture that is, for instance, kept alive in the Ramayana stories and performances, the Thais became Theravada Buddhists and the Javanese say that they are Moslems. Linguistically, of course, Thai and Javanese share an impressive Sanskrit-derived vocabulary, but often the individual words have acquired different meanings in the two cultural contexts. So, while the Thai *saksit* ('supernatural power') derives from the same *shakti* as the Javanese *kasaktèn*, the still related meanings have become specific in the divergent cultural histories. This also goes for other elements that derive from Indic civilization, such as the organization of the realm, the position of kingship, and religious conceptualization.

The Philippines remained beyond the influence of Indic civilization and never experienced a political organization revolving around a sacrosanct king. The few Sanskrit words that one encounters in Tagalog/Filipino have probably been carried there by the lively trade that made the South China Sea the Southeast Asian mediterranean before the Europeans disrupted communications. That trade also accounts for the very many common words between Malay, Javanese, and Tagalog that, as rather closely related languages, share many other roots and characteristics.

Communication across the seas may partly explain the similarities in religious thinking and the culture of everyday life that this book seeks to illustrate. These similarities may hint at some sort of 'Southeast Asianess' into which the various world religions and their civilizations had to be localized. This adaptation to Southeast Asia becomes apparent when one looks beyond Buddhism, Islam, and Catholicism that are the official labels of Thai, Javanese, and Filipino religious practice (Part I).

The most striking similarities appear when looking at the organization and ethics of life in the family. These seem to be very comparable among the three cultures (Part II). Yet, this compatibility may be much wider and not specifically Southeast Asian; it may also derive from the type of people whose thinking this book brings into focus. Virtually all the material presented derives from members of the educated, urban middle classes. It is among these people that I have done the bulk of my cultural research, in Bangkok and Chiangmai in Thailand, in Yogyakarta in Central Java, and in Manila and Lucena in the Tagalog-speaking part of the Philippines.

Perhaps it was accidental that I started to work among these people during my first research period in Yogyakarta in 1969-70. But ever since then, I have been concentrating on them, having found good reasons to do so. Cultural research among journalists, artists and authors, teachers, professors and other professionals, mystics, monks and clerics, civil servants, ideologues and social critics, brings to light the ideas of the actively culture-producing class, of opinion leaders and opinion-makers, who transmit, propagate and explain ideas to the rest of the population, especially to those who aspire to social mobility, to literacy, urbanity and modern education.

It is this opinion-forming function that is important. Ideas critical of government, about political renewal, about how to deal with modernity and social change, whether progressive or conservative, mostly originate from members of the educated middle classes who, at least in relatively open societies, also dispose of effective means of diffusion. Sometimes, of course, their voices are drowned out by the 'dominant' ideas of the political centre and big business, and it would be a mistake to see the middle stratum as the monopoliser of culture (Part III).

However it might be, the ideas presented in this book do not derive from the population at large, who may, however, orient themselves to these ideas with which they are also presented in the media and school. Yet I have the distinct impression that the mental worlds of educated Thais and Javanese also do connect with, or are at least related to, the more popular ideas of the lowly educated masses. Because of the long history of cultural colonization of the minds of the educated Filipinos, it is hard to say how revealing their thinking is of the mentality of the common man.

The ideas and interpretations presented in the following are admittedly sketchy. What ties them together is the introductory chapters to the various sections and the conclusions about the common cultural construction of social life; also the two chapters about the culture of the public world, namely 16 and 17, have been written from an integrated Southeast Asian perspective. The other chapters serve to illustrate the main points; these have been elaborated at greater length in my books and publications about Thai, Javanese, and Filipino culture, from which they derive.

Because of similarities, some themes surface regularly, and also the process of making comparisons leads to some repetition between chapters. Despite much thought, I have not found a good way to avoid this. However, one advantage of the present way of working is that chapters can be read as self-contained arguments. The context of these arguments evolves through the length of the book, Part I providing the wider world of ideas in which the everyday life observations of Part II are set. Both these segments provide the background against which the discussion of cultural change in Part III is elaborated. The conclusions then consolidate the main themes.

Major ideas

CHAPTER 1

Religious syncretism or Southeast Asian religion?

According to *The Concise Oxford Dictionary*, syncretism is the attempt to sink differences and effect union between sects or philosophical schools. In other words, effecting union is the higher goal, for which it is worth sacrificing principle and dogma. In anthropology and modern theology, the term syncretism is most often used to describe the blending of elements belonging to various religious discourses without resolving basic differences of principle; the Thai blending elements from Buddhism with Brahmanism and Animism, the Javanese their original religious practices with Hindu-Buddhism and Islam, and the Filipinos their pre-Hispanic traditions with Catholicism.

At first sight, it might seem that there is nothing wrong with the term syncretism that so aptly describes the act of blending, but sometimes its use smacks of derogation. Then it often seems to imply that Southeast Asians do not know principle, that their religious practices and thinking are hopelessly heterodox and exemplary of 'concrete' thinking which they are unable to transcend. In such cases the term is not very helpful and merely descriptive of the observer's conceit, missionary arrogance, or self-righteous dogmatism. If such observers are Westerners, they should reflect upon the origins of their names for days and months, the Christmas tree, the Easter bunny, or the dates on which these feasts are celebrated, and the myriad other living vestiges of Europe's heathen past.

The term syncretism, then, refers to mixing and blending, which is a universal outcome of culture contact. The question remains, though, what does the term really describe, what does it add to our understanding? Emphasizing mixing and blending may reveal precious little about the culture under study, perhaps no more than 'boats float' does as a statement about shipping. The revealing inquiry should rather be about what Southeast Asian religion means in a positive sense. What is it all about from a Southeast Asian point of view? In other words, we should try to discover and understand the essence that underlies religious syncretism. In the process, we may also learn about the characteristics of Southeast Asian thought.

Since the concept of syncretism is not particularly helpful or revealing, it would seem best to discard it and try to find out about Southeast Asian religion and thought by exploiting a more useful idea, that of localization. This highlights the initiative and contribution of the local societies in response to and as the ones responsible for the outcome of culture contact; in other words, it is the receiving culture that absorbs and restates the foreign elements, moulding them after its own image.[1] In the process of localization, foreign elements have to find a local root, a native stem onto which they can be grafted. It is then through the infusion of native sap that they can blossom and fruit. If they do not interact in this way, the foreign ideas and influences may remain peripheral to the culture.

The Filipinization of Catholicism is a case in point. When the Spaniards arrived with cross and sword, they had their ideas about Catholicism. What we find today is a statement about Philippine culture past and present. A few examples may help clarify this. The Spanish Catholicism of those days was well freighted with saints and miracles. This fitted nicely with the local belief in the active role of the recently deceased in the lives of the living. Even today, dead parents and grandparents are still supplicated for aid and supernatural intervention in human affairs ("Save water and pray for rain") is taken for granted.

The concept of localization also gives good grounds for disagreeing with the modern feminist position that the place of women in pre-Spanish days was entirely different, and that their second sex position of today is the result of the friars' attempt to Maria-Clarafy the Filipina.[2] While it is possible that virginity has a higher rating today than in the far-off past, it seems most likely that the position of the woman as mother was very similar to what it is in other cultures of Southeast Asia, such as the Javanese and the Thai. Because of her self-sacrifice in giv-

1 From a historian's perspective, the localization thesis has been elaborated by O.W. Wolters, 1982:52-5.

2 Maria Clara is one of the characters in José Rizal's *Noli Me Tangere*. Extremely coy, devout, obedient and will-less, she is a mere pawn in the hands of men. She is often thought to epitomize what Spanish friar Catholicism hoped to make of women.

ing life and nurture, she is entitled to the highest honour; mother is sanctified and placed on a pedestal.

What the Spaniards brought was a most powerful symbol that fitted the prevailing world of ideas. Consequently the Holy Mother could enjoy a tremendous popularity, chiming in with the pre-existing cult of the dependable and moral mother. In the process of becoming Mama Mary, even Her most popular representations changed from that of the Spanish Madonna-Queen Mother and Madre Dolorosa to the present serene yet kind and miraculous Lady of Lourdes, without the Child that had begun a life of its own as the Santo Niño (a non-Spanish devotion).

Ideas that did not find a root or stem to sustain them were the cluster sin, repentance, and atonement. Religion in Southeast Asia is typically future directed and serves to ensure a peaceful and blessed life; it is not directed to a sinful past, and certainly not if those sins consist of infractions of abstract principles and commandments. If there is sinful behaviour, it is located in tangible interpersonal relationships, with the relationship to the mother as the exemplary centre. To go against her, to betray her expectations, is hideous indeed, and also the transgression for which Filipinos, Javanese, and Thai agree that supernatural retribution will be inescapable. Not to know gratitude and obligation is to place oneself beyond the pale of civilized life.

In the course of its localization, Philippine Catholicism developed into a symbolic representation of family relationships, which is not so surprising since the family, in its communal setting, was then the core institution of Philippine society, and remains so to this day (chapter 4).

Thai cultural history also provides an illustrative case. Over the ages, the tension between the teachings of Theravada Buddhism and Thai animistic practice was resolved by appropriating those elements of the Buddhist doctrine that are compatible with animistic thinking and basic human experience. As a result, the institutional and ritual expressions of Thai religion appear to be very Buddhistic indeed, but its characteristic mentality is not so much interested in the Theravada message of moral self-reliance as in auspiciousness, worldly continuity, and the manipulation of *saksit* (supernatural 'sacred') power. Consequently, Buddha images became seats of such power and the practice of merit-making turned to ensuring prosperity (chapter 2).

The successful Thai-ification of religion parallels the Thai-ification of Indic thinking about statecraft, in which the king has become the protector, the patron, of religion. All this is expressed in the powerful *(saksit)* yet also morally exemplary centre, the palace cum temple complex in Bangkok. That core fuses and articulates the great traditions of Theravada Buddhism and Indic theory of state with the ordinary practice of life and the mentality that animates it. During this development, a distinct, self-confident Thai civilization has evolved that forms its own universe of discourse, while setting its own standards of exemplariness.

Javanese success in localizing several waves of intensive culture contact has been so impressive that the resultant philosophy of life became known as Javanism. In this, animistic, Hindu, Buddhistic, Islamic, and even theosophical and non-theistic elements fuse, and so it is seemingly correct to label it syncretism, but is it fair, or precise for that matter? The word Javanism is more appropriate because it emphasizes the uniqueness and specificity of Javanese thought, in which inspiration and intuition rather than dogmatic reasoning are the respected ways to truth (chapter 3).

To call Javanese religion Islam, or Thai religion Buddhism, or Philippine religion Catholicism is anthropologically misleading. This is not to say that there is not a great deal of Islam in Java, Buddhism in Thailand, or Catholicism in the Philippines, but it does invariably lead to the affixing of confusing labels, such as 'folk religion' as opposed to some hypothetical orthodoxy, or inept descriptions, such as statistical Muslims, bad Buddhists, or superficial Catholics. Those who are so arbitrarily labelled find their own practices perfectly righteous and congruous with their philosophy of life, and they are certainly not suffering from the tensions of unresolved contradictions that would be characteristic of syncretism. Like any of their other practices, their religion provides localized statements about their own culture.

Javanese, Thais, and Filipinos appropriated ideas selectively and in accordance with their own image. They did not take aboard lock, stock, and barrel whatever was offered, and never aspired to 'orthodoxy'. They merely made good use of those items that fitted their needs, and that were not in obvious contradiction to their beliefs about life. Thus, we need to know what these latter are, and to find out what those concerned want of 'religion', what they need it for. Which is why, in this search, the term syncretism becomes completely redundant.

Southeast Asian religion

While none of the formal adherents of the great religions in Southeast Asia will deny that living in accordance with the rules and obligations of the Faith is a way to salvation, progress along that path is deemed to be a personal matter, and furthermore, the avoidance of religious sin is not necessarily socially relevant. What life in society demands is respect for its order, and that is how a moral way of life is understood. Sometimes that esteem may be formulated in almost religious terms, such as when the Javanese say, "The person who honours his parents, his elder brother, his teacher and the king, honours 'God'", yet the crux of the matter is respect for the hierarchical order of society. This begins at home where it is exemplified in the morally unequal relationships of obligation between exalted parents and dependent child. By extension, the measure in which a person is thought to be moral depends on his way of handling the obligations inherent in his relationships with others, depending on the role he is playing. This way of thinking makes morality a social rather than a religious matter.

The focus of Southeast Asian religion is neither with morality nor with salvation or liberation. Religious practice is concerned with individual potency, with protective blessing, and with protection from danger and misfortune. In short, it is a relationship with power.[3] That power is located in the nature/supernature in which human life is embedded. In other words, that power, however concentrated and whether manifested in deities, saints, spirits, the recently deceased, or potent objects is very much part of the human situation and everyday life.

But implicit in this view of life is the belief that power is near, tangible, accessible, and that this potency is thought of in anthropomorphic terms. More importantly, it can be supplicated and manipulated, which is to say, humans know the attributes of the various manifestations of power, and how to deal with them. Whether this nearness, tan-

---

3 I like the way the Philippine anthropologist Prospero R. Covar formulated this idea. "Churches are neither for sinners nor for believers. They are the wellsprings that nurture religious potency and efficiency". From, General characterization of contemporary religious movements in the Philippines, *Asian Studies* 13/2:91 (1975).

gibility and accessibility of power demonstrates itself in Philippine intimacy with the Catholic saints, in the Javanese mystical attuning of the self to what is greater than man, or in magical manipulation, the point is that a relation to power is taken for granted. It is a part of everyday life that people live with as a matter of course.

This does not mean that all people have the same relation, are capable of, or interested in close relations to power and its manifestations. Generally, men are thought to be superior in such things to women, but individual differences are very considerable. Those who are so inclined may seek to enhance their potency in nature, to tap its power, so to say, in the practice of asceticism and meditation; others are ritual specialists who manipulate and cajole power to ensure protection and auspicious continuity; others still relate to power magically for curative or malign purposes. Mediumship is widespread and its practitioners mediate between the invisible and the concrete world; they may give predictions or transmit messages. Most people recognize a direct relationship between health and invisible power; they will rely on the expertise of their specialists and on the efficacy of amulets, prayer, ritual, offerings, and mild forms of ascetic practice to achieve their purposes.

Apart from the accessibility of power, the various exercises demonstrate the forward-looking nature of Southeast Asian religious practice. It is directed to achieving a palpable result here in this world, here among the living, who also include the recently deceased, especially parents and grandparents who have not yet cut their ties with those remaining in the visible world. As part of the invisible realm of life, they may still extend their protective blessing, and often they are also thought to be dependent at this stage on the honour and prayer their descendants dedicate to them.

The line between life and death is as fluid as the line between the visible and the invisible. These are not really separate realms but interpenetrate each other, religious manifestations being pervasive and present to the senses, at least to intuition or the sixth sense. This latter phenomenon is most developed in the Philippines and on Java, where it leads to trust in and acceptance of 'divine' plan and purpose, but it is not uncommon in Thai meditational practice either, or in the more common fascination with things mysterious, such as encounters with spirits, including those who have recently died.

Life is experienced as a whole, with religion an indwelling, insep-arable part. Since it is so much part of existence, it is life-directed, con-cerned with the present and the near future, while attributing a religious element to life in all its manifestations. Whether mystically expressed or not, the pervasiveness of religious phenomena and the possibility of intuiting, or feeling them, justify the more theological label 'immanence' to characterize religious thinking in Southeast Asia. This, at the same time, does away with the validity of such distinctions as sacred versus profane. Perhaps the best way to put it is that the most important locus of religion is in the individual, in personal feelings, and in an intimacy with invisible powers.

In such a conceptualization, that recognizes the prevalence of power, of a cosmic energy, as it were, in all kinds of things, and that also recognizes the validity of the personal religious experience, there is no place for dogmatism, systematic theology, or even momentous ideas and intense expectations about the afterlife. This belief system also expresses some of the basic characteristics of Southeast Asian culture, such as the value placed on tolerance, patience, compromise, plus the avoidance of conflict, and also the validity of, and respect for, personal feelings.

Seen from within, therefore, there is no question about resolving antagonistic principles, because the dogmas are uninteresting and peripheral at best. When the Buddha said that a preoccupation with the gods and the spirits is a waste of time for those seeking liberation, the Thai preoccupation with them merely demonstrates their quest for secu-rity by relying on the patronage of higher forces. When Filipinos seek consolation or efficaciousness through touching the statues of their saints, or when they go on Mount Banahaw pilgrimages in mystically enchanted nature, or seek cures through faith-healing, they merely express trust in invisible yet fatherly providence and care. When the Javanese pursue their ascetic exercises in the quest for direct, unmediat-ed 'divine' guidance, they merely express their intimacy with the invisi-ble, with the All-Soul, and their conviction that it is more appropriate to meet 'God' in one's heart than in Mecca. All this is life and near future directed, and poses no questions about liberation or salvation, let alone about the right path towards them.

If it is the above that is described by the label syncretism, the term is fine by me. I have the feeling, however, that the word in its current use belongs to a different type of religious discourse, in which the sacred is differentiated from the profane, in which man is confronted with a transcendent truth which makes the religious experience one of living by a doctrine that is beyond merely logical comprehension. In this, an all-powerful and unique godhead reveals conditions to be fulfilled in order to achieve salvation, a state that is apart from that of natural man. To reach that state of grace, he needs both revelation and dogma. To deviate from the prescribed path is to tumble into heterodoxy and mysticism: to fall prey to syncretism (a synonym for heresy).

Islam, Buddhism, Christianity?

Having said so much, I have not solved the problem of the labels Islam, Buddhism, and Catholicism for religion in Southeast Asia, labels that are no outsider's description, but used themselves by the Javanese, Thais, and Filipinos concerned. While some of them will concede that their practices are rather heterodox, all will call themselves Moslems, Buddhists or Christians. More than that, it is an important identity marker, as a sign of belonging to one of these world-wide religious civilizations. At a more direct and homely level, having religion sets man apart from animals; it is the essence of culture, it is the mark of being civilized. Following from this, it is felt there must be something wrong with people who claim not to have a religion.

Yet even given this recognized importance of religion, of having ulema who interpret the law, of having monks who hand down the precepts, of having priests who say mass, of qualified ritual officiants solemnizing family occasions and celebrating community ceremonies, some people do indeed still question the often vast discrepancy between orthodox teaching and personal belief, between the original theory and the actual practice. As a result, and especially with the advance of communications and modernity, religious reformers and fundamentalists dot the scene in Southeast Asia. According to them, if people take pride in calling themselves Moslems, Buddhists, or Christians, they had better be good ones and take their religion seriously. It is these religious activists who create consciousness of 'orthodox' practice, of scriptures and commandments, as opposed to magical and 'superstitious' accretions, in brief, of syncretism.

According to serious Moslems, Islam is about the submission of man to God, and his obligation to worship along the prescribed lines. For a long time, they have been irritated by Javanese ritual practices, the neglect of religious rules, the heresy of mysticism, and so forth, of their fellow countrymen, who sometimes even drink beer and eat pork. According to Buddhadasa Bhikkhu, the ways in which the Thais make religious merit is about as useless as "raising chickens in order to feed the eggs to the dogs".[4] According to Filipino priests, the Philippines is still missionary territory, where superstitions flourish and sin thrives, and where the message of the Mother Church is far from being understood.

So we find fundamentalism, reform, new sects and new interpretations, religious reflection of all sorts; but also a resurgence of magic, mediumship, faith-healing, esotericism. All are flourishing and vying with each other to attract the devotee in Southeast Asia at present. This very lively religious contention cannot be understood as a simple engagement between the representatives of orthodoxy and heterodoxy, of purism versus syncretism. It is definitely the case, though, that certain protagonists have succeeded to a modest degree in promoting their brands of reform and that, especially among educated people, knowledge about and sometimes the dedicated practice of formal religion is increasing. To go by the book, whether Koran and Shari'a, Tripitaka, or Bible, may even be a sign of modernity; it also goes against the grain of Southeast Asian religion, that validates personal experience, that is averse to dogma, that emphasizes the sphere of the dream, of the all-possible, and that is oriented to the present and the future of this life. And so it seems to me that the best Islamic, Buddhist, and Christian reformers can hope for is a syncretistic Islam, or a heterodox Buddhism, or a folk Catholicism, at least for a long time to come, because Southeast Asian religiosity will prove to be more tenacious and obdurate than the twentieth century vogue for purifying the faith.

---

4 For this and other reformers' observations in Thailand, see Modernity means criticism: reformers and identity. Mulder, 1995,a:125-129.

CHAPTER 2

Power and goodness in Thai symbolic representations

Analysis

In Thai thinking, Buddhism deals essentially with virtue and wisdom, which can liberate people from the common order of life. Buddhism shows the way out of the fetters of existence which, for our purposes, means the human condition that is characterized by impermanence, suffering, and an illusory self that is subject to the cycle of rebirth *(samsara)*. It transcends and relates to the trustworthy order of morality and goodness that is symbolized by the home, the mother, and the female symbols of Mother Earth and Mother Rice. Both the Buddha and also these latter three female entities are considered to have the highest *phrakhun* (goodness) towards us, its beneficiaries; together they constitute the domain of moral goodness, or what I call the '*khuna* dimension of existence'.

Next to this domain, we find the realm of supernatural power and, first, the area that the Thai classify as *saksit*. This realm is much less trustworthy and does not necessarily have moral characteristics; it represents the tenuous order outside the home. It is the subject of the most intensive religious preoccupation — concerning loss and gain, danger and protection — and there are very clear, almost mechanical, rules for dealing with it. Beyond the area of *saksit* power, we find the area of chaos and extreme unreliability, represented by the fearsome spectre of pure wickedness and immorality. Together, these latter two kinds of power form the '*decha* dimension of existence', while in between the *khuna* and *decha* dimensions of existence, we find an area of intermingling that affects the safety and continuity of the group. Schematically all this can be ordered as follows:

	Khuna ('moral goodness')			*Decha* ('power')	
Order	Pure order	Order of goodness		Tenuous order	Chaos
Symbol	The Buddha	The mother		*Saksit* power	Evil
Quality	Pure virtue; stillness	Deeply moral	Interpenetration	Amoral	Immoral
		Safety		Potential danger	

Domesticated area of existence

Decha

Domesticated power

Power is the most spectacular, beguiling, and central manifestation of Thai life; its cognitive elaborations and the way power is accommodated reveal the essentially animistic substratum of the Thai mentality. An understanding of *saksit* power will provide us with an ordering principle against which other classifications can be understood.

Power is primarily vested in *sing saksit* (holy objects), such as Buddha images, stupas *(cetiya)*, temple buildings, amulets, sacred words, holy water, the spirits and the gods *(phii saang theewadaa)*, and in the shrines in which they are immanent. Sometimes power is also vested in out-of-the-ordinary manifestations of nature, such as white elephants or deformed babies. *Saksit* power is also inherent in the position of the king, and as a matter of principle, in everything that has mysterious qualities. This power is both potentially beneficent and harmful; it lies all around us, like the atmosphere, and when it condenses in places or objects it results in *sing saksit*. People have to come to an accommodation with this sphere of power and must approach it on its own terms, in accordance with the laws that guide it. The power of *sing saksit* can be tapped for personal purposes, its protection may be sought, and its vengeful manifestations can be neutralized.

In almost every house compound, there is the small and attractive spirit shrine of the *phraphuum*. *Phraphuum* is 'the lord of the place' *(cawthii)*, that is, the local ruler whose presence should be recognized and respected. Just as all goods have their owner, all places have their local lord, not because of a higher order of legitimation, but as a matter of fact and natural right. The incidental human occupants of a compound therefore need to pay respect to the local potentate in order to be safe and to avoid its wrath, which can be provoked by negligent or non-respectful behaviour. If respected, well treated, and occasionally feasted, the *phraphuum* will be protective in return and care for the safety of the place. If untoward incidents still happen, these cannot be the fault of the spirit, and in such cases the causes need to be sought elsewhere.

Phraphuum is not the only local lord: in a village one will find at least two others, the *phiibaan*, that is, the ruler and protector of the village territory and also the *phiiwat*, or *syawat*, that is, the protective spirit of the temple compound. These lords should also be respected and honoured, and their beneficial protection needs to be sought periodically. Similarly, the wider territory of the province has its *saksit* ruler and protector, the *phiimyang* or *syamyang* that resides in or at the city pillar or *lakmyang*.

While the above might suggest that there is a hierarchy among the local lords, there does not appear to be any strict order of precedence among these potentates; they are simply there, exercising their right to rule. They all want to be respected and they all need to be supplicated in order to ensure the welfare of the human beings in their territory. The little *phraphuum* of one's house compound, being nearest, may easily be the most important of all since he is directly in charge of the protection of those who live in his immediate surroundings. A *phraphuum* is certainly not satisfied with respect paid to the *syamyang* or the *phiibaan* but wants to be respected in his own right. Because of his proximity, his subjects had best respect his wishes.

These guardian spirits are basically local rulers who have no power outside of their respective territories; in other places one needs to deal with other local potentates. But their power, too, is very much confined to their respective shrines, or ritual centres. One needs to go to these to supplicate them or tap their power since with increasing distance, it dissipates accordingly and they have no influence outside the borders of their realm. Some university students may seek success in examinations at the shrine of the *phraphuum* of the university compound, but there is little use in seeking the blessing of guardian spirits when one is outside their sphere of influence. In other words, it is not very practical or politic for a traveller to remain devoted to the guardian spirit of his village when he is away. As soon as he steps outside his village boundaries, he enters the realm of another local ruler who must be respected and worshipped.

While guardian spirits that care for the general peacefulness and protection of their territory are localized by definition, there are other entities which, for instance, see to the growth of rice and the falling of rain; these *theewadaa* influence and regulate specific processes. But however widespread their activities may be, these forces should be addressed at the right time and place if their blessing is to be invoked. There is little point in seeking the protection or curative properties of the miraculous relic of the Buddha at Doi Suthep Temple in Chiangmai without going there, and one does not ensure good luck by praying to the Four-Faced Brahma *(Thaaw Mahaa Phrom)* housed at the Erawan Hotel in Bangkok while one is up-country. The supplicant had better go to its shrine to propitiate a powerful spirit if he wants to feel any assurance. All these powers, be they guardian spirits, powerful Buddha images, or rulers of certain realms of activity, are basically localized and their protection should be sought at their particular shrines.[1]

In order to invoke the benevolent attention of *saksit* forces, the worshipper must initiate the transaction by paying respect and making a small offering. The supplicant then offers his terms of contract: if the concerned entity will fulfil his wishes, he will return and offer a feast, a pig's head, flowers, or perhaps even a theatrical performance. Most *sak-*

---

[1] Some Thais, especially those who travel abroad, hold the view that they can invoke the protective blessing of powerful *saksit* images, such as the Emerald Buddha, when they are far away. They may ask for safety or success in an examination and, if their wish is granted, they promise to redeem the vow upon returning to Thailand, preferably at the place of worship of the *sing saksit* concerned.

sit powers have known likes and dislikes: the Buddha image *Phra Chinaraat* in Pitsanuloke likes pigs' heads, *Phra Kaew Morakot* (The Emerald Buddha) loves hard boiled eggs, the spirit of the city pillar in Bangkok is fond of *lakhon chaatrii* performances, and the Four-Faced Brahma at the Erawan Hotel appreciates flower garlands, elephant statues, and a donation to the Erawan Hospital Foundation. Female spirits *(cawmae)* have a marked predilection for phalli.

The ritual of the invocation is always the same: one first pays respect and makes a small offering of burning incense in order to attract attention, then one states one's wish and makes a vow, and finally, after being granted one's wishes, redeems the vow. According to Phya Anuman, "If a *theewadaa* does not want to give what it has been asked for, but the ceremonial way in which it has been supplicated was correct, then it must without reservation fulfil that wish".[2] The contract between a supplicant and a protective spirit or *theewadaa*, or any other thing classified as *sing saksit*, is largely mechanical, for a specific purpose, and of relatively short duration.

The *saksit* forces respond to presentation, such as right ceremony, proper words, appropriate movements and formulae, and people generally know how to perform their side of the contract. Its efficacy is not inherent in itself but rather in their knowledge of the correct form that makes *theewadaa* and benevolent spirits respond. These entities may therefore be considered to be domesticated: people have clear ideas on how to handle them and are familiar with their behaviour; in this sense they are reliable and predictable. The same predictability is expected of the human participant in the contract. When a favour has been sought against a promise, the spiritual force concerned may become very irritated and dangerous if the vow is not redeemed in the correct manner and according to the terms of contract. In such cases, it turns vengeful and will punish negligent behaviour.

Insult to *sing* forces is by no means sinful, but merely stupid. One does not activate karmic retribution by defaulting on a businesslike contract but, in the manner of a civil lawsuit, the problem will be settled between the concerned parties. To honour the terms of contract is ben-

2 Translated from Sathian Kooseet, *Myangsawan lae phiisaang theewadaa.* Bangkok: Bannakhaan, 1972:309.

eficial, while the folly of not doing so will result in revenge, disaster, shame and loss of face. *Saksit* forces are highly sensitive about their power, rank, and prestige; they are easily insulted, yet also easy to please by a show of respect, an offer, or a bribe.

Summarizing, we find that the concept of *saksit* has the following attributes. The human life situation is encompassed by a realm of nature and supernature in which power is vested. Humans need it for protection, for blessing, for safety and auspiciousness, and for success in their personal and communal pursuits. In places such as shrines or other sacred localities, and in objects such as amulets, power is concentrated. This condensation becomes addressable and manifests itself as *sing saksit*. By knowing the proper method, such as the use of rituals, ceremonies, or incantations, these potencies can be induced to work for the needs of the human supplicants. Consequently, they may be considered to be domesticated. Contracts with such entities are defined by their purpose, have a relatively short time perspective, and need to be periodically renewed. *Saksit* forces are potentially benevolent and protective, but can be dangerous, jealous and vengeful if they feel slighted. In spite of these characteristics, humans feel the need to depend on them and seek their favour. To do so, the human partner must be the one to initiate the transaction.

Basically, *saksit* power is amoral, because it does not concern itself with motives and serves the good and the wicked alike. It is unprincipled and reacts to mechanical manipulation and an outward show of respect. Contracts with it are guided by a businesslike logic, and there is no higher moral principle that guides these. Moreover, these agreements are never fully reliable. If insulted, *saksit* beings may turn dangerous and seek revenge, but that revenge is escapable if its victim places himself under the protection of other more powerful *saksit* agents, takes refuge in the monkhood, or simply leaves their sphere of influence. Therefore, to attempt to take advantage of *saksit* power by, for instance, failing to redeem a vow is not considered to be sinful or subject to the moral law of Karma. In such cases one merely exposes oneself to revenge, which is plain stupid.

Nondomesticated power

Next to the *saksit* forces that are somewhat ambivalent but potentially benevolent, we find the inauspicious, wicked and evil representatives of the realm of chaos and immorality. These are the 'nondomesticated' or largely uncontrollable and often 'roaming' forces that are the carriers of bad luck. These evil spirits are unpredictable and essentially malevolent. They tend to act of their own volition rather than to wait until properly and ceremonially addressed; they resemble criminals and trouble-makers. Before they can be neutralized or mastered, they will usually have done some harm, having caused illness, death, destruction, or simply terror and fright. They can only be controlled with a strong counter force, such as a Pali incantation *(khaathaa)* by a Buddhist monk, or through the mediations of a spirit doctor. The latter specializes in localizing the spirit, and then subduing it by trapping it in a pot, or chasing it away by evoking strong annulling forces. These fiends can sometimes also be dealt with by politely placating them and asking them to go away in return for a gift — essentially a pay-off. But when all remedies fail, people had better lie low and be careful not to give further offence, in the hope that the carrier of inauspiciousness will roam on.

Some spectres are believed to be vaguely localized in places, such as cemeteries or forests, and are a nuisance or danger to the traveller beyond the protection of his guardian spirit or a *theewadaa*. To cope with such a threat, the traveller may surround himself with the portable *saksit* power of amulets, tattoos, and various protective formulae. Most often these amulets and words are of Buddhist inspiration, such as small Buddha amulets *(phrakhryang)*, medals *(rianphra)* of famous and spiritually powerful monks, and passages from Pali texts.[3] Protective tattoos are most often of mixed Brahmanic and Buddhist origin. Whatever the form, the protective power is not located in a person but in an outside agent that he has obtained. To acquire protection, invulnerability, or prosperity, one depends at least as much on these external *saksit* agents as on one's own skill, merit or plain good luck.

3 For elaboration of "the cult of amulets", see S.J. Tambiah, *The Buddhist saints of the forest and the cult of the amulets.* Cambridge: University Press, 1984.

The most effective means to confront evil, immorality and chaos, are the powerful 'white magic' symbols that derive from the realm of moral goodness (see *Khuna* below). Whereas protection against evil may be sought through propitiation of benevolent spirits and *thee-wadaa*, the most effective *sing saksit* derive from the symbols of moral goodness. Monks with psychic power and very charismatic laymen *(phuumiibun)*, by virtue of their accumulated merit, may produce powerful amulets, apply tattoos, or teach protective formulae. Similarly, relics of one's parents, and Buddha images infused with *saksit* potency, will normally protect against evil. Generally, Buddhist symbols are thought to be the most effective devices, and if a spirit doctor fails in his struggle against a representative of evil, the Buddhist monk is thought to be the ultimate agent to vanquish malevolent spirits.

In a similar sense, a village community may nurture auspiciousness and feel itself protected by the strength of merit that is generated and accumulated in the village temple. The discipline of the monks, their chanting and preaching, the merit-making ceremonies and the power vested in the Buddha image: all serve to increase the ambience of security, continuity, and auspiciousness in a life situation surrounded by potentially harmful agents. In contrast to the more transient nature of the purely animistic seats of power, the power that is vested in merit and Buddhist symbols extends over a longer time and is continuously reinforced by the presence of monks and the performance of ritual.

The power of Buddhism is most clearly demonstrated on the occasion of the supreme confrontation with chaos — death. While there are many animistic and Brahmanic elements in Thai death ritual *(phithii awamongkhon)*, the core observances to restore order and ensure the well-being of the deceased are clearly of Buddhist derivation.

As a religious practice, Thai animism is essentially a system that deals with power, whether of the amoral, ambivalent *saksit* or the immoral, evil variety. Such power encountered during the course of everyday life should be dealt with according to its own laws — laws which do not raise moral questions of good and evil. Whether the religious complexes that deal with such power are classified as animistic, Brahmanic, or Buddhist is irrelevant, because the way in which they deal with power is inspired by the same animistic mind-set. In that mentality, supernatural forces do not question intentions but react reflexively to a show of respect, to ritual prescriptions and to ceremonial form. They can be hoodwinked by pretensions, by a nickname or a mask; they do not distinguish between the genuine and the false.

The emphasis on proper form in the contracts with powerful entities makes it very understandable that attitudes of devotion, piety, and deep emotion are generally, though not necessarily, absent while relating to them. There is no value in these attitudes because transactions are mechanical and thus superficial. The strongest emotions that a representation of power can expect to excite are reverent awe and fear *(kreengklua)*. Yet to have the feeling of being protected may stimulate genuine feelings of loyalty and gratefulness on the part of the supplicant. On the other hand, equally heartfelt feelings of suffering from evil power also occur. But placating evil forces normally hinges on form and not faith, and the small, powerless man who can magically trick the powerful into favourable response may be much admired.

Power is there to supplicate and to grasp. In this way of thinking, man becomes a force in proportion to his ability to harness power. The dealings are businesslike, favour for favour, and revenge returned for insult. Power is not subject to moral restraints, because moral restraints play no part in it; it is there to be used, and the person who does not avail himself of a presented opportunity is merely foolish.

Khuna

Moral goodness

Power is complemented by moral goodness *(khunngaam khwaamdii)*. The realm of moral goodness is not antithetical to the realm of power, but the two mutually complement each other. Both are needed in life and both belong to everyday experience even though their essential characteristics are polar. Where power has a multitude of supernatural projections, goodness is essentially epitomized in natural and human manifestations. While power has its being in a tenuous amoral order and immoral chaos, goodness derives from moral reliability and stability. Whereas power is aggressive and largely masculine, moral goodness is powerless and its symbols are usually familiar and feminine, located squarely in this world.

The primary symbol of moral goodness is the self-sacrificing attachment of a mother to her children. She cannot help but be good, cannot but give and care; she is always benevolent and forgiving. She feeds and loves without expectation of return; she gives without asking and provides her dependents with stability and continuity in life. She is a refuge, a haven of safety, and the wellspring of the moral identity of her offspring. At mother's side one is safe and knows that one will always be accepted.

In a similar vein, the earth on which we depend for our existence, the rice that feeds us, the water that sustains life, and the guardian angel that protects the young child, are all represented as female: *Mae Thoranii, Mae Phoosop, Mae Khongkhaa,* and *Mae Syy.* All these life-sustaining manifestations are thought to have extraordinary goodness *(phrakhun)* towards their dependents. That benevolence engenders a moral debt that should be acknowledged; it is the fountain-head from which moral obligation arises.

In the group of representatives of moral goodness, we also find the figure of the teacher who shares the same qualities. The life-sustaining gift of the teacher is the knowledge and wisdom that his pupils need to lead a moral life. The teacher is also thought to be a source of *meettaa karunaa,* of sympathy and kindness, who makes considerable self-sacrifice for the good of his pupils, thus creating a moral debt on their part.

We have already seen that the *saksit* forces may have temporary *khun* (goodness, usefulness) towards people who place themselves under their protection, and that this *khun* also results in obligation. The figures of moral goodness, however, obtain enduring *khun,* that is, pure *bunkhun,* toward their charges; these wards do not need to plead but rather receive without asking. The recipients of this *bunkhun* need not fear revenge from the figures of goodness, because they will not — and cannot — avenge themselves. *Neerakhun,* that is, ingratitude or the refusal to acknowledge the moral goodness that one has received, is to sin against the dependable order of morality, and will automatically be punished by the principle of moral justice, called Karma. Psychologically, such negative behaviour is a source of guilt feelings.

The feelings that should guide the relationship towards all those people who have *bunkhun* to us, its beneficiaries, are trust, warmth, love, protection, dependence, gratitude, reverence, and acceptance of one's identity. Such profound *bunkhun* relationships are further expressed in the periodic rituals of honouring parents, elders, and teachers as the keystones of the unfailing moral order. Gratitude is also expressed in thanksgiving ritual for a successful harvest.

The complementary opposition of the essentially worldly and female figures of moral goodness and the figures of amoral power, between impotence and might, is further demonstrated by the ideas that guide the division of roles in everyday life. Females are supposed to avoid or shun the manifestations of *saksit* power. They should not touch a Buddha image or a monk, they should stay away from the potent *stupas*, and should not own powerful amulets or wear sacred tattoos, nor know powerful *khaathaa*. Women are thought to pollute and neutralize the power of *sing saksit* and are dangerous to the potency of man.[4] The male teacher does not, of course, share in these expectations; but if he is respected for his moral wisdom, people would certainly be surprised to find him equipped with lots of amulets, tattoos, and other protective paraphernalia: he is thought to be already protected by his own moral wisdom, unless, of course, he is a teacher of magic, which is to say, a specialist dealing with *saksit* supernature.[5]

The goodness of Buddhism

The goodness of Buddhism reflects the order of pure virtue that lies beyond the human order of *kilesa* (passion and prejudice) and rebirth *(samsara)*. This pure order represents the realm of truth and the

4 In 'village Thailand' this thinking is still demonstrated by the taboos that guide the washing and the drying of clothing. Preferably, feminine clothing should neither touch nor be on the same line as male clothing. Moreover, feminine clothing should never be hung to dry above the head of a male. Similarly, a female stepping over a male is thought to be highly inauspicious for the male and a threat to his potency.

5 It is true, however, that there are female witches who deal with or manifest evil power. There are also some Buddhist 'nuns' *(maechii)*, technically in the sexually neutral *samanapheet* category, who practise healing. Further, most spirit mediums, irrespective of whether they mediate between humans and either *saksit* or evil powers, are female.

highest *khun*, such as exemplified by the qualities of the Buddha. These are pure virtue *(borisuttikhun)*, the highest compassion *(mahaa karunaathikhun)*, and wisdom *(panjaakhun)*. The Buddha is the highest refuge *(sarana)*, and His Teaching *(Dhamma)* directs towards liberation from the fetters of *samsaric* existence; the Noble Eightfold Path leads towards that liberation. This Buddhist Path is essentially a way of morality and wisdom that is indifferent to whatever is *saksit*. Its message is focused beyond the human order, not domesticated as it were, and its way needs to be cultivated in the individual.

Buddhism is not a supernatural manifestation of goodness — although the Buddha as a person is sometimes seen as such — but is rather a path that cultivates goodness and morality as instruments leading to wisdom, equanimity, and ultimately to liberation. The gift of Buddhism is like the gift of the mother or the teacher, a benevolence that does not require any return, and as such it is exemplary of the symbols of goodness in this world. Yet, for all its beneficence, Buddhism does not promise forgiveness and mercy, but places the burden of moral behaviour squarely on the shoulders of the individual, each and every one of whom remains subject to the impersonal law of Karma. Salvation is not a gift but a task, and the Buddhist Path is merely suggesting how to go about it. No wonder that in everyday life the highly tangible figures of mother and teacher remain the very centres of goodness, because they directly help and guide the individual.

The common understanding and practice of Buddhism remains animistic in the sense that merit-making is generally understood as a mechanism to ensure safety and auspiciousness, and thus the institutionalized Buddhism of the masses has become a powerhouse for individual and communal protection. Some people, though, are genuinely interested in following the morality and wisdom of the Buddhist Path and, especially in old age, many practise seriously; such people are no longer interested in the *decha* dimension of existence. To most Thais, however, accruing merit is a technique to ensure safety in a world that is replete with power, and such a use and interpretation of Buddhism can best be described as "Buddhist Animism" (Terwiel, 1975).

Interpenetration of *decha* and *khuna*

The interpenetration of the realms of power and moral goodness is embodied in the role of the 'good leader', who is expected to know his way around in both. Such a leader symbolizes, and should personify, goodness and reliability, but also masculinity. This ambiguity is clear in the incumbent role expectations for the father, the headman, the elder, the reliable patron, and ultimately the king. All these should combine benevolence and authority; this duality, however, does not appear to culminate in a central cosmological representation that fuses existential contradictions.

The clearest representation of the interpenetration of power and goodness is in the Sukhothai era ideal of the king as a 'father of the people', or in modern times as a *thammaraja*, a just king. When the king, under the influence of the 'Khmerization' of Ayudthayan times, came to be perceived as a *devaraja*, a Lord of Life, he became clearly identified with the realm of *saksit* power; nowadays the moral imperatives of kingship are strongly emphasized once again. The power and morality of King, Religion and Nation are celebrated in the 'civic religion', along with its identity bestowing symbols, whose centre is in the here-and-now; it is not represented as a cosmic or supernatural principle. The hub of the contemporary Thai cosmos, if there is one, would of necessity be of this world.

Ritually, this civic religion is most clearly expressed in Brahmanic state ceremonials that are intended to ensure the continuity and prosperity of the nation, coordinating the country with the cosmic forces of auspiciousness and the blessings of the *theewadaa*. Its functioning, like animism, is highly mechanical and incorporates all the symbols of auspiciousness, whether Brahmanic, Buddhist, or animistic in origin. The cast of mind that inspires it is essentially animistic, having safety within the tenuous order of saksit and chaotic forces as its goal.

At the level of the small community, the moral unity of the group is still expressed in the rapidly eroding worship of the collective ancestor spirit *(phii puujaataajaaj)* that still exercises a mild social control in parts of the Thai countryside. This depersonalized collectivity of spirits is the guardian of tradition as a moral way of life, and becomes upset over infractions of the rules of social harmony, such as illicit sexual relationships. Nowadays, this collectivity constitutes a minor guardian spirit that can be satisfied by simple ritual which imparts the information that 'all is well'. The ancestors' role in protecting the moral relationship that should exist between all those linked by the bonds of communality is still expressed in marriage and some other life-cycle rituals.

Other ancient ritual enactments, that still persist from the times when the Thai were full-fledged animists, are the *khwan* ('life essence') ceremonies to facilitate the incorporation into the community of strangers, of members who have ventured outside and been in danger, and of members who are in some transitory stage of their life cycle — for instance, marrying, or ordaining as a monk. It is no wonder that these primeval ritual expressions to ensure continuity and auspiciousness have acquired Brahmanic elaborations.

Reflections

Human experience is characterized by basic dualities that can be formulated as complementarities, oppositions, or contradictions, but that nonetheless all belong to the totality of man's state. There are always 'we versus they' situations, insiders versus outsiders, enemies contrasted to friends, trusted intimates and distant strangers, power and powerlessness, order and chaos, safety and danger, and other opposites without end. Within our own experience, we recognize and classify accordingly. Naturally, every philosophy of life, whether of religious inspiration or not, needs to come to grips with these basic dualities and to give them symbolic expressions.

In Thai thinking, the sophisticated elegance of a universal principle combines with the primordial directness of the animistic outlook; somehow Theravada Buddhism and the pre-Buddhist animistic heritage have collaborated in an enduringly harmonious marriage. The Buddhist message does not endow this universe with a comforting centre, but characterizes worldly and cosmic existence as impermanence, suffering, and non-self, imbued with the impersonal principle of Karma. For the contemporary Thai, the pleasant prospect of a heaven peopled by ancestors has been replaced by a long cycle of rebirths, and the knowledge that to do good improves one's karmic position, and that to do evil worsens it. The tribal centre of 'insiders' is somewhat diminished by the introduction of these universal Buddhist principles, but otherwise Buddhist thinking about this life and the universe does not conflict with original animistic cosmology, since both are convincing religious representations of the experience of everyday life.

Thai thinking does not attempt to resolve the contradictory, opposed, or complementary experiences of daily existence, but leaves them side by side just as they are: contradictory, opposed, and complementary as they come to us day by day. Yet, in order to assess (and deal with) the problems of existence in an acceptably optimistic perspective, moral 'inside' classifications versus power-related 'outside' ones have remained quite strong, though not all-pervasive, with the most basic of these considered as 'being safe', in opposition to 'being in danger'. These two complementary experiences are equally integral parts of life.

Ultimately, life is conditioned by the law of Karma, and the only way to overcome this *samsaric* cycle of birth-death-rebirth is to overcome karmic conditioning by the cultivation of morality and wisdom, so escaping from this impermanent and illusory existence into a sphere that is not of this world, and about which we have no knowledge. There is no lasting centre to our world other than the individual person, and there is no cosmic equilibrium of contradictory principles beyond each person's balance of karma. This Buddhist thinking comes very close to explaining existential experience in a convincing perspective, and because Buddhism shares this quality with the very existential explanations of animism, which it does not contradict, the two can exist together, explaining the same reality by similar logic but from a different viewpoint; this at least seems to be the case in Theravada societies.

One of the basic characteristics that Thai animism shares with Theravada Buddhism is the recognition of impermanence, instability, and insecurity, at least in the outside world. The animist recognizes that his life passes among all kinds of unpredictable forces that he needs to find some accommodation with in order to create temporary order. He achieves this by ritual, and by employing a wide range of talismans.

To the animist, the centre of the world is his group, and that centre ensures continuity, stability, and safety. His order lies close to home, the outside being chaotic and capricious, and he only takes the trouble to subject aspects of the outside to temporary order as the need arises. The inside and the outside remain distinct, and the animist's notions of order and disorder — and the means to deal with them — remain distinct, too. This schism being a fundamental attribute of the human experience, it is no cause for surprise that this bifurcation has been elaborated into separate institutionalized religious complexes that can easily coexist. This division is nothing other than an institutionalized reflection of the complexity of experience. The point left to ponder is why other religious thinking has sought to transcend, or at least unify, the basic dualities of existence by suppositions of a single god or a principle of cosmic equilibrium.

In the Thai frame of mind, animistic expression, 'magic', and popular Buddhism deal essentially with the tenuous order of *saksit*, plus the chaotic realm of evil powers, and these religious expressions should be understood as one complex. Brahmanic expressions (including state ritual, civic religion, and *khwan* ceremonies) are essentially concerned with the continuity of the group and auspiciousness in a hazardous environment; such expressions are directed toward mediation between the moral inside and the amoral outside. These latter expressions serve to ensure and sustain auspiciousness, and thus they are, apart from calendrical and life-cycle rituals, most typically manifested in astrological calculation.

The cult of the order of goodness enjoys little overt religious expression, but is tangibly expressed in the mother-centred ideology that teaches dependence on parents, elders, teachers, and on tradition — the obligation of the younger generation to recognize the *bunkhun* of the older generation. Respect for the order of goodness is most strongly reinforced by the feelings of guilt and the social and karmatic consequences attendant on the sin of *neerakhun* — the failure to recognize the obligations of gratitude. The cult of goodness is also propagated in the rituals directed to Mother Rice and Mother Earth.

The quest for salvation is expressed in the earnest following of the Buddhist Path and is generally a preoccupation of old age; this self-centred quest turns its back on the vicissitudes and onuses of daily life. While symbolically beneficial to the stability of the group, the Buddhist quest for merit in old age should not be equated with the popular merit-making practices to gain safety and protection. Everyday merit-making is offered in the hope of a rather immediate return, whereas in old age, Buddhist practice tends to be a quest to realize the hope for a better rebirth and for liberation, the aim being less to 'buy' protection for oneself than to hold devoutly to the practice of morality as a refuge leading to ultimate rewards.

This recognition of various realms of experience is reflected institutionally in a similar variety of religious complexes. The acknowledgment of a multifarious cosmos would seem to be closer to life's reality than is a reduction of everything into one integrated concept to explain the often contradictory experiences of life. Because the postulate of Karma easily accomplishes this, and since Buddhism recognizes and explains Dharma as a broad stream that encompasses life in all its variety, the Thais have no difficulty in calling themselves or their world 'Buddhist'.

CHAPTER 3

The Javanist perspective

The deep and very pervasive substratum of Javanese culture is often called *kejawèn*,[1] translated as Javaneseness or even Javanism. The suffix *-ism* is felicitous because it suggests that *kejawèn* is a teaching and a praxis. As a philosophy of life, it is remarkably elaborate, containing a theology, a cosmology, a mythology, a metaphysics, and an anthropology. Together these inspire a widely shared Javanese world view that, as a system of thought about social relationships, informs the ethics and common sense that legitimate the conduct of life.

Before the elaboration of some cardinal characteristics of Javanism, it should be made emphatically clear that Javanism is not a religion,[2] although it may give rise to certain 'religious' practices. Theologically, it recognizes a Divine Principle *(ke-Tuhanan)* rather than a 'personalized' or transcendent God. This essence, often referred to as Life *(Urip)*, encompasses and pervades all existence; it constitutes the origin and destiny of all that is.

Cosmologically seen, all belongs together, not in a haphazard way, but as a coordinated whole that is subject to preordination rather than volition. The former is known as the *ukum pinesthi* or *kodrat alam*, that is, the principle of necessity. The outcome of preordination, *kebeneran*, translates as truth, manifestation, and co-incidence. This cosmology is often illustrated by the *wayang purwa* mythology that contains the Javanese elaboration of the Mahabharata cycle, with the Bhagavad Gita at its core.

Anthropologically, man is part of it all, but in a special way. First

---

1 Roughly speaking, *kejawèn* are those ideas that belong to the deep-rooted Javanese tradition that is mainly inspired by Hindu-Buddhist and primordial animistic thought. In the literature, the Javanese who attribute meaning to life according to these uniquely Javanese ideas are known as *abangan*. These latter contrast with those Javanese who adhere to more orthodox Muslim ideas (*santri* or *putihan*).

2 For a different position, equating Javanism with *Agami Jawi* (Javanese religion), see Koentjaraningrat, 1985:316-79.

of all, he can choose, he has a will, and his choices may be uneducated (stupid, emotional, immoral) or educated (wise, conscious, moral). Secondly, man is considered to consist of two parts, a phenomenal *lair* and an inner *batin*; to the phenomenal part belong the five senses, and the capacity for rational thought; the inner part is secretive, constituting the line to his origin and containing a spark of Life itself; to it belongs the sixth sense, the intuitive inner feeling *(rasa)* that is the instrument for deep insight and revelation.

At the level of the world view, social relationships, like cosmic ones, should be well-ordered and coordinated. In the Javanese view of society, such relationships are hierarchically organized, people being the occupants of certain status positions that relate to each other in morally unequal ways. This order of society is a part of the total cosmic order.

From these considerations follows the *kejawèn* ethic, such as the imperative to seek *budaya*, that is, knowledge and wisdom. With that, one will know one's place in the social order and in that of Life; one will also know the task and the ethic that belong to one's place. One should live attuned to both orders. In one's phenomenal existence one should respect the order of society, honour one's elders and superiors and be considerate of inferiors by 'taking the measure of oneself' *(tepa slira)*. In other words, do as you would be done by. One should care about harmonious relationships, at least outwardly so, and avoid all open conflict. To be able to do this, one should not only have knowledge but be able to master oneself, one's drives and emotions, and cultivate and strengthen one's mind or inner self *(batin)*.

In its widest sense, this cultivation of the mind or inner self is known as *kebatinan*, or as *olah rasa*, which means the training of the inner feeling. A strong *batin* enables one not to be disturbed by whatever happens in the *lair* world, to be patient and wait for the right moment to act; it also enables one to accept life as it comes and to adjust oneself to it. It is a training in sensing and feeling, to know when the right moment to act has arrived, to feel oneself attuned to cosmic happenings, to seek to be in step with the Divine Principle, or Life, and eventually to seek union with one's origin and destiny, thus realizing the Truth in oneself. It is only in this last, mystical, sense that *kebatinan* has clear religious overtones, in all other senses it being rather the epitome of the *kejawèn* way to wisdom and an ethical life.

Whichever the case, to live attuned to what is greater than oneself, be it the order of society or cosmos, cannot but be moral and wise. The disturbance of it is immoral and foolish. Since society is part of the totality, respect for its pattern may already signify reverence for the system of Life and a way of honouring 'God'.[3] One's moral obligation is to fulfil one's life and position in the world, therefore eschatological speculation and expectations are only weakly developed. Life is essentially in the here-and-now.

The *kejawèn* stress on *kebatinan* leads to a strong self-centredness. In one's *batin*, one is important; the reality of society, its rules and sufferings should be accepted, but the real truth is contained in the deep self. A person's moral and ethical task is to cultivate the mind, seek wisdom, and fulfil his place in a universe of unequal positions. Harmonious relationships with others guarantee an undisturbed *batin*/inner life, while at the same time, conflict avoidance, self-centredness, and self-fulfilment foster a great measure of tolerance vis-à-vis other persons. In one's *batin*, everybody is potentially free in a restrictive, hierarchically ordered society.

People who cultivate their *batin* by way of ascetic exercises may do so for all kinds of secular purposes, such as concern *(prihatin)* about one's immediate course in life or the future of one's children. It is an expression of taking life seriously, of taking care. Some people practise *kebatinan* for a religious purpose, such as mysticism. Because there is no dividing line between the secular and the sacred in *kejawèn* thinking, it is hard to say whether the *kejawèn* way of life is in itself an expression of *agami jawi*, as the Javanese religion is called.[4] This much is certain, the *kejawèn* philosophy of life fosters a religious attitude, mysticism, and self-centredness, while at the same time it devalues expectations about an after-life, institutionalized religion, and the fulfilment of the latter's religious obligations.

---

3 In single quotation marks, 'God' refers to the more immanent *kejawèn* concept; without them, God refers to the more transcendent Middle-Eastern idea.

4 If Javanese religion can be defined by its practices, I suggest that the observance of the *slametan* rituals, the paying of respect and prayer to deceased parents (also rulers and religious personalities) at their graves, and periodical offerings *(sesajèn)* to spirits may be considered as defining characteristics.

Rasa

Naturally, the *kejawèn* perspective allows for the analysis of reality at a number of levels, which was noted above, for instance, in the division of a phenomenal *lair* world and its inner *batin* core, as also in the recognition of a world of rationality and a less volitional world of mystery. All these seem to combine at the level of *rasa*. Mystically and practically, *rasa* may be described as the intuitive inner feeling that is an element of everyone, some people having a more refined *rasa* than others, thus being sensitive to things that escape the latters' attention.

In its most common sense *rasa* means 'taste' and 'feeling', such as the taste of rice or the feeling of sickness; it means the physical sense of touch, as well. Yet it also stands for the fundamental nature of a substance, or its true being. It is the personal instrument leading to true insight, being one's essence and one's part in The Essence. Often it is interchanged with *rahsa*, *rahasya*, meaning secret, hidden, mysterious, and in one of its meanings, semen, it may stand for 'vehicle of life'.

Often Javanese juxtapose *rasa* and ordinary common sense *(nalar; akal)*, or the instrument for understanding the phenomenal world and its mundane affairs. Such rationality, though, cannot reveal the essence of that world; this can only be grasped by the personal intuitive inner feeling. In the *kejawèn* perspective, real knowledge is both mysterious and subjective; it is personal insight into the true nature of things that cannot be formulated objectively. It is in and from oneself that 'truth' can be grasped through training in intuitive sensitivity. Consequently, the *kejawèn* quest for knowledge is informed by fascination for mystery, and the elusive knowledge of 'God' is no better than a personal experience. No wonder then that there is an absence of dogma and generally accepted theology. These latter will naturally be absent from an essentially open-ended idea of knowledge that emphasizes the development of the personal *rasa*.

It comes, therefore, as no surprise that Javanese teachings should be full of symbolism and esoteric knowledge *(ngèlmu)* that stimulate fantasy and reflection. Such teachings are also contained in the old *wayang purwa* mythology that is inspired by the Mahabharata, in which life on earth appears to be a mere reflection, a shadow of higher truth and realities. The illumination so attained can only be intuited rather than reasoned, which contrasts sharply with the themes of the modern *wayang* shadow plays that have, for instance, the birth of Christ as their subject. That Catholic innovation attempts to communicate a message through scenes that spell out an explicit orthodoxy, which by its nature cannot stimulate a variety of interpretations, nor foster free association around its symbolism; it thus does not stimulate the Javanese predilection for mystery. True *wayang* is subjective, transcending historical truth, while opening visions of personal recognition in a symbolic idiom. Somehow, things are not so interesting nor so much fun if they are plain and clear.

This contrast between the interest in objective versus subjective knowledge is also borne out by the experience of a European Catholic priest working as a long-time missionary in Java. Teaching in seminary, he told me about his frustrations in explaining the importance of the historicity of Christ. The fact that Jesus had been there, that he was a historical person who had really been on earth, was the keystone of his faith. Yet he complained that his Javanese students were not impressed by such facts, being far more interested in the mystical significance of Christ. I think that no Christian Javanese will take it as a mere coincidence that the European priest's name was Thomas.

Order

The unity of existence is essentially mysterious, yet it constitutes a regulated order of which life on earth is also an expression, a shadow *(wayangan)*, as it were, of higher truth. This unity is subject to cosmic law, the *ukum pinesthi*, which states that all creation has to run its preordained course. Life, while setting limits to experience, purpose and volition, is also an inevitable, inescapable progression for all without exception. It is an ordered and coordinated whole, which people must accept, and to which they should adapt themselves. After all, it can only be wise to live in tune with that which is greater than oneself.

Consequently, people have the moral duty to respect life's order. They should acquiesce in life as it comes while cultivating a state of inner peace and emotional calm. Impulsive actions, or yielding to one's lusts and desires by giving free rein to passions, are reprehensible because they upset personal, social and cosmic order. Therefore one should master oneself, inwardly and outwardly, while trying to shape life beautifully.

Accepting *(nrima)* means knowing one's place, means trust in fate and gratefulness to 'God', because there is satisfaction in fulfilling one's lot in the consciousness that all has been destined. One should consciously follow the path of destiny from which, anyhow, there is no escaping. This does not mean that a person should not strive to make the best of it, because he can only know the results of his lot by the outcome of deeds. It thus makes sense to be active in shaping life in the consciousness of fulfilling one's task in the great order.

This notion of task, or obligation to station in life, is illustrated by the well-known episode from the Mahabharata cycle in which the hero Karna has to face Arjuna. Karna is the half-brother of Arjuna and the other Pendawa — the five brothers who symbolize order, righteousness and justice. In the great war of the Bharata Yudha, they have to fight their cousins, the Kurawa, who stand for the forces of disorder, passion and desire. It is Karna's lot to serve on the side of the Kurawa, thus facing his half-brothers in battle. After having killed Gathutkaca, Bima's favourite son, he knows that he will have to die at the hands of Arjuna. As a noble warrior *(satriya)*, he is true to his position in life, his fate and obligation to his king, fighting valiantly until he is killed. It was his opponent Arjuna who hesitated and wavered, reluctant to accept his duty to kill Karna. Upon turning to his divine counsellor Kresna, he is urged to carry out his duty, this wavering being weak and condemnable, because it is his destiny to kill Karna.

While both finally fulfilled their duty in implementing the course of history, to many the real hero is Karna, personifying the moral example of a man who follows his duty and destiny without hesitation; his fate is in the hands of 'God' and the best he can do is to accept it and shape it beautifully. Such is a true hero; such is also a moral man. Life and destiny are ordered in a scheme that is beyond human volition, and in which moral choice means faithfulness to position and obligation.[5]

5 For elaboration and other interesting interpretations of *wayang*, see Boediardjo, Wayang: a reflection of the aspirations of the Javanese (H. Soebadio and C.A. du Marchie Sarvaas (eds), *Dynamics of Indonesian history*. Amsterdam, etc.: North-Holland Publishing Co., 1978:97-122).

The fact that life is subject to cosmic law and part of an inescapable order stimulates fascination with prophecy and projective action. Because the cosmic design has been 'fixed', it may also be known and it remains a matter of discovering its coordinates to know the future. Prediction is thus possible if one has access to the great scheme by way of meditation or mystical practice, magical calculation or knowledge of horoscopy.

For example, when walking the streets of Yogya, one may come across a group of tricycle drivers squatting on the pavement, one of them scribbling figures and lines on the ground. They are busy discussing the meaning of a revealing symbol that has, perhaps, been published in that day's newspaper; they are calculating the outcome of next Saturday's lottery. They are searching for the truth, as it were, for the hidden shape of reality to come. Part of that secret has already been revealed in the published symbol. It is up to them to interpret it and to calculate the number that is predestined, although not yet visible. Theirs is a very utilitarian attempt to discover the as yet unrevealed course of the future.

Events do not happen because of chance but manifest themselves because of hidden forces that bring about each co-incidence *(kebeneran)*. A new event is a cross-road, a co-inciding, in which the shadow of inevitability becomes a fact. This notion of causality is at the same time both extremely pragmatic and deeply mystical, giving reason to activity and the endeavour to uncover the coordinated structure of events to come. Therefore, one needs to calculate auspicious days to start a venture, and marriage partners should be matched on the basis of characterological and horoscopical singularities to ensure that they fit *(cocog)*. Once the right formula or the right coordinates have been established, action may be initiated in the expectation that it will develop auspiciously, in other words, without causing disturbance of good order.

Sometimes conditions and events may be recognized as threatening and potentially disturbing, in which case they should be constrained by ceremony and ritual. Basically, such constraining *(ngruwat)* is an attempt to change inauspicious coordinates to orderly ones, to undo the evil spell that hovers over persons who suffer from involuntary states of affliction (who are *sukerta*). Long lists can be drawn of inauspicious birth constellations and other circumstances that attract danger, thus calling for ritual intervention, which demonstrates that the coordinated nature of the unity of existence is two-sided: man plays as much a role in the working of order as any of the other impersonal forces that influence it. Naturally, this idea stimulates the desire to make order transparent. Yet even if momentarily crystal clear, order, much like the knowledge of it, remains shifting and elusive; it thus makes sense to influence its course by ritual and projective action. Whatever the case, the disturbance of good order is basically sinful, as it is also to upset it by emotion or magical practice. On the other hand, action that is directed at redressing order, or its auspicious continuation, is right in itself.

Slametan

The core ritual to sustain, maintain, or promote order is the *slametan*, a communal socio-religious meal in which neighbours plus some relatives and friends participate. Their purpose is to achieve the state of *slamet*, which is "a state in which events will run their fixed course smoothly and nothing untoward will happen to anyone" (Koentjaraningrat, 1960:95).

Such invocations are held on the occasion of all life crises and of communal cyclical events in order to ensure undisturbed continuity. They are also held on all sorts of occasions when well-being and equilibrium have been affected. In theory, all participants enjoy the same ritual status, each person contributing equally to the spiritual power of the event. The *slametan*, therefore, serves to demonstrate harmonious community *(rukun)* which is the prerequisite to invoke effectively the blessing of gods, spirits and ancestors (Geertz, 1960:11-5, 30-85).

They also demonstrate the desire to be safeguarded from danger in an unruly world. They do not aim at a better life, now or in the future, but rather at the maintenance of order and the constraining of danger. It also appears, however, that humans play an active role in maintaining this order and can influence its course, well-ordered social relationships being a means and a condition to promote the state of *slamet*.

Continuance of life

The social pattern is often thought to be the microcosm of the order of Life, the basic model of which is the family. It is the normal task of every adult to seek the continuation of life within Life, to marry and to have offspring. Parents, having been born before their children, are in a superior moral position and have the duty to care for their children from before birth until they are married, when the latter take over the task of continuing the lineage.

Apart from being givers of life and moral superiors, progenitors are also an important source of blessing *(restu)* for their children. At the end of the fasting month of Pasa (Ramadan), they should present themselves before their parents, kneeling in front of them *(sungkem)* in order to ask their forgiveness, while seeking their blessing. But also after their death, children should visit their graves during the month Ruah that precedes Pasa. There, the merit *(jasa)* of parents is thought to flow as a protective magical force out to their descendants who will pray to them and seek their guidance.[6]

Parents, as representatives of life and its order, are entitled to the highest honour, and children should *ngabekti*, that is, pay homage and service to them as a quasi-religious act. To respect their moral superiority is honouring Life, which is often further elaborated in the notion that honouring elder siblings, parents, teachers, and the ruler is equivalent to revering 'God'. This notion very clearly demonstrates the hierarchical concept of order, in which the inferior should respect all those who are closer to the sources of life, moral wisdom and power. To live in harmony with the encompassing order is moral behaviour per se.

In consequence, it is sinful not to honour one's parents, not to accept their advice, or to hurt their feelings. Such behaviour is thought to establish a serious infraction of the moral order and will invoke automatic supernatural retribution *(walat)*. This powerful sanction, that is especially relevant to understanding the inviolable and exalted character of the position of parents, is one of the best safeguards for the mainte-

---

6 Many serious Muslims will also visit the graves of their parents but they will, of course, not pray to them; they will pray to God to receive and bless the souls of their parents. This tallies closely with the *kejawèn* notion that the well-being of the souls of parents is dependent on the honour and offerings they receive.

nance of ordered relationships conducive to the state of *slamet*.

Social relationships beyond those with one's parents are generally not thought to be protected by supernatural sanctions, although the quest for *slamet* and serene propriety in the here-and-now naturally places great emphasis on the maintenance of good relationships with one's fellows. For ritual efficacy, one is dependent on the goodwill and participation of neighbours when holding a *slametan*, even if these primarily serve personal and familial purposes. Therefore, it is imperative to cultivate good relationships by practising *rukun*, respecting others' feelings, and being tolerant in matters of religious opinion. Moreover, one should contribute to common rituals, such as communal *slametan* and burials.

Kebatinan

However imperative all the foregoing, nonetheless the vital core of *kejawèn* is thought to be in *kebatinan*, by which is meant the cultivation of one's inner being and covert self. It is that deep self that really constitutes the quintessential microcosm of all-encompassing Life. In many characteristic similies, the experience of life itself is described as a journey from origin to destination, from conception to reabsorption with the All. In the *kejawèn* perspective, this self-training should move from the outside to the inside, from the mastery of the *lair* to the cultivation of the *batin*, from becoming fully aware of one's social surroundings to becoming sensitized to the presence of Life and the realization of it in one's inner being; it means coordinating the self with higher truth until one fuses with it.

This idea of the journey on one's way to truth and self-realization is vividly illustrated by the well-known Dewaruci story of the Mahabharata mythology. That story relates Bima's quest to discover the secret of life. Soon after setting out, he is led astray by false advice, while later on meeting with all kinds of dreadful dangers and the trials in the wilderness that he has to undergo before he is taught that he will find the secret — the water of life — hidden in the profundity of the ocean. When, after overcoming further challenges, he finally reaches the depths of the ocean, he meets with a miniature double of himself,

Dewaruci, who instructs Bima to enter through its ear in order to find the secret of life. This story symbolizes the lonely mystical quest of man who has to overcome himself before he is led to the source of truth and wisdom, that he can only discover by descending into the depth of his own inner being. After conquering his passions and delusions, it is there that 'God' can be found, the unity of existence ultimately being realized in one's deep self.

The basis of Javanese culture lies in self-mastery and, deriving from this, in the capacity to shape life beautifully. In its deeper dimensions, it centres on the cultivation of the self in order to realize the perfection of life, irrespective of one's social surroundings. It is an ethical way to wisdom and perfection that need not be religiously expressed, although it always entails the cultivation of the *batin* and the exercise of refining one's intuitive inner feeling, or *rasa,* to sense the true dimensions of existence. To follow this path, one should be trained: "When one is young and ignorant, father is needed as the first teacher. Then one seeks for a teacher *(guru)* who knows more, or other things, then on to others, until ultimately Bathara Guru ('God') takes over". At that last stage, of course, each person is alone, the discrete individual becoming the centre of insight in life, and its order.

In a more mystical perspective, this thinking is expressed in the idea of achieving unity between servant and Master *(manunggaling kawula-Gusti).* To reach this, one has to overcome the fetters that tie each individual to phenomenal existence, such as passions and worldly rationality, that only lead to a delusive perception of truth. In the same vein, the mystical adept should be free from egoistic motives *(pamrih)* in training his inner self to be attuned to Life. Social life and its ritual exigencies, including the ceremonies of formal religion, become mere outward requirements that are useful as disciplinary practice, but far from profound experience. The latter is the truly important dimension of life, giving access to truth, guidance, and revelation from 'God'.

The practice of *kebatinan* is an individual-centred endeavour that places the deep self, that is, the "true I" *(Aku; ingsun sejati)* at the very centre of all evaluation. It is the development of one's *rasa* that becomes the measuring rod of inner growth. The ultimate stage is to realize the conviction that one lives in step with Life, and that one has access to truth in a direct and unmediated way, drawing power from

'God' at the same time that one is independent from sources of truth outside the deep self. The practice of *kebatinan* may thus be seen as a personal pursuit toward self-realization by building up strong inner resources so that finally one is guided by divine revelation *(wahyu)* and ultimate truth *(kasunyatan)*. Its basis is the conviction that individual life and inner feeling constitute the valid centre of all experience, and the ultimate empirical and self-validating testing ground for truth (Geertz, 1960:318).

CHAPTER 4

Filipino religiosity as an expression of

family relationships

This chapter seeks to clarify the way people think of their relationships with near others and with religious representations. As such, it is the analysis of a mentality, a way of viewing the world, as it was found in research among members of the educated, urban middle classes of Tagalog Filipino society. That is not to say that everybody thinks this way or, especially where religion comes in, that there would not be people whose thinking is secular, or who are doctrinal or rational Catholics. What is presented is a typological description of a dominant mentality in which individual people share to a greater or lesser extent.

In this mindset, relationships with family members and near others are thought to be really intimate. What this implies will be described as the positive mentality that guides these relationships. It then becomes evident that the same world view inspires lowland 'popular' religiosity. The relation to things religious is intimate *par excellence*, and religion seems to be a 'natural' part of everyday life. In the process of its localization religious representations have been domesticated, so to say, and they are readily accessible. This will be described in the second part.

Thinking about relationships with near others

According to Enriquez's *sikolohiyang Pilipino* (Philippine psychology), the notion of personality as elaborated in western psychology does not correspond to the way individuals are supposed to function in the Philippines. In consequence, he proposed the notion of *pagkatao* as an appropriate counterpart. While on the one hand, western psychology sees personality as the expression of the individual in and by himself, in isolation as it were, on the other, *pagkatao* would correspond with the Philippine situation in which individuals do not define themselves as separated from others, but include *kapwa* ('the other') in their identity definition. *Kapwa* is the unity of 'self' and 'others', and expresses ego's awareness of shared identity (1989:26,43).

At the time that Enriquez began to formulate the characteristics of a Philippine psychology, he was especially irritated by the interpretations of Philippine behaviour reached by the researchers associated with the Institute of Philippine Culture (IPC). Their notion of *pakikisama* (to get along with others) drew his ire as being far too facile and, in addition, only descriptive of a certain type of relationship. In its place, Enriquez developed a scale to describe the intensity of relationships, ranging from *pakikitungo* ('transaction/civility with') through *pakikisama* ('being along with') to *pakikiisa* ('being one with'). While the lower levels of intensity, including *pakikisama*, are descriptive of relationships with *ibáng tao* (outsiders; literally other/different/strange people), the higher levels concern the *hindî ibáng tao* or near others, with whom identity sharing becomes deep (*ibid.*:31-3).

Some form of identity sharing would seem to be the normal occurrence in relationships among Filipinos. According to Enriquez, people refusing to take positive account of others somehow lose their *pagkatao* ('personhood') and *pakikipagkapwa* ('shared inner self'), that is, their essential human quality; in doing so, they place themselves beyond the pale of civil society (*ibid.*:35,45). "We Filipinos really care about the feelings of others."

Here it is not an apposite point to observe that 'identity sharing' is mystical and mysterious, since it lacks objective verification, nor does it matter that it can be criticized as psychological theorizing that appears to be completely out of date. The interesting thing about Enriquez's work is that he attempts to develop culturally relevant concepts on the basis of current Tagalog vocabulary, and that his work may therefore be relevant to this attempt to understand how people think about their relationships. In a slightly different way, such thinking also surfaces in the works of his Filipino colleagues who phrase their psychology of 'the Filipino' in the more general (western) conventions that Enriquez protests against.

According to Bulatao, family-type relationships, socialization practices, and inescapable togetherness all foster the intensive experience of oneself as a member of a closed group rather than as a separate self. He describes this phenomenon with the comparative notion of 'unindividuated ego' (1964:430). As a result, one's interpersonal world becomes the primary source of emotional gratification, the successful negotiation of interpersonal affairs with family and friends bringing reassurance, recognition, and material rewards, thus gratifying the need for security and acceptance (Lapuz, 1978).

The need for security and acceptance leads to the observation that a person's self-esteem derives from how he is perceived by others, thus making for conformity to group opinions, timidity and unassertiveness (*Signal*, 1985). It also inclines individuals to seek security in role enactment. In Bulatao's opinion, this often results in an 'inferiority complex' for which the educated person "will blame colonial powers for imposing upon him a 'colonial mentality'", but that more accurately should be seen as the product of the suffocatingly close ties that allow for insufficient development of the self (1964:434).

Therefore, Bulatao describes the Filipino as somebody whose individual core is identifiable but whose ego-boundaries blend with those of others (*ibid.*:431), an interpretation that Arellano-Carandang refers to as a relative degree of differentiation (1987:66-7). Filipinos perceive themselves as members of groups and have group-dependent identities. So the basic unit of society is not the individual, but the closed group (Bulatao: interview 1988).

While I can sympathize with Enriquez's quest for positive, Filipino-based terminology to describe Philippine psychology (Enriquez, 1989:47-66), the basic interpretations of others are remarkably similar. Even though the idea of identity-sharing appears to be inaccessible to empirical observation, and cannot be operationalized, Filipinos seem, and believe themselves to be, highly dependent on their family for identity, reassurance, and psychological well-being.

Whatever the ensuing psychological interpretations, we can certainly accept the above as statements about lowland Christian Philippine culture, about a shared system of perception and 'knowledge'. This is, for instance, apparent from the Civil Code that states, "The family, being the foundation of the nation, is a basic social institution which public policy cherishes and protects".[1] It is also apparent from the title of a collection of articles about family roles that is unwittingly or deliberately called *Being Filipino,*[2] as if to be a member of a family is the Filipinos most striking quality. According to the authors of the 'Shahani Report',

> To the Filipino, one's family is the source of personal identity, the source of emotional and material support, and one's main commitment and responsibility... This sense of family results in a feeling of belonging and rootedness and in a basic sense of security.[3]

Belonging, rootedness and identity, emotional support and security, are located in deeply felt relationships. The high emotional charge of these relationships may lead to the ideas of identity sharing, of direct participation in each other's *loób* (inner being), and thus to the widespread idea that people who are near and dear to each other easily empathize. We may formulate this as the dependent experience of the self, as dependent subjectivity.

Dependent subjectivity makes for a high degree of sensitivity to the quality of interpersonal relationships, for vulnerability of self and others in those relationships, and thus for a measure of insecurity and the desire to please the other in order to be accepted. It also causes people to see others as extensions of themselves. This may be especially so in the relationship of parents with their offspring.

Children are generally seen as a blessing from God and the inspiration of life; an enormous amount of emotion is invested in them. Parents tend to identify with their successes and failures, the child becoming their substitute self. No wonder they may think that they

1 According to the Constitution of 1987, Article II, section 12, "The State recognizes the sanctity of family life and shall protect and strengthen the family as a basic autonomous social institution". The idea of this autonomy as the foundation of society makes the family very much the exemplary centre of social life in the Philippines.

2 Hilda Cordero-Fernando (ed), *Being Filipino.* Quezon City: GCF Books, 1981.

3 *Building a People, Building a Nation. A Moral Recovery Program.* A report submitted by Senator Leticia Ramos-Shahani to the Committee on Education, Arts and Culture and the Committee on Social Justice, Welfare and Development. May 9, 1988. Published by the Instructional Materials Corporation for the Department of Education, Culture and Sports, Republic of the Philippines. Page 2.

know their child inside and out, that it has no secrets from them. This rationalises their interfering in the child's affairs, a constant meddling *(makialám)* that the child should understand as an expression of concern, love and acceptance.

People's emotional dependence on their progeny reinforces the authority structure of the family: parents require unquestioning obedience. It is also expressed in possessiveness and the overprotection that they extend, especially to their daughters. Needless to say, such impositions do not foster the growth of psychological independence in adolescence. The contrary is the case, resulting in a circle in which lowly individuated parents, especially mothers, rear lowly individuated children (Bulatao, 1964:436).

In the emotion-charged setting of the family, a child will be kept in line by the threat of non-acceptance, the withdrawal of love. Psychologically dependent on others, with parents in full control of its conscience, the growing Filipino child will particularly develop the right section of his brain. According to this theory of Bulatao, in that lobe the ego is not prominent and the self gets lost, leading to an unself-aware individualism that orientates itself on outside others.[4] A person belongs to and lays claims on others. It is these others, with the members of the family, the household, at the centre, that delineate a person's moral universe. In this way of thinking, one's conscience is located in tangible relationships with other known people; one's conscience is consciousness of them and their opinions. The most important of those links involve the recognition of goodness received and the ensuing moral obligations. To renege on these is not merely shameful but comes close to committing sin, and activates feelings of guilt.

To develop an independent self-esteem, a child needs first of all to distance itself from its parents. This seems to be very difficult in such a context. Psychiatrist Lourdes Lapuz muses, "Perhaps, some day, the time will come when a Filipino no longer has to cross miles of ocean and continent to emancipate himself from his parents" (1978). The

---

4 Bulatao speaks about a 'jeepney-driver individualism' that is oriented to the outside, guided by 'radar' as it were, in which the self is not the source of action or judgement. In cultures that foster the development of the left section of the brain, individuation, or the development of a prominent self, would lead to a greater degree of independence. Such a person would show the characteristics of a 'gyroscope' (interviews 1987, '88).

Filipino's self-definition is profoundly relational; he is bound to a group, a family and his parents to such an extent that even when married, his mother will be accorded precedence over his wife (Lapuz, 1977:57-8, 60-1).

It is from these bonds that a person may derive his psychological, material and moral security. He is not alone in the insecure wider world surrounding his primary group of near others. Within his group, he is accepted, cared for, and will be forgiven, all the solidary inner relationships providing a safety net against his lapses or transgressions. Because of this, his mutual loyalty in return should be unquestioning.

So far, this presentation of relationships in the world of intimates has not taken much account of the negative aspects of closeness and togetherness (chapter 10). This has been done in order to present the positive side of a mentality guiding familial relationships, while describing its psychological and moral underpinnings and consequences, because it is these that are expressed in lowland Christian Philippine religious symbolization. As its salient characteristics, we found the ideas of low degree of individuation, 'identity sharing' and empathy, dependent subjectivity, primacy of family and moral obligation, emotional and moral dependence, and the validity of emotions.

Religious representation of family relationships

One common widespread Asian belief is that concerning the role which souls of the recently dead play in the affairs of their surviving kin. The ones that are particularly important are those of parents and grandparents whom one has known personally. As trusted near and dear relatives, one can be sure that they have the interest of their offspring at heart, that they listen to their prayers, have a continual interest in family affairs,[5] and will be present at family reunions.

---

5 "Filipinos also believe that spirits of their dead kinsmen take an interest in the needs of the living relatives and feel hurt when they are not remembered" (L.N. Mercado (ed.) *Filipino religious psychology.* Tacloban: Divine Word University, 1977:26). Consequently family-centred church ritual, such as marriage, is often seen as a means to inform dead relatives (J.M. de Mesa, *In solidarity with the culture. Studies in theological re-rooting.* Quezon City: Mary Hill School of Theology, 1987:196).

The occasion on which this becomes especially evident is *undrás,* that is, *Todos los Santos* on the first of November when people congregate in the cemeteries for a festive picnic with food, candles and prayer offerings to the dead. Their souls are not only accessible, but actually participate in the family party, and so it is not so strange that the most prestigious cemetery in Lucena puts up some masts with loudspeakers from which pop music blares to mark the festive occasion (1-11-89).

When asked, "How come that you people celebrate All Souls' Day on All Saints' Day?", a quick-witted Filipino answered that everybody in heaven is a saint and that people cannot imagine their dear ones to be any place else. But wherever the souls may be, they can be addressed and will respond to prayer. For instance, on a day when one has to go out into the rain, having forgotten 'the good old umbrella', a short plea to one's deceased grandpa may often help to stop the shower. Psychologically, this continued concern of such souls for their descendants is very reassuring, and so they are particularly invoked when people are troubled because of the anger of others. The spirits of the departed can console the supplicant and ward off any threat of revenge.

Besides these souls, the presence of saints whose images stand on house altars, as well as in churches and chapels, is also taken into account. Often such figures are well cared for, being provided with a change of dress at the appropriate times, and at home they may be treated as trusted relatives whom one caresses and touches. This tangible presence may express more than mere fondness or the desire for nearness. Many statues are believed to harbour *bisà*, a potency that may cure illness, protect from harm, or strengthen psychical resources. It is through touch that this potency is transferred to the devotee.

The central and most important personage in the pantheon of saints is the Virgin Mary. The Philippines is a Marian country and the Holy Mother is its patroness. This special relationship is also expressed at the individual level and ritual practices and prayers addressing her are very common and widespread. As a good mother, she is dear to most Filipinos, and she is supposed to care for and help all those who invoke her name. Although her cult is also a reflection of the familial cult of the mother, the most popular statues of the Holy Virgin, for instance, of the apparitions at Lourdes or Fatima, are those without a child, which radiate purity, calm and grace. Besides these ubiquitous effigies, her picture as the Mother of Perpetual Help, always represented with child, is most commonly seen. How deeply she is adored and venerated in the Philippines is perhaps best demonstrated by the initiative of the local hierarchy in celebrating the year 1985 as her 2000th birthday. During that year, Marian devotions were intensified and the anniversary itself was celebrated with huge birthday cakes, their appearance greeted by the strains of "Happy Birthday Mama Mary".[6]

Through her intercession, the Holy Mother responded to the intensive prayers. Shortly after the Marian year celebrations had ended, the dictator Ferdinand Marcos was ousted in the 'revolution of the rosaries', and then fled into exile.[7] It was obvious that God cared for the Philippines and had intervened in its destiny. The event was subsequently declared a miracle, and the Eucharistic year celebrations of 1987 could rightfully be proclaimed to be taking place in the *bayang pinili ng Diyos* (God's chosen country).

The Philippines is a place of miracles and wondrous things are an accepted commonplace occurrence. God's power and grace are manifested by mediums and faith healers, by apparitions and the sun spinning over Manila,[8] by power-laden images of saints and the mystical nature of Mt. Banahaw, where holy history is re-enacted in pilgrimages that bring a person closest to God.[9] Stones from the crater are thought

6 All this is beautifully illustrated in H.Q. Dee *et al.* (eds), *Bimillenium. 1985 Marian Yearbook*. Metro Manila: Bahay Maria, 1986.

7 Because of the great role of religious symbolism and prayer it seems appropriate in this context to refer to the events of February 1986 as 'the revolution of the rosaries'. It was "Flowers against bullets. Rosaries against tanks. Love vs. force" (Joseph Sta. Maria, The Immaculate Heart and the Philippines, *Ave María* II/2:23 (1986)).

8 Interest in miracles, apparitions, saintly intercession, etc., must be strong if we consider the amount of newspaper space devoted to such things in the English language press.

9 It is often held that Banahaw and Rizalista cults are the exclusive preoccupation of simple, mostly rural folk. This does not seem to be the case. My contacts with Banahaw mysticism came through four university-educated professionals in Lucena City, who regularly participated in a Tayabas-based medium-centred cult. My experiences with faith-healing have been with thoroughly middle-class people, too. This point is also made by Takefumi Terada in his UP dissertation, *The spirit cult of Santo Niño: an anthropological study of popular religiosity in the Philippines*, "Many economically well-off, educated, intellectual individuals are also participating in the activities as principal supporters" (1987:223).

to make efficacious amulets with curative properties. The devotees of the Iglesia ni Cristo hold their founder to be an angel of God, while to the folks around Calamba, the national hero and martyr José Rizal has become the equivalent of the Holy Spirit of the Trinity. They expect him to reappear and to free his people from injustice and oppression, thus inaugurating the millenium.

The supernatural in all its aspects appears to be entwined with nature, to be directly involved in human affairs, to be very much a part of daily life. What's more, its major manifestations seem to be protective and benign. So people automatically turn to things religious when looking for help. According to IPC research, trust in God even outranks obedience to parents, and is asserted to be the most important child-rearing value (Porio *et al.*, 1981:27-8). When feeling alone or worried, when others are out of reach, people will pray, 'talk with God', and they may forgo pleasures in a personal sacrifice as a special offering just to please God. God can and should be trusted. After all, everything is in His hands; "He is not mad and knows what He is doing".

This trust in the divine presence is pervasive, and especially expressed in attitudes of intimate dependence. In this context, it is of interest to consider the similarity in the opinions of a professor-procurator of a seminary and a charismatic, yet simple-minded leader of a popular mystical cult. In a well-humoured way, the learned priest expressed his reliance on God's bounty, at the same time that he underlined God's caring responsibility for man:

> I agree. In the Philippines, miracles happen every day. Think about this seminary. Every week I need 10,000 pesos to feed the people here and I can only account for a thousand or so. Yet, the money is there, every week. Obviously God provides. Well, He should, because if we are expected to carry out His work, then He had better see to it that the money is there to do it.

The mystic functions as a medium in typical all-night waking sessions. Then he impersonates both God, the Santo Niño, and other holy personages. During Holy Week he leads his flock up along the power-laden stations (*puwesto*) on the slopes of the Mount Banahaw. Then the continuous invocation of *Amá* (Father) is guaranteeing the safety of the worshippers in negotiating the hazardous passages that are an intrinsic part of that purifying pilgrimage. He expressed his trust in God thus:

> God is our Servant, a servant upon whom we can depend if we approach him by way of personal sacrifices. It is the Devil who is out in the open, who is the lord *(panginoón)* who wants to be served by us.

God is invoked at the beginning of almost every type of endeavour, whether the opening of a session of the Senate, at the outset of a voyage, the inauguration of a snack-bar, or a social event at the tennis club. His presence is seen as a matter of course, and is manifested in the multitude of religious symbols, from the "God bless our trip" sign in a public conveyance to the omnipresent Santo Niño, from the space devoted to religion in newspapers to the national postage stamps, from jeepneys named "Immaculate Concepcion" and "St. Peter" to the halo on the figurine of Jesus in an up-country bus lighting up in white when speeding, or His holy heart gleaming in red when stepping on the brake.

This ubiquitous symbolization hints at nearness, intimacy, accessibility. In poetry, one may find sentences about "God my Brother", in advertising about "friendship between God and man", on a sticker in a vehicle above the driver's seat "God is my co-pilot". A progressive action group is called "Friends of Jesus", in the Ateneo high school they talk about *Kuya Jess* (Older Brother Jesus). It seems that people feel not only friendship but even sometimes kinship with the holy family.

This intimate relationship is expressed in the feelings of dependence already hinted at, and in the emotional identification and empathy with the suffering of Jesus and His Mother. Naturally, this suffering comes very much to the forefront during Holy Week when the emotion-charged passion of Christ is re-enacted all over the country, but it is also present when visiting a church, or while praying to and touching the image of the tormented Christ. Extreme identification appears on the part of the flagellants during Holy Week when they embark on this task in order "to help Christ and share in his ordeal", their participation in His once-a-year torment making them His bosom friends.[10]

10 Fernando N. Zialcita, Popular interpretations of the passion of Christ. *Philippine Sociological Review* 34/1-4 (1986):59.

The most domesticated personage is the Holy Child. Over the past thirty years His popularity has grown by leaps and bounds, and His image has been adopted by all and sundry. He is the protector of both the gays and the firemen, is dressed as a fisherman in villages along the coast, in *barong tagalog* in night clubs but, by contrast, was portrayed in his birthday suit as the *Santo Niño ng Kalayaan* (Holy Child of Freedom) during the first anniversary celebrations of Marcos's flight. Normally, the Sto. Niño is dressed up in rich 16th century European garb, in red or green, and he may be found on the house altar, as also at the pay-desk of many a shop since, apart from all kinds of blessings ascribed to the Holy Child, he is especially thought to attract money "because people like to give to a child". Being a child makes the Sto. Niño easy to please and often people cajole Him in hopes He will grant their wishes.

The intimacy with the holy family, the Trusted Father, Mama Mary and Older Brother Jesus/Santo Niño, makes them seem an extension of one's own family, part of one's identity as it were, with whom one feels in direct emotional contact. Since they symbolize the positive aspects of these relationships, such an intimacy emphasizes trust, protection, dependence, consolation, and even playfulness in the case of the Sto. Niño.

This closeness to the holy family is not marred by feelings of sin. Sin and guilt are specific to concrete links with known persons. So it is, for example, insolence to one's parents that needs to be atoned for.[11] Sin and guilt are not located in the idealized bonds with God as a fatherly friend and protective father, or with Mama Mary as a pure, caring, and forgiving mother, or with Jesus as a reliable elder brother or friend. They understand and accept human weakness. As long as one tries to be a good son or daughter, as long as one proves to be a reliable friend, misdeeds will be smoothed over and one can be sure of acceptance, as long as one sticks to the basics of the family code.

Family relationships, whether idealized or actual, are subjective,

---

11 Zialcita's research among flagellants provides interesting detail: whereas adults engaged in the practice to redeem a vow and to ensure health and physical strength, and thus sacrificed for a future objective, young adolescents felt obliged to submit to the ritual because they had wronged their kinsmen and could in this manner publicly express their repentance (1986:60).

personalized, negotiable and emotional. They do not represent a fixed moral order. On the contrary, because of intimacy and emotional identification with the holy family, as well as with one's own, people may remain little individuated and judge each other by the quality of their interpersonal relationships. So, as a result, sin as the infraction of God's law, and its confession — which means self-assessment by external criteria and which involves an exercise in painful, individuating self-criticism — are not deeply meaningful categories in the religious mentality.[12]

The absence of any deep sense of sin does not mean that one expects to be free from suffering. It is impossible to know God's reasons and plans, but one knows that He can be trusted. Moreover, suffering seems to be an intrinsic part of life, dramatized in the passion of Christ and the grief of Mary. Suffering is the lot of the righteous, a way of purification that may give the courage to struggle on. The way out of it, if any, appears to lie more in prayer and personal sacrifices than in repentance and seeking forgiveness; such religious practice is future directed and not intended to redeem a sinful past.

In summary, emotional participation in the sphere of religion goes hand in hand with a low degree of individuation. People are intimate with their religious representations — their holy family and saints — that seem to participate directly, in a literal and tangible way, in their lives. Fascinated with and trustful of supernature, miracles are only to be expected, and prayer must be effective, an attitude which often results in a childlike faith but also in naive credulity.[13]

12 Priests complain that people who come for confession tend to explain their 'sins' in terms of circumstances, of being pushed into a certain action by family or friends, blaming others for their transgressions. Consequently, a sense of repentance often seems to be lacking. The concept of sin was introduced by the Spanish missionaries who coined a word from the root *sala*, which means mis-take, missing the target. Yet to miss or err is merely human, and is perceived as no good reason for extreme sanctions. Moreover, priests err also, they are human, too. So why go and confess to a fellow human being who may commit the same errors? (The notions of sin, guilt, and repentance are, of course, known and often even alive among those who attended Catholic schools for many years.)

13 After giving a long list of utterances that may be referred to as instances of magical thinking, psychiatrist Lourdes Lapuz emphasizes, "These were not utterances of provincial or rural folk, of the unschooled, or of psychophrenics. They were spoken by persons who were literate, enlightened, mostly professionals (includ-

Conclusion

If religion is to be vital, it needs to connect to everyday practice and experience. Its representations and symbols must be close enough to life to be easily recognizable. In this sense, the Filipinization of Catholicism has been very successful: the predominant religious mentality is very similar to the positive one guiding family life. Religion idealizes, legitimizes and sanctifies familiar relationships with kin and other intimates. Its symbols strengthen and express the private and morally binding realm of life.

Popular religiosity does not appear to transcend the family. It is not really concerned with great ideas, such as the relationship between man and the universe, cosmology, or even the afterlife. God is an individual, personalized God, and it is personal trust in God that legitimizes the conditions in the wider world outside. The practice of religion is not church-centred, and people do not regard themselves as members of the institutional Church. The prevailing religious mentality focuses on individual and family needs, thus making the family its own closed moral universe.

Catholicism has greatly contributed to shaping lowland culture; conversely, it has also been permeated by social experience and the prevailing world view. This process of Filipinization is continuous and probably accelerating due to the loosening hold of the priests over the beliefs of the faithful. Nowadays, the authority of the priest is questioned, and he has come to be perceived as essentially human. Because people at large generally take a strong interest in such matters, an extraordinary religious supermarket appears to be flourishing that offers something for every taste, so inspiring more and more people to go their own ways.

---

ing nurses and doctors), who read current literature on psychology, child rearing, and personality development. They were not spoken in the course of jesty banter or meaningless chatter, but during serious discussions of personal psychological difficulties" (1977:110).

CHAPTER 5

Individual and society in modern Thai and Javanese

Indonesian literature

Modern Thai fiction

After the end of the Second World War, several Thai authors began to write socially critical novels which were intrinsically modern in the sense that they strove to raise the awareness of their readers about the structural and cultural conditions of Thai social life. In their elaboration and search for solutions, however, such novels are clearly the heirs to an older moralistic tradition of Thai writing, which emphasized right moral behaviour and wise personal ethics as the foundations of a good society. From the tension between the modern and the moralistic approach arose the idealistic progressive novel. The two outstanding representatives of this genre are Seenii Sawwaphong (the pen name of Sakchai Bamrungphong, a retired diplomat) and Siibuuraphaa (the pen name of Kulaab Saajpradit who died in exile in Peking in 1974).

These two authors were preoccupied with intellectual and moral emancipation. They strongly believed in the possibility of a better future that would bring freedom from oppression, so long as people grew conscious of their circumstances and became motivated by humanitarian ideals. It is no wonder, then, that they were taken as heroes by the student generation that overthrew the Thanom-Prapaat dictatorship in the October uprising of 1973. For the students, the idealism of these authors provided a guide for their own desire to establish a better, more equitable society.

Both authors produced precursory novels set in a foreign environment before moving on to tackle the problems of inducing change and modernization in Thai society. Seenii Sawwaphong's first humanitarian novel, *The Love of Wanlajaa* (*Khwaamrag khǫǫng Wanlajaa*, 1952), was set in Paris, with a cast of Thais and other people of diverse social backgrounds and preoccupations. Wanlajaa, a female student of lower middle class origin, is the pivot around whom these characters circulate, while discussing their views of life. She is the progressive figure who holds the view that it is not enough merely to live and struggle to establish one's own position, but that one should devote oneself to building a positive future for one's fellow men.

Wanlajaa's 'love', as used in the title, is love for humanity and its struggles. Her selfless passion is contrasted with motives of egoism and egotism, exemplified by the career motivations of a young Thai diplomat who sacrifices his wife and child to his ambitions. Social consciousness is illustrated in the story of a young Thai seaman who, through his contact with a Spanish labourer, is made aware of class solidarity, and the bright future that awaits proletarians of all countries if they unite. Seenii further raised the question of the social relevance of art in the person of a lonely surrealist painter. When confronted with the ideas of Wanlajaa, he switches his allegiance over to the social realist school, a shift which subsequently brings him friends and companionship.

The Love of Wanlajaa is at best a theoretical treatise on idealism. It elucidates the social consciousness and personal ideals of the author, and it is therefore very comparable to Siibuuraphaa's *Until We Meet Again* (*Conkwaa Raw ca Phobkan iig*, 1950). This latter novel is set in Australia, where a privileged Thai student gradually develops a sense of social responsibility through his encounter with two young women who question the world in terms of justice, and demonstrate a dedication to humanity in their work.

Both Seenii and Siibuuraphaa subsequently dealt with their preoccupations in a Thai setting. It is in *Evil Spirit* (*Piisaat*, 1953) and *Look Forward* (*Lae Paj Khaangnaa*, 1955, 1957), respectively, that they unfold their visions of Thai society and the ways in which it should develop into a better one. The fascination of both novels is that the authors tried to develop a full picture of Thai society, and the perceptions and ideas that inform it. In the power of their social imagination, both books were ahead of their times, and these pioneering 'modern' novels are still relevant to a contemporary understanding of the development of Thai society.

In *Evil Spirit*, Seenii introduces Saaj Siimaa, who is the son of a poor peasant family. Due to his intelligence, and through the patronage of a monk, he finally becomes a lawyer. In spite of conflicts of loyalty, he consistently sides with the plight of the poor and exploited villagers of his background, and devotes himself to the task of making Thailand a just society. His relationship with a high-class girl makes her aware of the conceited view of the life of her peers. Saaj thus becomes the embodiment of the 'evil spirit' of change, responsible for the awakening of the common people that threatens the position of the entrenched and privileged ruling class.

Evil Spirit opens perspectives into Thai life as seen from the positions of both the underdog peasants and the self-indulgent yet stagnating ruling class. The main characters are a group of university students of divergent backgrounds and ethnic origins (Thai and Chinese) who come to know each other during the course of their rejection of the dominant Thai values of hierarchy and willing submission. The development of the novel clearly implies a protest against the Thai social order, yet no programme for political action emerges. Society is clearly unjust, but injustice and the arrogance of the elite are seen as being fought by the personal example of lone idealists. Consequently, all the main characters act out their idealism by devoting themselves to the betterment and enlightenment of the poor and deprived people of Thailand.

Though Siibuuraphaa's *Look Forward* is very similar to Seenii's novel, his characters are set in a more precisely defined historical period, from the absolute monarchy through its overthrow, and then on into the period of fledgling democratic ideals up to the early years of the Phibun Songkhraam dictatorship. *Look Forward* is a novel in two parts, the second being left unfinished. In the first volume, *Youth* (*Pathomwaj*, 1955), we witness the vicissitudes and good fortune of Canthaa. The son of poor and suffering peasants, he arrives in Bangkok to further his studies, supported by the sponsorship of a monk. Subsequently, he is enabled to study at high-school through the patronage of a ranking aristocrat, in whose compound he comes to live as a kind of a privileged servant. Later, he becomes an official in a ministry as a result of the same high backing.

Canthaa's life story enables the author to provide glimpses into the life of peasants, and their exploitation at the hands of both officials and gangsters, into their suffering from natural events and bad health, and into the poverty and the exacting but upright life in a temple in

Bangkok. Through such techniques as the portrayal of status competition among the retainers clustered together in the compound of the aristocratic patron, by his depiction of the interaction between teachers and pupils of the most diverse origins at an elite school in the capital, and in his elaboration of all kinds of situations that cut across class lines, the author gradually fleshes out a full picture of Thai society.

The second volume of the novel, *Middle Age* (*Matchimmawaj*, 1957), has a more explicit political content, which describes the deceptive evolution of Thai political life after the 1932 'revolution'. As in the first book, the development of the protagonist, Canthaa, remains vague, the turbulent ambience of the changing times being personified and acted out by the secondary characters that surround him, such as former classmates, fellow students at Thammasat University, teachers, and other associates. This strategy suffices for the author to develop an elaborate panorama of the ideas and thought patterns of the progressive and democratic generation of that period. These enlightened ideas contrast with the reactions of the aristocratic class, and the ascendent military, who were to become the decisive new factor in Thai political life. Towards the novel's end, Canthaa has become an up-country assistant prosecutor, in the hope of serving the peasant class from which he came in its quest for justice.

Siibuuraphaa was a utopian socialist who believed in the possibility of the emancipation of the people. If — he speculated — everybody could enjoy equal opportunity, especially in education, while simultaneously developing a sound political consciousness, then all social problems would necessarily evaporate, and the end result would be an ideal society. This was why he lamented a hierarchical society's suppression of personality development and individual consciousness. In his view, structural barriers between the classes prevented communication, suppressing the lower class while isolating the upper class, and leaving both guided by 'false consciousness'. Confined by their limited social experience, people appear to be doomed to self-centredness and narrow-mindedness, which in their turn are the main causes for the lack of social justice.[1]

---

1 Some of the socially critical views of Siibuuraphaa are finally available in translation. It is the "other stories" in Siburapha, *Behind the Painting and Other Stories*. Singapore, etc.: Oxford University Press, 1990.

Both Seenii and Siibuuraphaa were moralizing authors who pre-sented their pictures of society in strong stereotypes, with their charac-ters representing ideas, rather than flesh-and-blood people who come to life on the page through embodying psychological motivation. Individual experience is explained by social setting, and by the formula perceptions and expectations that belong to it. Twenty years later, we still find these qualities in the autobiographical works of another major novelist, Bunchoog Ciamwirija (the pen name of Nat Suphalaksanasyk-saakon, born in 1933).

Bunchoog is a prolific author who writes about circumstances with which he is intimately familiar. Highly educated, with a master's degree earned in the United States, he became a District Officer. If it had not been for his remarkable personality, inspired by honest idealism and compassion for the people he had to administer, his potent talent as a writer would perhaps never have emerged. He became disaffected, however, with the corrupt and exploitative practices of government and, fired by his indignation, he left the civil service in disgust to go his own way.

His first and, to date, most successful novel, *The Revolutionary District Officer* (*Naaj Amphoe Patiwat*, 1975), relates the experiences of a District Officer, and the moral dilemmas inherent in that position. Written in an ironical tone, the book delineates the tension between integrity and power, contrasting respect for human dignity with syco-phancy and career motivations, fair administration with exploitation of the poor, and similar dichotomies. The book's focus is the life and prac-tice of the provincial civil service and its relationships with influential Chinese merchants and the powers-that-be in Bangkok. Because the District Officer's moral integrity is at odds with the greed and self-inter-est of the civil service, the protagonist cannot be kept in his position. He is deemed 'revolutionary' because he is honest and committed to the welfare of the people that he has come to serve. These themes are fur-ther elaborated in *Black Sky* (*Faa Siidam*, 1977), a subsequent attempt to explain the moral choices of the 'revolutionary' District Officer. Both of these works seem to have struck a chord with Thai readers, and have become unprecedented best-sellers.

Bunchoog's most penetrating novel is his voluminous *The Human Element* (*Thaadmanut*, 1978). Its themes are the same, namely the injustice and exploitation perpetrated on people who are just, sincere, and earnest in a society where amoral and immoral power reigns supreme; where 'justice' can be bought, the honest suffer from oppression, and hypocrisy leads to reward. The setting is a vast urban society, Bangkok, and the world of unscrupulous publishers and impoverished struggling authors, the pirating of copyright, and the vagaries of the justice system. Altogether, *The Human Element* constitutes a powerful indictment of urban Thai society, with its selfish mentality and overwhelming indifference to the plight of the powerless.

In his latest writing, Bunchoog describes his youth in the trilogy comprised of *Born in the Countryside* (*Koet Baansuan*, 1979), *To Be Born Means to Fight* (*Koet laew Tǫǫng Suu*, 1980), and *The Young Student* (*Nisit Num*, 1981). In some passages, this series of novels exhibits remarkable similarity with Siibuuraphaa's *Look Forward*; the main character, Klaa, however, is more independent and learns more quickly from life's experiences than his counterpart Canthaa. Yet both are products of the poor countryside and both find patronage to further their studies, and it is through their confrontations with a great variety of people and situations that the authors succeed in evoking a picture of Thai social life in all its diversity.

These three novelists provide a critical yet somewhat stereotyped analysis of life in modern Thai society. Their novels belong to an older moralizing tradition, in which characters embody qualities and traits rather than becoming convincing living personalities. While such abstractions may be a concession to Thai taste and perceptions, it often makes for tedious reading when compared with the more penetrating and immediate descriptions of life by the extremely gifted short story writer Laaw Khamhǫǫm (the pen name of Khamsing Srinawk, born in 1930 and now working in Khorat province).

Khamsing is of Northeastern peasant origin and also writes about the underdog in Thai society, especially about their limited aspirations and the bitter fruits of their striving, their naivety and suffering, plus the reasoning and personal motivations that characterize life in the countryside. The strength of his stories derives especially from wonderfully evoked empathy and from exceedingly keen observation. His compelling interpretations and implicit social criticism are clear, yet he leaves it entirely to the reader to draw his own conclusions.

Khamsing expresses his commitment in the titles of his collections. The first, *No Barriers* (*Faabokan*, 1958; latest and enlarged edition 1979), voices his conviction that the high and the mighty do not have the right to suppress the poor and downtrodden of Thai society. Yet suppression is exactly what happened to his stories; Marshal Sarit Thanarat showed his displeasure upon the publication of his first collection, which was consequently not reprinted for quite some time. His writings were also disapproved of by the Thanin government that came to power in the counter-revolution of 1976, when Khamsing felt it prudent to go into voluntary exile. The title of his second collection, *The Wall* (*Kamphaeng*, 1975), refers to the wall that separates the urban Thai from the rural Thai, the powerful from the powerless, the privileged from the exploited. A selection of these short stories has been translated into English as *The Politician and Other Thai Stories* (1973).

In his succinct, and sometimes very brief, stories Khamsing reveals his mastery by saying a great deal in a very few words. In an intricate and subtle style coloured by a touch of mocking humour, he bares the matter-of-fact atrocities and self-centred motivations that lurk beneath the ideally smooth surface of social life. This revelation of underlying motives, of the fundamental conditions of poverty and ignorance, of baseness and suffering, have not helped to make Khamsing's writings widely popular. For the urban, educated Thai reading public, Khamsing's depictions are just too powerful; his caustic style and perception expose realities which most readers would prefer to deny — or at least to avoid.

Such fastidious readers find it easier to empathize with the society-confirming works of minor authors such as Nimit Phuumthaawon. Once an up-country headmaster, he is one of the most prominent popular writers. He obviously identifies himself with peasant life and the school situations he writes about. His stories consistently exploit the conventional cognitive classifications that underly the Thai 'social construction of reality'. Mothers are self-sacrificing and good, teachers are either generous and righteous or else they turn into irresponsible drunkards who cannot adjust to the hardships of country life, village leaders are firm and protective of their villagers and do not shy away from the use of the gun when danger threatens, and village abbots are moral and wise. A major theme of Nimit's is that the relative peace of village life is threatened by dangerous gangsters and other quasi-criminal and power-hungry outsiders. Such characterizations pervade his novels *The Fragrant Smell of Grass* (*Hǫǫmklin Dǫǫgǫǫ*, 1975), and *Headman Phoo Choenchaaj* (*Kamnan Phoo Choenchaaj*, 1977). A very similar picture of life in the countryside, and more authentic for that matter, is drawn by Prajuab Thirabutana in her charming autobiographical recollections, *Little Things* (1973; in English).

In a similar vein, the awareness of the educated urban upper middle class comes to life in the novels of Duangcaj (the pen name of Prathumphon Watcharasathian). An associate professor of political science at Chulalongkorn University, she explores female reactions to a male dominated society. Her mildly progressive novels capitalize on the typical perceptions that inform the life of her class, yet they are nonetheless worth reading for their useful insights into the dilemmas of modern Thai women, and the problems of family life. Her most perceptive novels are *Stagnant Time* (*Huangsutthaaj haeng Kaanweelaa*, 1975), and *The Light of the Candle* (*Thian Sǫǫng Saeng*, 1977).

Modern Thailand, being a relatively open society, allows the publication of a vast quantity of socially critical fiction and non-fiction. Social commentators, former political prisoners, politicians, disaffected civil servants and monks are among those who publish their thoughts and memoirs. Especially since the student uprising of 1973, a spate of short story writing has erupted, which aims at telling the 'true' conditions of Thai society. While analytically useful, most of these stories have been written from a 'social realist' perspective that often makes them quite dull as literature. The first full length novel along these lines is Rom Ratiwan's *The Fighter from the Northeast* (*Toontheewadaa Nagsuu caag Thiiraabsuung*, 1980). This novel contrasts with his earlier stories, *Pujnun and Duangdaaw* (1965), which are far more convincing in their authentic depiction of the meaning and experience of life in the countryside.

Modern Javanese-authored Indonesian fiction

Pramoedya Ananta Toer is without any doubt the outstanding giant of modern Indonesian prose-writing. His early works develop from reminiscences of his childhood through the havoc of revolution, armed struggle, and imprisonment to the vacuous situation of post-revolutionary life in Jakarta, where the fruits of political freedom appear to be merely cynicism, loss of ideals, and corruption. In his autobiographical *Stories from Blora* (*Tjerita dari Blora*, 1952), he reveals the cruelty and hypocrisy that are the dark side of Javanese decency in the story "Inem"; in "Circumcision" ("Sunat") he describes the destruction of his hopes of belonging when he realizes that he will never be a good Muslim, because he will always be too poor ever to make the pilgrimage to Mecca.

His early vision of life is most saliently recorded in his novelette *Life is not a Pleasant Happening* (*Bukan Pasar Malam*, 1951), in which he describes his visit to his dying father and remaining family in Blora, after his detention by the Dutch and subsequent struggles in Jakarta. Everybody appears to be alone, subject to his own suffering and incapable of relating in a meaningful fashion to others. "In life we all come alone and die alone. Life should be a pleasant party where we come and go together", but life is not a pleasant happening, husband remaining stranger to wife, child growing up alien to its parents, while even brothers and sisters can only vaguely relate to each other.

Pramoedya's analysis of the revolution is given in the collections *Dawn* (*Subuh*, 1950) and *Sprinklings of the Revolution* (*Pertjikan Revolusi*, 1950), and in his novel *Guerrilla Family* (*Keluarga Gerilja*, 1950). These writings penetratingly reveal the madness of the times, the egoism of motives, the cruelty, the powerlessness of the individual, the total destruction of family life, integrity, and every humanitarian quality. People merely appear to be the victims of a life beyond their control.

His later *Stories from Jakarta* (*Tjerita dari Djakarta*, 1957) elaborates the same themes. They deal with the lives and experiences of the poor and suffering rejects of society. The revolution has run its course; what remains is disappointment, meaninglessness, and disorientation. Pramoedya's vision is basically critical of life itself and not really addressed to social conditions. People are powerless and eternal losers, everybody being alone, outsiders to each other and mere observers. For the poor, the price of belonging is too high, everybody having to fend for himself. "In our neighbourhood poverty killed all ideals."

All these early works are individual-centred, their wider social setting being a cataract of events severing all ties, which leaves the individual as a helpless victim without will, responsibility, or perspective. It is a bleak interpretation of the human predicament: life happens to the individual, it is pleasureless, and everybody ends up alone. Pramoedya eventually became conscious of the social irrelevance of the work he was producing. After 1957, he virtually stopped writing creative fiction, instead producing essayistic work about the position of *The Overseas Chinese in Indonesia* (*Hoa Kiau di Indonesia*, 1960), and the symbol of women's struggle for emancipation, Kartini, *Just Call Me Kartini* (*Panggil Aku Kartini sadja*, 1962).

Pramoedya's frustration with the state of creative literature in Indonesia became apparent in his intemperate opposition to the Cultural Manifesto of 1963, in which many of his colleagues pressed for artistic and intellectual freedom against Pramoedya's arguments for the social relevance of art and a 'social realist' approach to creative fiction; art should serve to edify the people and raise their consciousness. The coup of 1965 landed him in jail and the penal colony on remote Buru; for a long time nothing was heard of him. During his imprisonment, however, he conceived his momentous historical novels, thus fulfilling his premise of the social relevance of art. Given their later date, we should first review other works written by ethnic Javanese that have appeared between the revolution and the present.

It is true that the sociological relevance of these latter novels is almost negligible, and that descriptions of society as it is, or as seen from an ideological perspective, are virtually absent. Most authors are seemingly always concerned with personal experience and the individual predicament, irrespective of the social setting, which tends to remain vague. A partial exception to this general tendency are some works by Harijadi S. Hartowardojo, Y. B. Mangunwijaya, and Nh. Dini (Nurhajati Suhardini).

In his novel *Exile* (*Orang Buangan*, 1971), Harijadi contrasts the perceptions of isolated villagers with the modern rationality of a teacher. During an outbreak of epidemic disease, the villagers are convinced that the teacher is the cause of misfortune and death. He remains in the village, however, until a medical team from the capital moves in to fight the disease. Upon meeting his former love, who is a member of that team, he leaves, the clash between modern and traditional perceptions remaining unresolved. The structural conditions of village life remain vague, but this novel at least constitutes an attempt to relate perceptions to social background and conditions.

Mangunwijaya's first novel, *Weaverbirds* (*Burung-burung Manyar*, 1981), is apparently built up along the lines of the Javanese *wayang purwa* shadow play but, at least in its first part, gives a convincing analysis of the relationship between moral choices, social place, and personal history. Its early theme is to show how and why certain Indonesians 'chose the wrong side' during the revolution against the Dutch; in its further development, however, romantic considerations, and the very Javanese cyclical motive of the quest for origin-and-destination *(sangkan-paran)*, gradually come to predominate. But despite that, it remains an important book in its treatment of the theme of collaboration, which has only seldom been discussed: Toha Mochtar's *Home-coming* (*Pulang*, 1958) being another example.

In contrast to Pramoedya's autobiographical works, Nh. Dini's reminiscences of her childhood are basically optimistic, relating the warmth and goodness of family life against the background of vicissitudinous times. It is their setting against the experience of life in Semarang in the later days of colonialism, the period of the Japanese occupation, and the time that the town was reoccupied by the Dutch, and then during early independence, that lends these novels some socio-historical worth. The four novels concerned are, *A Lane in my Town* (*Sebuah Lorong di Kotaku*, 1978), *The Wild Grass Field behind the House* (*Padang Ilalang di belakang Rumah*, 1979), *The Sky and the Earth are our Friends* (*Langit dan Bumi Sahabat Kami*, 1979) and *Sekayu* (1981).

If we seek for further interpretations of the social experience of life, we should either consult non-Javanese authors or read the works of lesser artists, who depict life in a stereotypical and milieu-bound fashion, Titie Said's *Don't Take my Life* (*Jangan Ambil Nyawaku*, 1977) being a good example. We could also read some of the better 'pop' novels that invariably have the outrageous life of Jakarta's 'golden youth' as their subject matter. These novels are set in the milieu of parvenu bourgeois society and describe the lives of alienated or corrupted individuals who revel in their irresponsibility. They are often interesting because of their complete reversal of Javanese values. With *Arjuna in*

Quest of Love (*Arjuna Mencari Cinta*, 1977), Yudistira Ardi Noegraha (Massardi) established himself as the foremost exponent in this field.

Focusing on serious fiction again, we may first of all note the new but characteristic genre of the mystical novel. When Danarto published his prize winning story "Rintrik" (1968), it was hailed as an important innovative 'trend' in short story writing that shared some characteristics with the absurdist novels of the Batak Iwan Simatupang, for instance *Pilgrimage* (*Ziarah*, 1975). It became a movement, with Danarto's collection *Godlob* (1974), Kuntowijoyo's *Sermon on the Mount* (*Khotbah di atas Bukit*, 1976), and Harijadi S. Hartowardojo's *Date with Death* (*Perjandian dengan Maut*, 1976) as outstanding examples.

These latter writings deal with intensely personal experiences set within the weird sceneries of mystical fantasizing. Their direction is away from social life, and turned inwards to mystical experience, the quest for death and detachment from life, with a strong emphasis on determinism and fate. Since they are so characteristic, it may be useful to illustrate this genre with Kuntowijoyo's *Sermon on the Mount*.

This author, who is a practising Muslim, told me that he wrote his novel at a time when he was very disappointed with developments in Indonesian society. Also under the New Order, the hoped-for solutions of a democratic, just, and prosperous society had become as utopian and beyond reach as under the previous government.

The main character of the novel is Barman, a former diplomat and man of the world. When he retires to a provincial town, he soon finds his life intolerably dull. His son arranges a solution, finding him a villa on the slopes of a mountain, together with a beautiful, devoted, and relatively young mistress (Popi), his evening of life thus promising to become a paradise.

One morning in his garden, he briefly meets a strange man who is not particularly respectful. Without introducing himself, the trespasser bluntly asks, "What is your work?" and when Barman asks in return who he is, the stranger answers that he is "the guardian of the mountain". Later on they meet again; his name is Humam and he lives in a house a little above Barman's. During their walks, Humam talks in riddles. "Our relationship is no relationship"; "Don't worry about me; the burden [of life] I have already let go"; "My being is my non-being, or the opposite". He also gives mysterious answers as in the following dialogue:

"What is your purpose?"
"There is no purpose; I merely am, the greatest joy."
"And when we die?"
"Well, then we do not move any more."
"Aren't you afraid?"
"Of all things, that is just what does not make me afraid at all."

Initial attraction to Humam gradually becomes fascination with this strange recluse, who seems to know a secret and is not afraid of death. Little by little, Barman detaches himself from Popi, her good care, his house, and the enjoyment of the beauty of nature. When Humam dies, Barman moves into his house where he lives alone, cutting all links with his former way of life. His solitary existence, however, arouses the interest of nearby villagers: they have discovered a guru, a man who knows the secret, and after a while people come crowding into his yard day and night.

Barman, however, knows that he knows nothing and that he has nothing to say. When he tries to flee from the crowd, he is stopped. "Don't leave us, Father! Please speak to us. We are afraid. We suffer. We are confused." When Barman finally speaks, he only says, "We shall go to the top of the mountain." In a long procession, they start moving, Barman riding a horse. Upon their reaching the top, the night comes down, it gets cold, and the crowd grows restless. "We want happiness! Do show us the way!" Suddenly, Barman has disappeared, and when his body is eventually found, they bury it on the very peak of the mountain. He did not speak; he was detached and vanished into the void.

The characteristic themes of the mystical novel, such as the individual quest for knowledge about origin-and-destination, detachment from social attachments, and deep questions about life, are by no means restricted to that genre. They are so pervasive as to show up in one form or another in all kinds of Javanese fiction, the 'pop' novel being no exception. In *Vaingloriousness* (*Sok Nyentrik*, 1977), Eddy D. Iskandar introduces a family of humble origin and their daughter Ichik. Upon winning the lottery, the family moves to Jakarta, where the rural Ichik soon becomes the fashionable and extravagant Inge. After living all the adventures a secondary school girl can have, she is finally overwhelmed by her own ostentatiousness, while growing increasingly con-

fused. When she falls ill, she returns to the Sundanese village of her origin, back to her grandmother and former peasant boyfriend, becoming
Ichik again; there she finds peace and dies.

Also Moh. Diponegoro's *Cycle* (*Siklus*, 1975), which is a kind of a
'pop' novel for grown-ups, dwells on such matters as purpose, death
and inevitability. Men are but puppets in the hands of fate, and what
they may perceive as coincidence and mystery is really the expression
of a divine plan that forces people to move on, whether they want to
believe in predestination or not.

The second predominant genre has individual loneliness in society
as its subject. One is lonely because one fails to relate meaningfully to
others, because of the dictates of the fate that one has to fulfil, because
of the failure to live up to traditional expectations, or because one feels
powerless and poor in a big corrupt world that conceitedly pretends to
be the bastion of righteousness and honourable tradition. It is of interest to note that protestations against the compulsion of tradition are
elaborated far more by non-Javanese Indonesian authors, such as the
Batak Armijn Pané in *Fetters* (*Belenggu*, 1940), the Sundanese Achdiat K.
Mihardja in *The Atheist* (*Atheis*, 1949), and the Balinese Putu Wijaya in
Telegram (1973). Javanese somehow appear to know that life is a lonely
affair, and are seemingly more inclined to accept things as they come to
them. At the hands of gifted authors, such as Pramoedya and Subagio
Sastrowardojo, this experience of existential loneliness has been most
penetratingly described.

In Subagio's collection *He-manship at Sumbing* (*Kedjantanan di
Sumbing*, 1965), prowess and will to live are intimately related with
death. All his characters are forced to fall back on themselves in their
confrontation with life, where the other person is always just, or totally,
beyond reach. This lonely quest motivated the poet Rendra to give to
his only collection of prose writing the programmatic title *The Young
Roamer* (*Dia sudah Bertualang*, 1963), reflecting his conviction that
everybody has to seek his own solution to the riddle of life.

Loneliness within tradition, and the consciousness that to fulfil life
is to fulfil fate, have been elaborated in Umar Kayam's female characters, Bawuk and Sri Sumarah. In these two novelettes, that were combined under the title *Sri Sumarah dan Bawuk* (1975), he describes two
apparently contradictory female characters who both follow the dictates

of fate. Bawuk is somewhat obstinate in going her own way. As the daughter of a high-class family of government administrators *(priyayi)*, she gets involved in a misalliance, eloping with a hard-headed fellow who becomes a communist leader. During the terror of 1965, she comes back to see her relatives, who are greatly worried about her fate, yet later leaving them again in order to rejoin her husband in his futureless struggle. Her decision and dedication are respected and respectable. She follows her fate to its ultimate consequences, surrendering herself, equating her being with the fate of her husband.

Sri Sumarah is a different character, and entirely within the confines of tradition. From her earliest days, she has learnt that the fulfilment of a woman's life lies in devoting herself to her husband. She is nothing but a mother and wife, and surrenders *(sumarah)* herself gracefully to circumstances, husband, and 'God'. In accepting life as it comes, while finding satisfaction in her subservient role, she performs the mystical practice of self-surrender in everyday life.

The poet Linus Suryadi AG also focuses his lyrical prose on the inner world of Javanese women. In his *The Confession of Pariyem* (*Pengakuan Pariyem*, 1981), a female servant of a noble family relates the story of her life, which is completely bounded within the confines of the traditions of the court town of Yogyakarta. It is these latter, with their emphasis on the fulfilment of her task within her station in life, that make her existence meaningful, and from which she derives her satisfaction. Although this prose poem has been hailed as a penetrating analysis of culture that is revealing of Javanese social life, it is basically an idealization of a system of values that belongs to the past.

Umar Kayam and Linus Suryadi are men and write their stories from a male point of view, traditional expectations being their guideline. Modern female Javanese authors appear to have a different perspective, their emphasis being on conventional religious expression, such as prayer, instead of the mystical acceptance of fate. Predictably, their novels treat the theme of marital relationships that fail, the promise of happiness not maturing when, after the birth of a few children, husbands become infatuated with younger women.

The original husband, however, remains to dominate the emotional lives of these women. The authors describe the process of drifting apart, of unfulfilled hopes, and their liaisons with new suitors. Yet they remain lonely because they are incapable of surrendering themselves to a substitute husband. While devoting themselves to the education of their children, they also learn to fend for themselves and to rely on their own resources, which they simply must, because they are invariably deceived in their expectations if they hope for support from their parental families. These themes are well elaborated by Titis Basino in *Harbour of the Heart* (*Pelabuhan Hati*, 1978) and Sri Rahaju Prihatmi in *On the Ruins* (*Di atas Puing-puing*, 1978). They also figure in Nh. Dini's first novel, *The Quiet Heart* (*Hati yang Damai*, 1961), in which inevitable fate and the spectre of seduction illustrate the insecurity of marriage.

Iskasiah Sumarto's seemingly autobiographical novel *Astiti Rahayu* (1976) adds to this picture from a non-married perspective. To be unmarried is shameful, to herself and to her parents. In her student days, she fails to build a meaningful relationship with either her suitors or the men she is interested in. Upon meeting an Australian, she does not dare to commit herself to his love. A Javanese girl should mix with Javanese. Moreover, he is a Christian and she a vague Muslim. While a religious reason is given as the grounds for incompatibility, the basic reason is his being a foreigner; deceived in her expectations by Javanese men, willy-nilly she ends up living alone.

After years of imprisonment on the island of Buru, Pramoedya was finally heard from again in 1980 with the publication of the first two volumes of his prison-conceived, great historical novel. In *This Earth of Mankind* (*Bumi Manusia*, 1980), and *Child of all Nations* (*Anak semua Bangsa*, 1980), the reader is introduced to the colonial environment around the turn of the twentieth century through the novel's main character, Minke.

When we first meet him, he is one of the very few Indonesian pupils at a Dutch secondary school in Surabaya. This important intellectual experience in an alien environment sets him free from the fetters of his high-born Javanese background. While eagerly absorbing advanced European ideas, he also discovers through bitter experience that he is a second class citizen in his own country. This stimulates him to excel in his mastery of Dutch, which he demonstrates by writing for a Dutch-language newspaper. Upon travelling into the interior of Java, he is confronted with the truth of colonial exploitation and the injustice that is perpetrated against the suffering peasant masses. Indignant about what he has seen and heard, he writes a series of articles for his newspaper that is not accepted by its editors. Slowly it dawns upon him that the newspaper is owned by the almighty sugar interests, and that all the time he has been working for one of the tools of colonial exploitation. More importantly than that, he slowly begins to realize that he himself is culturally colonized, that he has become a little Dutchman, and that his freeing himself from 'feudal' Javanese thinking has only led him to fetter himself to another style of perception that is equally inadequate to understanding what is going on in his country.

When he is goaded into becoming aware that he does not know his own people, and that he is even unable to write for a Malay-language newspaper, the foundation has been laid to develop the story of his further emancipation and the discovery of nationalist ideas. This theme is further elaborated in *Footsteps* (*Jejak Langkah*, 1985), when Minke becomes fully aware of the colonial predicament at the time that the first modern native associations are organized. Actively propagating the emancipation of the colonized, his writings increasingly get him into trouble with the Dutch authorities, however sympathetic a few of them may be to the highly accomplished Javanese.

The last volume, *Glass House* (*Rumah Kaca*, 1988), tells about the efforts of the colonial government to control the population, its budding nationalism and political aspirations. These efforts make the country like a house of glass in which the authorities can monitor and manipulate any movement among the population. At the hand of an indigenous intellectual who works for the Dutch in suppressing the national wakening, we are further made aware of the perfidy of colonialism in its ability to subvert the minds of the people as one of its instruments of control.[2]

These four volumes span the period from 1890 to 1918, and are inspired by the biography of R.M. Tirto Adhi Suryo, an influential journalist who played an important role in the early period of national awakening. Their great interest lies in the clarity with which a new view of the human condition is developed. Even though the characters are naturally conditioned by their past experiences, they are no longer will-

---

2 Pramoedya's quaternary novel has been translated by Max Lane and is published by Penguin Australia Ltd.

less victims of their times and circumstances but develop an awareness of their conditioning, and can thus develop hopes, future perspectives, and political ideas. While the structural argument of the exploitation of a people under the yoke of colonialism is clearly developed, the main emphasis is on the consequences of this for the subjugation of the spirit. Contrary to most other novels discussed, these latest works by Pramoedya expose the realities of society, and are a great step forward from the characteristic tradition of escapism and self-centredness. In the words of *Kompas*'s Parakitri,

> With this novel Pramoedya breaks through the stagnation of recent Indonesian literature that was merely obsessed by technical innovation while wandering in confusion and psychological emptiness, isolating individuals from social issues, or that was merely reduced to the cheap entertainment of 'pop' novels. This novel digs down to the roots: (Javanese) culture itself.

Pramoedya's historical novel makes one think of the comparable works of José Rizal in the Philippines at the end of the nineteenth century. With *The Social Cancer* (*Noli Me Tangere*, 1887), and *The Reign of Greed* (*El Filibusterismo*, 1891), he published a convincing indictment of the colonial situation at the end of the Spanish reign, aimed at awakening the readers to their oppression and mental subjugation. In this, Rizal was remarkably successful and he is now recognized as a hero because of it, the father of the national awakening. Pramoedya's penetrating historical-sociological analysis also has the potential for awakening people to their situation. So, after wavering for almost one year, during which the first two volumes were printed in unprecedented editions, the authorities concluded that the works were 'Marxist analysis' and should be banned.

Comparative conclusion

The social scientist may draw tentative conclusions about the indigenous perception of social life from all sorts of written sources. Modern Thai fiction is an especially valuable one because Thai authors seem to 'address' their society. Their characters are always socially defined in types and roles that leave little room for psychological development. In a sense, this confinement contradicts the interpretations of an earlier generation of anthropologists who were impressed by a measure of Thai individualism (Evers, 1969). In the writings of Thai authors, individuals are almost always placed in clear and recognizable social settings that define them. If we contrast this with the depiction of the self-centred individual prevalent in current Javanese Indonesian literature, we may suggest that Thai individuals are more inclined to define themselves in their social setting and to see themselves more in terms of their status positions than as independent personalities.

The strong tendency to perceive other persons in terms of social types results in the tendency to symbolize certain social positions. With the exception of one atypical character in Duangcaj's *Thian Sǫǫng Saeng*, mothers are invariably compassionate and benevolent, sacrificing and forgiving, personifying the perfection of moral goodness *(bunkhun)* vis-à-vis their dependents. Mothers are portrayed as the very embodiment of virtue, and many Thai authors devote whole stories and even novels to this quality of the mother, P. Inthrapaalit's *Mother (Mae*, 1976) being an example.

Similarly, the character of 'teacher' embodies important values. Often the teacher appears to be the male equivalent of 'mother', but as a man he may function as a bridge between the homely world of trust and the vast and daunting world outside. Combining the roles of goodness and wisdom (both sources of *bunkhun*) with masculinity, teachers are often depicted as the white heroes who oppose a wicked world. Fighting evil single-handedly, such as in Khammaan Khonkhai's *The Teachers of Mad Dog Swamp (Khruu Baannǫǫg*, 1978; English translation, 1982), they often perish in the end, strongly suggesting that righteousness cannot win against amoral power.

In the writings of Bunchoog, Nimit, and Duangcaj, an inner world of trust and goodness appears to be systematically opposed by an unreliable and threatening world of power. Authors such as Seenii, Siibuuraphaa and Bunchoog protest against it, while Khamsing and the early Rom seem simply to acknowledge its existence. In all cases, life is unstable and informed by the fear of uncertainty and unreliability. Thus it is wise to seek safety and security in the inner world of family, relatives and community, as described by Nimit and Duangcaj. In the novels discussed, this dualism is elaborated as a question of moral choice. The reading public appears to appreciate this identification of personal conduct with ethical behaviour. The good person applies the ethics of the inner circle to each and all, the 'revolutionary' District Officer being the perfect example in his protest against double standards and moral particularism.

All the authors discussed emphasize individual-centred ethics. Even in the more 'sociological' approach of Siibuuraphaa, society is not pictured as an organic, interdependent whole that is amenable to social engineering. To Siibuuraphaa, individual moral development is the well-spring from which good order is to flow. If, he seems to say, everybody enjoys an equal chance to better himself, and if we learn to have compassion for our fellow man, a just society will inevitably result. In *Look Forward* it is precisely the status order of Thai society that is seen to be the root of all its ills. In this, characters are depicted as the occupants of status positions who look out for themselves and their own self-centred interests. Yet what might be a better society of thinking and enlightened people remains unclear and undescribed, because its impulses are identified in individual moral and ethical behaviour. Therefore society appears as an aggregate of individual statuses that relate to each other in pains, and no consolidated view develops.

Most Javanese authors who write in Indonesian are given to describing individual-centred experience against the background of an amorphous but cruel society that it is beyond human volition or hope to change. Their descriptions of it remain vague, and often contrast with their elaboration of natural setting. Their characters travel through time rather than through social space, often having recourse to religion, mystical experience, or resignation to fate.

These authors tend to focus on the individual predicament, their characters relating to themselves rather than to their fellow men. Most often they write about individuals who turn inward, exploring their own course irrespective of others, or the society they live in. Theirs are novels of personal suffering in which individuals should find their own solutions. While lacking in social characterization beyond the relationships with near others, the Javanese Indonesian novel emphasizes the possibility of living with one's self, reflecting the powerful *kebatinan* tradition in Javanese culture. This is also exemplified by Rendra's credo,

Kemarin dan esok	Yesterday and to-morrow
adalah hari ini	occur to-day
Bencana dan keberuntungan	Catastrophe and good luck
sama saja	are the same
Langit diluar	Heaven outside
langit di badan	heaven inside
bersatu dalam jiwa	are united in the soul

In spite of individual-centredness, characters remain psychologically unconvincing, while descriptions of their motivations tend to remain as weak as the vague social settings in which they are placed. The best exception to this is probably Titis Basino's *Harbour of the Heart* in which, towards its end, the main figure of the novel is described in a convincing psychological perspective. Overall, however, Javanese characterization is 'flat', allowing for little or no psychological depth of characters, their actions seemingly being guided by fate and inevitability.

Historically, we may perhaps understand this emphasis on inevitability by the experience of war and revolution that brought about an absolute rupture with the colonial and predictable past. When the Indonesian Revolution had run its course, society and political ideals became vague, with a clear future receding ever further beyond the horizon. It is against this situation of confusion and hopelessness that Javanese Indonesian self-indulgence and the self-centredness of its creative fiction may be interpreted.

In such novels, individuals appear to stand apart from society and do not appear to have roles that are integrated in or that function as parts of it. The authors appear to be preoccupied with individual experience rather than with social description. Sometimes, they give as the reason for these self-centred choices the strong pressures to conform to the exigencies of social life. Subsequently, they will depict the latter's hypocrisy and shortcomings that impel the individual to go his own way. By writing such stories, these authors dissipate the myth of social harmony that is 'official' Javanese reality, while revealing an atmosphere of lost hopes and resignation.

For the Thai authors, the social stage is the centre of the world that defines their characters, who are logically outwardly directed in their quest for a meaningful existence. Their writings are often critical of society, while religious considerations are conspicuous by their absence. So far, comparable, socially relevant Indonesian literature has characteristically been produced by non-Javanese authors and only very rarely by ethnic Javanese. Javanese social commentary up till now has mainly been the concern of playwrights, and surfaces in all kinds of theatre productions. Yet it may be expected that Rendra's recent theatre scripts and Pramoedya's impressive quaternary novel may stimulate the writing of books that dissect and examine social processes, problems and changes. The fact that this will certainly be frowned on by the authorities may confine social satire and criticism to the stage for the time being.

PART II

Everyday life

CHAPTER 6

Basic principles of everyday life

Thai, Javanese, and Tagalog Filipino society are characterized by a bilateral kinship system, that is, descent is reckoned both through the male and the female line with relatives on both sides being equally important. The preferred way of living is in nuclear households that may, at some time or other, take in near relatives, such as a spinster aunt, aging parents, a nephew or a cousin, or whatever.

Siblings stick together out of loyalty to parents and meet at family celebrations, and also to discuss common concerns. Normally, however, they do not act as a corporate group in economic matters: the parental inheritance is divided and each nuclear family goes its own way. So, while there is a pervasive norm and an impressively common practice of assisting siblings or relatives, there is a great measure of voluntariness and no enforceable obligation to this assistance.

The basic social grouping consists of the parents and their offspring, or, to put it differently, of the siblings grouped around the parents. More distantly related kinfolk are quite important for reasons of identity, emotional and other support, so relatives are often known to each other up to the second and even the third degree. Yet in spite of that, these more far-flung relationships differ in importance for each individual, everybody having a different network of relationships with preferred aunts, cousins, nieces, and so on. In other words, the extended relationships are not all-embracing but, seen from the position of individuals, dyadic, meaning that specific pairs relate to each other individually. Given the popularity of creating bonds of ritual kinship with patrons and friends, such dyadically structured networks can grow extremely extended among Catholic Filipinos.

Though, in terms of descent, fathers and mothers are equally important, households tend to be matrifocal, revolving around the mother more than the father, with the former, and in the long run her relatives, providing the primary source of stability and continuity for the children. The house is clearly her domain, the world outside of it being male territory. Matrifocality is further fostered by the cult of the mother, the children being indoctrinated with the ideal of the moral exemplariness of the mother. She is so, not just because of giving life and nurture, but also because of her self-sacrifice and unconditional love.

According to the Javanese, "Heaven is located at the feet of mother", meaning that to be devoted to her is one's basic and ultimate fulfilment. As the Thai have it, "The goodness of the mother overflows the world", and that worth, overwhelming as it is, results in eternal obligations. In the Philippines, maternal inviolability is powerfully expressed in the symbol of the Holy Mother. Submission to mother, honouring her, expresses respect for the moral hierarchy that She epitomizes.

Of course, fathers should also be honoured but, however moral, caring, and wise they may individually be, they represent another domain of life, namely the hierarchy of the external sphere in which they are supposed to know their way around. That outer world is not necessarily a moral place; it is primarily an arena of contest for material goods, prestige, and power.

So, children are taught to honour their parents, to remember their goodness, and to feel obliged, but additionally the figure of the mother becomes even more special because the seat of morality is vested in her. What's more, she is close and available, where fathers tend to remain rather distant figures. In consequence, she becomes the primary superego representative and foremost reference point of her children's conscience.

As recipients of goodness, care, and guidance, children are placed under a debt of gratitude vis-à-vis their parents that obliges them to follow their advice, not to talk back but to be obedient; children should also be loyal to their family and jealously guard its reputation. To be a disgrace to the dignity of one's family is directly hurting the feelings of those who matter most in one's life; it is a betrayal of trust, a denial of one's moral identity, and thus deeply disturbing. Such behaviour is sinful, also, in the sense that it will invoke inevitable supernatural sanction.

The sociological importance of all this is that the model the family provides is the same basic one for Thai, Javanese, and Filipino social organization. Its cardinal elements are hierarchy, moral inequality, debt of gratitude and obligation, and conscience located in concrete social relationships. Hierarchy implies consciousness of status, that is, of one's relative station vis-à-vis others. Status obliges: the relative superior should provide protection and guidance, the inferior should accept these and render honour and obedience in return. Being the recipient places the beneficiary under a debt of gratitude (*nii bunkhun* Th; *utang budi* J; *utang-na-loób* TF) that cements social relationships, and which gives them a moral quality. Therefore, conscience and self-esteem are dependent on how one handles one's relationships.

Seen in this perspective, social relationships form a highly personalized world where one is tied to specific individuals. These bonds imply obligation, and although links to some always remain highly unequal, in those with near-equals the balance of obligations may oscillate. The fact remains that most relationships have a hierarchical dimension from which it is difficult to escape, and that a moral element is inherent in such relationships. Basically, hierarchy and its concomitant inequality are moral in themselves.

The above thinking makes the wider world comprehensible and provides the rationale for action. Its strength derives from the family, and the personalized perception of social relationships. As a model for society, it is expressed in the widespread phenomenon of patronage, in which an inferior seeks the protection and favour of a known superior. In the Thai and Javanese contexts, this model is enlarged to the dynastic realm of the monarch.

Just as in the family, patronage structures crosscut the divergence of individual or class interests, the basic idea being that all share in the available resources and thus have a common interest. While the patron is naturally entitled to a lion's share, his advantage coincides with that of his lowly servant, who also partakes in the patron's resources. As long as he gets his portion, the subordinate should be loyal and serve faithfully. This dominant view of patronage is diametrically opposed to any form of class analysis, the patronage model being moral, and one that posits mutually antagonistic interests being immoral per se.

It is for this reason that the culturally dominant approach to social questions remains a-sociological. Society is not seen as an arena of conflicting interests among classes and institutions, and politics is typically a contest for resources among patrons and their factions. Beyond that, society appears to be an aggregate of individuals, or of individuals who cluster in families and patronage groups.

A central ethical concept of hierarchically organized society is that people have unequal rights and duties, and that the good order of society is best served if everybody behaves in a manner befitting his station in life. This ethic has to be learned, one has to become aware of one's place; thus unbecoming behaviour shows that one is not conscious of one's relationships to others, that, as the Javanese have it, one has not learned enough *(kurang ajar)*.

In the hierarchical mind cast, the root of social problems must be sought in individual moral decay, in people who have lost their sense of honour, who no longer know shame, who do not conform to their station in life. Governments consequently feel urged to teach good citizenship, which until recently was called 'the duties of the population' in Thai schools; moreover, they think that religion, too, serves as a useful means to curb waywardness and impropriety. Many people seem to agree with this, since they enthusiastically respond to the call of fundamentalist and reform-oriented religious sects (chapter 12).

Gender

A social model that derives from the family may be expected to be rather conservative, especially as it is a moral paradigm. Such an ideal goes largely unquestioned; it is the ideology of the family, and it is sacrilegious to probe into it. Thus, it exerts a very forceful pressure in prescribing the roles that keep the sexes in their proper place, even though the role expectations are not always the same.

As far as the 'cult of the mother' goes, and all that it implies, Thai, Javanese and Tagalog Filipino thinking appears to be very similar. Yet the male role is enacted differently. From the material presented in this section, it will appear that the enactment of gender relationships is very similar in Thailand and the Philippines, and reminiscent of such relationships in other cultures that are characterized by a virility cult. This element is largely absent in Javanese culture. Whereas Thai and Filipino men very much need their social environment for their self-expression, Javanese men are expected to seek satisfaction in their inner being, in the cultivation of a *batin* that can either absorb or offer an escape from the frustrations of life in and outside the family.

Being inward-oriented, many Javanese men make a subdued impression, also tending to give in to their wives, who are supposed to be more emotional, earthy, and spiritually less mature. Consequently, the men express themselves apart from society, and are supposed to be able to take care of themselves emotionally. They are distant husbands and remote fathers. Yet, materially, they are presumed to be female dependent and incapable of caring for themselves.

In other aspects, the gender relationships appear to be comparable. Each gender has its specific domain in life, and prescribed complementary, yet equivalent roles that show little overlap or interpenetration. Also for the Javanese male, sex is not a moral issue but rather a simply physical necessity, which contrasts with the expectations about the moral mother, and thus the moral wife. It is this infusion of morality in the female role that may act as an obstinate conservative force in gender relationships. So, even though the relative exclusiveness of gender domains leads to a high degree of mutual dependencies of varying kinds, it may also probably lead to a low measure of sharing and communication because activities and experiences remain gender specific.

In the following five chapters, the basic principles for living one's social relationships, that have been sketched hereabove, will be illustrated. Then, in the next section, we shall take the opportunity to ponder the forces of change that are impinging on them.

CHAPTER 7

How to be a mother in Thailand

Thailand, 'The Land of Smiles', is known for the charm of its women and is also thought to be a bachelor's holiday paradise. It is known for serene Buddhist temples and also for Thai boxing, probably the toughest form of pugilism. As is often said, the Thai have a smile for every emotion, and whereas the gracious smile of one woman may underline her unassailability, it may be another woman's invitation. The peaceful temple preserves the Buddhist Path, and may also serve as a training ground for kick-boxing.

All these contrasts can be understood by reflecting on the remarkable separation of the male and female domains in life. The Thais like women to be beautiful and charming, virtuous and unassailable. Yet, simultaneously, the men also seem to have a strong need for other women to express their virility. They also box. And become monks.

Whereas women seem to represent beauty and virtue — the two elements are almost fused in Thai thinking — men are supposed to be able to dominate the wider world and express their manliness in the brothel and the ring, in politics and religion. In that last area, women need them most.

As monks, men are representatives of the virtue of Buddhism, and of the sacred and its power. Monks provide a receptive 'field' that enables people to gain the merit they need to enhance their chances for a better rebirth, or even for the improvement of their current circumstances. Though gaining merit is not an exclusively female preoccupation, women are thought to gain tremendous merit by having a son ordained in the temple.

But why should a young man bother to engage in the disciplined life of a monk when there is so much more fun and excitement in the world outside? Of course, there may be many reasons, such as poverty or the quest for an education, but the traditional motivation will also hold for most, namely, to make merit for one's parents, especially for mother.

In Thai education, the idea is inculcated that mother is the most important of persons. She has given life to the child, suffering for and feeding it at great psychological and physical cost to herself. What's more, she is the source of love and care, and she gives all freely. This tide of goodness results in a moral debt on the side of her child, a debt that it is never able to repay.

The only thing that the child can do to reciprocate is to love its mother. This love is expressed in being obedient to her, in considering and anticipating her feelings, and in showing gratitude and respect. Not to do so would imply the denial of the goodness of the mother, a repudiation that would come closest to the western notion of sin — also because such behaviour is believed to invite immediate supernatural retribution. No wonder that mother succeeds in imprinting herself very deeply on the emotional life of her offspring. Which is why making the sacrifice of becoming a temporary monk is an expression of filial devotion.

As a source of goodness, mother symbolizes virtue and selflessness. She is the pivot of one's moral obligations that revolve around the family. Her purity symbolizes the wholeness of the home. It is thus not too far-fetched to conclude that mother easily becomes the foremost reference point of one's conscience, that conscience is consciousness of her, and that she is the primary superego representative of most Thais.

This way of thinking may shed light on a curious phenomenon, the vast production of mother-centred literature. When I first ran across the collection *Mother Dear*, I was truly amazed at finding some sixty short stories and poems devoted to 'Mother', written by all kinds of notables, such as army officers, medical doctors, government ministers, well-known nobility, and so on and so forth. Soon I found out that almost all Thai authors write one or more short stories, and sometimes whole novels, about mothers, presumably their own.

Needless to say, this literature is really boring. Apart from eulogizing mother, it invariably depicts her in the terms the Thai ideology requires. She is not a person any longer, but the symbol of virtue and sacrifice, of goodness and forgiveness. Yet, also in the general literature, it is very difficult indeed to find flawed mothers, mothers of flesh and blood who act as normal living people.

Thus I was very happy the day somebody told me about a collection of short stories written by a practising female psychiatrist.[1] Five of the six stories are about the mother-child relationship, and indeed, the author tries to bring more life to the character of the mother, some of whom she describes as cruel, non-caring and non-protective. But even she does not dare to go clear against the grain; on the contrary, toward the end of her stories it is the children who recognize that their mothers are the best of persons, and that it was their own perceptions which were at fault.

Obviously, the mother image is inviolably sacred. Having been virtually canonized, the ideological fog surrounding her position seems to be particularly dense. By becoming the symbol of Thai morality, she is placed beyond the ordinary world of men and everyday life. There she presides alone, she is the Holy Mother on earth, where Catholics have the Holy Virgin, or the Chinese their Kuan Yin.

Ideologically, mother stands on the lonely pedestal that seems to be her place in many societies that cultivate a virility complex, whether it is Mexican macho or Latin he-manship. In that nexus, it is men who compulsively strive to steal the show, not so much to outdo women, but in competition among themselves. They like to indulge in boastful behaviour, demonstrating their masculinity by drinking and fooling around with women. They relegate their wives to the home, where she should fulfil the role of moral mother, who is not supposed to be a lover. The area of erotic adventure is completely outside the home, where one finds a 'different type of woman'.

It appears that roles are firmly prescribed and that people find their security in conforming to role expectations. For the Thai husband, these expectations focus on his duty to provide for his family, while the other expectations about his virility should be proven in the world outside. And whereas Thai women occupy all kinds of positions in public life, they are supposed to find their fulfilment in the roles of mother and wife. In these positions, they should defer to men and accept the latters' privileged status. Inevitably, this separation of domains keeps men and women at a distance from each other, a distance that marriage most often maintains or even reinforces rather than bridges.

---

1 Suphathanaa Deechaatiwong na Ajutthajaa, *Here I Am... Beloved Enemy (Chan Juu nii... Satruu Thiirag,* 1977).

In Thailand, the competition for status and power appears to be intense, often giving rise to a lively political spectacle. Beyond the smile and female gracefulness, one finds the authoritarian ethos of a highly hierarchical society characterized by the struggle for power and personal prestige. It is conflicts of interest, and the fact that 'face' can so easily be lost, that make the country a rather violent place, with an unusually high murder rate.

So, in parallel with the serene Buddhist temples and the mother-centred home, one finds the male area of contention and strife, that contrasts with the dependable area of existence that is symbolized by things female. The good things in life, such as the earth on which we depend for a living, the rice that nourishes us, the water that sustains life, and the guardian angel that protects the young child — all of them are represented as female, such as Mother Earth, Mother Rice, and Mother Water, among others.

It is not really in question whether an ordinary Thai woman can even begin to aspire to live up to the image of goodness and morality that the Thai ideology assigns to her. In daily reality, she is firmly of the world, and in the mundane realm she should above all be reliable. This is the role that Thai culture assigns to her: to be dependable as a wife and a mother, to be the stable point in a world that allows males to gamble and gallivant, to seek adventure and self-aggrandizement.

The male world means risk, politics and prestige. Men are consequently vulnerable, easily offended, liable to loss of face in their quest for glory. Basically, theirs is a competitive world, and where the risk of disappointment is so high, they need the compensation of a stable home to relax in, and to nurse the injuries to their self-esteem that they suffer in the world outside. Emotionally, they therefore lean far more on their mothers and wives than the latter do on them. In a way, many men remain boys, a kind of grown-up son *(luugchaaj khontoo)* to their spouses.

In practice, the woman is thus one-up on the man, and this substantiates her title to him, gives reason for her possessiveness. By serving others, the woman stakes out her claim to be their 'conscience', so, in effect, it is her reliability that constitutes her bargaining power vis-à-vis her male, who depends on her psychologically to provide the secure base for his forays into the external world. As the Thai say, she functions as 'the hindlegs of the elephant', through her strength sustaining the great show of masculinity that would crumble without her support.

Most Thai women are quite pragmatic about all this. Where many men often appear to be wishy-washy, spoiled, cocky, and carried away by the greatness of their schemes, the women are generally hard-working, responsible and conscientious. They can, and do, take a lot. In spite of this, they normally maintain their good humour and their grace, contributing to the mystique of Thailand as 'The Land of Smiles'. Let nobody be mistaken, though. In the male dominated world of Thailand, a smile may mean anything, from defence to submission, from politeness to subservience, and behind smiling female grace and elegance, one often finds powerful, go-getting women. Nevertheless, even given all that, the Thais appreciate grace and elegance; things should be beautiful to be in order, yet this order also requires hard work and dependability. Which is why it is women who are at the heart of Thai life.

CHAPTER 8

Living with conflict among Javanese and Tagalog Filipino's

This chapter seeks to explore how educated, urban people live with conflict in everyday situations. Of course, daily life includes many more circumstances than can be considered here. In order to limit the discussion, the face to face relationships that have a marked moral content will be brought into focus.[1] This largely excludes the areas of life that are businesslike, that is, the amoral or technical-legal areas where conflicts arise because of power and property, the rather anonymous spheres of politics and economics.

The moral, personal sector of everyday life is exemplified by family relationships, but also includes relationships with neighbours and friends, sometimes extending to cover a local community. Beyond these boundaries, one finds the contest for power and possessions, where relationships are subject to different rules, which seem to be at odds with those of solidarity that should characterize life in the moral area. And so everybody knows that one should avoid doing business with relatives, that one should leave politics outside the home, and that inheritances are potentially divisive and threatening to the unity of the group.

The generic element that sets the area of moral action apart is the commitment to solidarity; it is the individual links to each other, in which the attachments themselves are valued. So any conflicts arising from these are different in kind from conflicts involved in the competition for power and things. Conflicts of solidarity involve persons per se, and thus have remarkable moral and emotional dimensions.

---

1 Anthropological literature about conflict in the moral segment of life is rather scarce. I have, though, found Hildred Geertz's analysis of conflict situations in Java most useful. Of course, on the positive side of *rukun* much more literature has been produced. The most relevant literature about friction and strife with near others in Tagalog/Philippine society has been written by psychologists, such as Bulatao and Arellano-Carandang, and the psychiatrist Lapuz. Lynch's classical article on smooth interpersonal relationships also remains useful.

The nature of the most primary relationships

The exemplary mother

Both Javanese and Tagalogs have a bilateral system of descent, and a preference for living in (extended) nuclear households. As far as the children are concerned, these households are matrifocal, meaning that they tend to be organized around the mother and her relatives. Mother is the prime source of nurture, goodness, dependability, teaching, and authority; she is considerate, anticipating the feelings of her children, and knows what is good for them.

This cultural convention portrays the child as always on the receiving end. Mother has given it life, she sacrifices herself for its welfare, she is the person it can always return to, she accepts her child unconditionally. All this places the child under a moral obligation, one of gratitude that is primarily expressed in obedience. Although Javanese and Tagalogs will generally be reluctant to describe this relationship of love in terms of an *utang budi/utang-na-loób* (moral debt), as is common in Thai culture, there is no doubt that the growing child is taught to recognise the validity of this claim, and that it is impossible to repay.

Going against the mother is equated with not knowing gratitude, being morally defective, denying goodness, and is thus thought to be the worst of actions. Such behaviour is believed to be punished by unavoidable supernatural sanction *(walat/mabusong)*. So, even though the mother is the nearest, the closest of persons, she is also the moral pillar of the universe, demanding unwavering loyalty. Going against her is sinful indeed. Consequently, she succeeds in fixing herself deeply in the emotional sphere of her children and evolves into the primary superego representative. In this thinking, a child's relationship to its mother is not only the most special of all, but also the most exemplary, from which we can derive a few principles about relating to others that are definitely relevant to an understanding of how people live with, or resolve, conflict. The child's bond with its mother is one of moral dependence on an actual, living person and contributes to the formation of a dependent conscience, one that is other-directed; a consciousness of others, of their eyes, ears, and opinions.

To be a good or a bad person depends on how one deals with

individual kinfolk, neighbours and friends, and is therefore highly particularistic. Primary relationships are obligatory ones, demand (unequal) reciprocity, and are thus not morally neutral. Since every individual is enmeshed in a network of such particular ties, it makes sense to keep them in good order and to avoid situations that may disrupt them. Thus pleasant manners, sensitivity for the feelings of others, consideration, indirectness, withdrawal, and dissembling make sense.

The distant father

The good order of the family is headed by a normally authoritarian father, in most cases an emotionally distant person with a great claim to respect. He represents order and hierarchy, he is also the embodiment of life outside the home which, for the Javanese, is well structured, having a clear hierarchical order, though for the Tagalogs, it is a rather loosely structured and often unruly wider world.

Also father's claim to respect is backed up by supernatural sanctions, but his remoteness makes him very different from the approachable mother. In Java, this distance is underscored by the child's use of High Javanese *(krama)* in addressing him, plus institutionalized avoidance behaviour; matrifocality in the Philippines is reinforced by that emotional gulf and the sheer amount of time that males spend outside the home. Both Javanese and Tagalog husbands generally prefer to leave matters of the home in the hands of their wives.

Respect for parents' authority and goodness is an intrinsic part of the principle of respect for age that prevails in all family relationships, thus also in relative age rights that spell out the obligations due among siblings, and impart a mild hierarchical flavour to their mutual relationships. Such a clear pattern of relative authority may be conducive to creating order and avoiding conflict.

Living with conflict

However well structured these links may be, in the closeness of the family conflicts arise, and have to be faced and solved. Quite early in life, people learn to suppress their negative feelings and to master their emotions so as not to disturb each other unduly. The initiative is with the nurturing mother, or her representative, who takes very close care of the child, sheltering it from disturbance and indulging it at the slightest signs of displeasure. As a result of this, autonomy is late in arising, dependency is regarded as positive, and attuning one's sensibilities to the presence of others becomes innate.

In other words, people not only learn to side-step confrontation but also give it little opportunity to arise. Siblings learn to share, to play games for the sake of playing and not of competing, and if arguments break out, most likely all involved are punished. Quarrelling among siblings is disgraceful, and possible negative feelings should be suppressed.

Conflicts with parents are viewed as almost sacrilegious and characteristically their very existence is denied — but if one should burst into the open, it is experienced as socially most shameful and destructive of one's self. Discord among siblings should also be muted, although the feelings of resentment it gives rise to may often be vented in the private company of a good friend. Since mutual avoidance in the family is almost impossible, in cases of strife parents may take an active role in reconciling their children with each other, and in restoring the semblance of peace and harmony. However, where suppression of conflict is a norm, a veneer of normalcy may hide true feelings and tensions simmer on long. "Yes, we forgive, but never forget."

While this is somewhat more so in Tagalog than in Javanese society, nevertheless people in both learn to experience themselves as members of a solidary group that defines part of their identity, and from which they derive a good deal of their self-assurance. Within that group, they enjoy a rather low degree of ego autonomy, and accept hierarchy and deference for age as unquestioned moral criteria. Consequently, they equably tolerate a measure of interference in 'their' affairs, including criticism from relevant others.

The relatively dependent identity and other-directedness make for a high measure of vulnerability at the hands of others, of the easy arousing of feelings of shame and wounded dignity. Since people know this of themselves and of each other, they are given to caution, to avoiding and tolerating frustrating behaviour, and to being wary of each other. Sensing the feelings of others thus becomes an art, the art of staying out of trouble and, of course, of getting one's own way.

Emotion and feeling, intuition, empathy and sympathy, self-con-sciousness and appreciation of each other's dignity, these are the valid guides in interaction, along with the suppression of conflict, the denial of frustration, and the mastery of one's negative emotions. Often one's own strong dark feelings are felt to be as threatening as the presumed critical opinions of others.

Yet despite all that, tensions and frustrations may build up and need to be released. While Javanese may have recourse to talking with friends about negative experiences, their culture also fosters a more self-centred way of releasing tension in the practice of *kebatinan*, the cultivation of the inner self and a calm mind. By declaring the inner self to contain a truth superior to whatever may be the reality of the social world, many Javanese are able to handle their bad experiences, learning to accept *(nrima)* rather than letting themselves be overwhelmed by them. Their safety valve, so to say, is within themselves.

Tagalogs need more social space to release their frustrations. To them, friendships are a truly vital element in organizing life and restor-ing disturbed equilibrium. Gregariousness is especially celebrated in friendship groups *(barkada)* that allow for the letting off of steam and the voicing of opinion, normally encouraged by a generous helping of liquor and a great measure of tolerance. A second way of dealing with the frustration caused by conflict is to seek help and guidance in prayer to the saints or the Holy Mother; the consoling power of deceased grandparents and parents is also thought to be efficacious.

Avoidance

In a private world that is conceived of, and experienced, as highly interpersonal and interdependent, it pays to spend much attention to the avoidance of open, solidarity-threatening conflict. People develop great skill in interaction, perceiving others' sensitivities, measuring these against their own sentiment, anticipating trouble and thus withdrawing, and controlling deep anger through inaction. Often, they stay out of trouble by not involving themselves at all, by indifference. If, on the contrary, they are involved, it may make sense to avoid contact with the adversary, to behave as if that person is thin air, to refrain from all unnecessary dealings.

Although avoidance behaviour is especially suited to people who do not live under a common roof, silence may also be practised within the home as a way of either softening or carrying on a conflict. To talk about it, or try to deal with it by discussing the problem, is usually felt to be too confrontational an approach to the resolution of such tensions. In all sorts of relationships, one may find that people are rather inhibited, guarding themselves, and normally unable to pin-point what precisely plagues them emotionally. Generally, negative feelings need to be left to soften up over time — avoidance and the use of intermediaries being excellent means.

Wives may avoid husbands, refuse to talk to them for days on end, or retire for some time to mother's. Often there are a plenty of reasons for such sulking behaviour; infidelity, trouble with in-laws, conflicts of loyalty (to own parents or to spouse), spending too much time away from home, 'affairs' and drinking parties, all being the roots of much marital discord and conflict. Yet, in the marital abode the need for reconciliation, or at least peaceful co-existence, is high, and thus many wives choose to confine themselves to their roles of housekeeper and mother (rather than spouse and lover), while men opt to be mere providers rather than emotionally involving themselves with their wives and the affairs of the children.

Hildred Geertz reported the case of a young married Javanese man who did not talk much with his wife, which was, according to him, a good way of avoiding trouble. My Filipino girl friend remarked, "We never seem to agree", and has grown very reluctant to broach any subject that she thinks may be controversial. Some Javanese colleagues almost mocked my efforts to get at things Javanese by way of interviewing, which they found extremely naive. "We are closed, we never show what we think. At best we'll give you the information that [we think] you want to hear". Quite a few of the Filipino colleagues I have known over many years, and who know that I am sincere in my efforts to understand Philippine culture, found it very difficult to discuss a paper that I circulated and that they found negative in tone.

Discussing problems appears to be difficult, because it can be felt to be confrontational. If it occurs, it is top down, parents telling children what to do, and so on, though children are not supposed to answer back — as with subordinates outside the home. Criticism or rebuke of children should preferably be done in private and never in front of others — and so it should be in other extra-familial relationships. People are very vulnerable over 'face' and may feel that their dignity, in which the eyes, ears, and opinion of others are vital, is at stake. A small request — "See to it that there is always a rag hanging here for wiping my motor-cycle" — caused so much panic in the servant of my Javanese housekeeper that he left the house the same day. A midnight request, through the intermediary of one of the floor staff at my Lucena hotel, asking the lower floor neighbour to turn his radio down, resulted in so much hullabaloo that my life was threatened.

Direct interaction carries the seed of conflict, and yet people need to work together and cannot avoid associating with each other. Keeping each other at a certain distance helps, and so do good manners, indirectness, shyness and giggling, sensitivity to the mood of others, respect for authority, tolerance and low privacy requirements, conformity to expectations, and fear of gossip and backbiting. Altogether, to keep relationships in good order and operational takes a lot of conscientious effort. Neither Javanese *rukun* (harmonious relationships) nor the famous Philippine SIR (smooth interpersonal relationships, Lynch) come for free, and people are very conscious of, and sensitive to, the quality of relationships.

In brief, the way in which Javanese and Tagalogs live with conflict in the moral sphere of everyday interaction is very much coloured by the effort to avoid it, and not to involve oneself in situations that may provoke or challenge others. The anger of others is often felt as physically or magically threatening, in the same way as bad words, or talking about an inappropriate subject, may cause upset. But while gossip falls in the category of bad words, it is sometimes also positively appreciated as a means of getting to know of the neighbours' irritation about one's behaviour, in which case the offense can be avoided in future. The best thing, of course, is to give no cause for gossip, and people feel virtuous when others have no bad things to say about them.

Strategies

A common strategy for dealing with, or avoiding, conflict is (unconscious) denial of its existence, which sometimes leads to psychological problems that are subsequently drowned in over-activity or (excessive) gregariousness among Tagalogs, or side-stepped in the self-centred practice of *kebatinan* among Javanese. Another way, cultivated among both groups, and particularly by women, is to live up to one's obligations, even in adversity, by complying with the wishes of others, which is known as *sumarah* among the Javanese, and the *inâng martir* (self-sacrificing mother) syndrome among Christian Filipinos.

Other strategies favoured for coping with potential confrontation that are less overtly psychological are staying away from where one has no business, being tolerant of or indifferent to what happens around one, withdrawing from contact when anticipating trouble or controversy, denying its existence by behaving as if everything is normal, acknowledging the moral right of superiors and following their wishes (*turut/sunod*, literally, to follow, and thus, to be obedient), or passivity and inaction even in the company of others. In most of these things, Javanese and Tagalogs behave in a very similar manner, and both societies are familiar with the person whose self-defensive strategies have failed, his bottled up frustrations exploding in the frenzy of *amuk* (in TF also known as *huramentado*).

Differences

Apart from the often different personal reactions to discord that are expressed in *kebatinan* versus over-activity/gregariousness responses, the Javanese limits to tolerance, even in near relationships, seem to be more firmly marked than in Tagalog society, which has sometimes been commented upon as having a great measure of 'ambiguity tolerance'.[2] Recourse to avoidance behaviour is highly institutionalized and

2 The idea of 'ambiguity tolerance' was voiced by Frank Hirtz in the discussions about his Philippine research at the University of Bielefeld (1988-9). It seems to correspond to Alfredo V. Lagmay's findings that the Filipino has an "improvisatory personality that allows him to cope and be comfortable and adapt even in unstructured, indefinite, unpredictable and stressful situations" (Enriquez, 1989:62).

to the forefront in the consciousness of the Javanese, so divorce is a most common occurrence and, when the limits have been reached, repudiation, even of a child, is not uncommon.

Often, the Javanese explain this unforgiving attitude with reference to the *wayang* stories from the Ramayana and Mahabharata. In *wayang* one wins or loses, one kills or is killed, and that 'solves' the conflict. They also emphasize that the supernatural punishment *(walat)* that follows on the infraction of parental expectations is automatic and unavoidable.

This relative rigidity of the Javanese contrasts with the more compromising attitude of the Tagalogs, whose moral universe is less severe. The repudiation of a child is a thing difficult to conceive of, and acceptance in the circle of the family seems unconditional. The extreme consequences of going against parents are talked about as "God will withdraw his blessing *(pagpapala)*", which is thought to be unavoidable. But still, the Christian God can and does forgive, and thus the more lenient, 'understanding' attitude of Filipinos in matters concerning near others may be related to the influence of Catholicism.

Epilogue

In this chapter conflict in the inner, moral circle of life was related with the nature of familial relationships and early socialization. This latter makes for a slow development of individual autonomy, and places individual security in group membership and the ability to handle relationships carefully and considerately. Such a cultural device fosters the experience of the self as a member of a solidary group, while placing self-esteem in the hands of others whose acceptance of one's person is psychologically important. This other-directedness also guides one's conscience; one's superego seems to be located in relationships, in the consciousness of others. Consequently it is there, in these relationships, that one is vulnerable and thus it becomes imperative to avoid conflict and promote solidarity.

Conflicts that arise are side-stepped rather than faced, and although there is a lot of satisfaction in handling one's relationships skilfully, as also in reducing tensions by elegant, almost intuitive means and avoidance strategies, for some, perhaps less skilful or particularly powerless people, the side-stepping of conflict and the repression of feelings may lead to typical, culturally induced psychological problems.

It may still be helpful to clarify further by drawing a contrast. In much of the western world, children are trained to make a nuisance of themselves. They are under constant pressure to prove their autonomy and independence, which may often be quite vexatious all around, but they finally learn to achieve a measure of self-sufficiency. Consequently, self-esteem and self-confidence are less dependent on the judgement of others, while conscience is not confined to concrete social relationships but is also located in more abstract principles that transcend them.

As a result, contemporary Westerners enjoy a measure of moral autonomy and self-awareness, tolerate a considerable amount of non-conformity, and are unfazed by a measure of confrontation. In married and family life, as also in friendships, anger and quarrels are anticipated, and normally faced squarely. Within bounds, they are not felt to be particularly threatening to relationships, but rather a means of deepening them, since they are typically dealt with in an active communicative fashion. The side-stepping of conflict is thus considered less adept than solving it, and 'getting it out of your system' through a meeting of hearts and minds.

CHAPTER 9

Status, manners and conscience in Yogyakarta

The mark of the adult is that he has internalized the forms of social order. Conscious of, and identifying with, his place in society, he respects the position of others, while living up to the expectations that are intrinsic to his station in life. All this is recognized to be demanding and obliging, and is coloured by a greater or lesser degree of anxiety about performance. On the other hand, accomplished presentation and style are sources of satisfaction that are self-validating.

The cultivation of good manners and appropriate expression is the art of a civilized person, whatever his station in life. This is clearly illustrated by the story of an acquaintance. He himself is a highly accomplished person but having spent most of his life in Jakarta, Indonesian became his customary language, and his manners spontaneous and relaxed. While on a visit to his relatives in Surakarta, he wanted to take a pedicab to their home.

> I really felt ashamed that I did not know how to answer the driver when he spoke to me in beautiful Javanese. After all, I am a Javanese, but when I was a child we spoke Dutch at home and my knowledge of Javanese never fully developed. Upon coming back to the town where I was born, I felt uneasy about not being able to respond correctly and politely to that fellow whose language was so refined *(alus)*. I answered him in Indonesian.

Graceful presentation in language and gesture should be combined with modesty and politeness *(andhap-asor)*. The art of indirectness, of dissembling motives, and of keeping one's opinion to oneself are implicit in the foregoing. Of course, one's house should be open to others, and there is satisfaction in acting as a congenial and hospitable host, yet contacts should remain indirect and polite while observing the propriety and good form that makes the ensuing interaction a quasi-ritual experience.

On meeting, people do, of course, pursue their own intentions, but will avoid confronting each other when trying to convey the things that relate to their personal interest. Sensitive to innuendo and minor details, they try to keep the conversation superficial and pleasant while holding each other at arm's length. While the purpose of the meeting seldom remains hidden, the style of conveying it is such that each partner may claim misunderstanding by just taking the content of the words exchanged at their face value. The host has been left the freedom to agree with his visitor that "rice is terribly expensive these days" without swallowing the bait that the latter is fishing for a loan. Each partner should be allowed his own way out, feigning misunderstanding while politely talking about irrelevant subjects.

Similarly, an offer of hospitality does not mean that the payment of rent is not expected, although the subject may never be broached; in such cases it may take some time to find out the appropriate rate by seeking precedent or the opinion of non-connected outsiders. Expressions like, "I leave it to you", or "Whatever you think is right", are almost always accompanied by very definite expectations, and sometimes even unrealistic hopes about the generosity of a comparatively affluent person. To name a definite price is just coarse manners, disturbing and not even appropriate in the market-place, where a mutually satisfactory compromise should be sought in a gentle process of bargaining.

That things are not what they appear to be, everybody knows. Yet it is wise and pleasant to uphold appearances in order not to suffer disappointment and defeat. After all, to say, "The prince of the Netherlands visited Indonesia, paying homage to our nation; when did one of our ruling sultans ever visit the Netherlands?" sounds much better than stating that he came on a business trip to negotiate the repossession of his family plantations. An outsider might call it hocus-pocus or self-deceit, but for those involved, the art of maintaining good form is satisfactory in itself. In interpersonal contacts, this art also keeps individuals separate from each other, mutually according respect while avoiding deep contact or any possibility of confrontation.

There is safety in avoiding these, even when one needs the other person's help badly in order to accomplish one's plans. The standard technique for overcoming any problem caused by interpersonal distance, both vertically and horizontally, is the use of intermediaries, for instance, in seeking a favour, the repayment of a loan, or for sounding out the possibility of a desired marriage contract. The intermediary should have easy access to both parties but also enjoy the advantages of being neutral and not being emotionally involved in the issue at hand. It saves the parties concerned having to directly confront each other with its inherent risks of disappointment and loss of face. This difficulty in approaching the other person whom one needs is felt as *pakêwuh*. The feeling arises when one has to seek assistance, even if it is from people with whom one entertains relatively close relationships; it is the feeling of reluctance when one is squeezed between the desire not to disturb the other and the necessity of doing so. The best way out is by humbling oneself, while advancing one's request in refined and polite words, practising the art of indirectness.

In order to gain perspective on Yogyakarta manners, I sought the opinion of some long-time Sumatran residents. Invariably, they lauded the openness and spontaneity of their compatriots as compared with the Javanese. "We speak our mind and stand upright, looking the other in his eyes. But here, in Yogya, people hide themselves behind a mask of smiles and mannerisms. You never know what they are up to; they tell you one thing, yet do the other." To them, people in Yogya were tricky *(semu)* and hiding behind appearance, their outspoken opinion being, "If they have so much to hide, they must be insincere." They even doubted whether people in Yogya could have true friends, although, interestingly, at least two of my Sumatran informants were married to Javanese women, with whom they appeared to live happily.

In Javanese, the word *semu* does not have the negative connotation it has in Indonesian, but means those signs in face-to-face communication that convey (unintended) hints about real purposes and feelings. Among themselves, Yogyanese will understand these indications, such as smiling as a sign that one feels insulted, or kicking the cat because one is angry with one's elder brother. In that sense, the comments of East-Javanese informants were more revealing. They certainly did not doubt that people in Yogyakarta were communicating, but rather accused them of being too much concerned with form and showing so little in their reactions, thus lacking spontaneity. According to them, people in East Java are more open in speaking their mind, in striking up friendships, while at the same time they are less afraid or inhibited in showing their true emotions. They found Yogyanese manners an impediment to friendships and free flowing communication.

Yet to the people of South Central Java, refined manners and indirectness are important. They are signs of self-mastery and patience, protective of one's self while slowly moving to one's goal. Often they jokingly observe, "Suppose that you want to go to Yogya, that's your purpose. In that case, you should go to Surabaya first, then to Jakarta, back to Semarang, and by way of Banyumas you will surely get to Yogya." It is not important that you get there as soon as possible, the important thing is that you get there, precisely and on target. Look which way the cat will jump before you make your move, take your time, and be alert to the intentions of others while remaining discreet about your own.

With all this in mind, it is small wonder that ethics are largely formulated in terms of don'ts rather than of do's. Its cardinal command is 'to measure by oneself' *(tepa slira)* what result one's words and actions will have on the feelings of others. In other words, do as you would be done by. In practice, this usually comes out in terms of, "Do not irritate the other", "Be careful not to hurt the other's feeling", "Do not insult the other but show respect for his position", "Do not cause trouble to others", "Stay away where you have no business", "Be careful not to cause the other loss of face", etcetera, which all boil down to a self-protective strategy of restraint. Not to involve oneself is wise and good.

This rather self-centred ethic combines with a sensitivity about the honour due to one's person and position. For that, one is of course dependent on the perceptions of others. Moreover, being well regarded and receiving honour also carries obligations, since one's status depends on the personal effort one makes to live up to expectations. Especially if sufficiently high up, "One has no place to hide one's face", and irrespective of (possibly disastrous) financial consequences, the need is felt to demonstrate status by throwing a big, lavish party on the occasion of major life-cycle rituals, especially for circumcisions and marriages. When I remarked to my landlady that it was quite an impressive wedding at one of her neighbours houses, possibly two hundred people having gathered there, her spontaneous reaction was that she had entertained at least five hundred people at her daughter's wedding, thus belittling the status of the next door family in contrast to her own.

One should assert personal status, having no place to hide one's face, and even poor people will go into debt to contribute an appropriate present at their superiors' celebrations in order to be well-thought-of. The acceptance of their gift naturally obliges the better-off to care for the poorer segment, while these in turn will take pride in their community, and thus in themselves, over the generosity and recognition of their superiors. As members of society, they belong each to the other and so it is important to validate oneself in others' eyes.

With status considerations and acceptance apparently so central to life in Yogya, the question of self-respect became even more intriguing when I checked on Wojowasito's Dutch translations of self-esteem *(eigenwaarde)* and self-respect *(zelfrespect)*.[1] In Indonesian, he glossed self-esteem as *harga diri*, while rendering self-respect as *harga diri yang wajar*, 'genuine value of the self', which is a constructed translation. Subsequently, I went in search of Javanese equivalents.

The vast majority of my *kejawèn* respondents thought the Indonesian notion of *harga diri* corresponded with *praja*, the prestige that results from one's status position *(pangkat)*. In trying to differentiate this from the Dutch notion of self-respect, almost all of them stuck to the Javanese idea of *praja*, some of them explaining that the idea of *harga diri* was typical of Sumatrans, who could not appreciate the important value of humility *(andhap-asor)*. In their view, self-esteem and self-respect both meant the same thing, namely to be well-regarded, to care for one's reputation, and to receive the honour due to one's status position. In other words, self-respect appeared to stand for what other people consider a person to be; outwardly the individual is a social being who is defined by the prestige that others attribute to his position, which becomes his identity on the stage of life.

Of the twenty informants questioned about self-respect, three gave *kebatinan*-related answers, differentiating the notion of the "true I" from the visible person, while only three others differentiated it in a clear social perspective. Two of them were members of the Muhammadiyah (a modern Islamic reform movement), the other being well-known as a flagrantly independent-minded artist. Although these three agreed that to most the idea of *harga diri* was dependent on status recognition and

1 S. Wojowasito, *Kamus umum Belanda-Indonesia.* Jakarta: P.T. Ichtiar Baru-Van Hoeve, 1978.

attributed honour, they also recognized a more personal variant of self-respect. This latter idea they conceived of as *kaprawiran* or *kasatriyan* which to them was a clear and important concept that meant 'having the courage to go one's own way irrespective of the opinion of others, following one's own convictions and mission in life'. They referred to the Prophet or the Javanese Muslim saints *(wali)*, or to the *wayang* heroes Bima and Karna as the examples to follow.

In a further attempt to clarify the issue, I made another outsider's approach by trying to find a functional equivalent for the western Christian notion of conscience. This idea is often translated as *suara batin*, inner voice, and relates basically to mysticism, intuition, and one's contact with 'God'; it certainly does not convey the idea of a personal superego. Although the Javanese notion of *rumangsaning ati* seems to come somewhat closer, it clearly remains a form of sensitivity regarding others or, as an informant explained, "It is deeper than shame *(malu)* and has to be trained in order to acquire a finer feeling as to what might hurt others". Along with several people later interviewed, he disagreed that it would be reluctance to do wrong per se or in the eyes of 'God', and also rejected the idea that actions are good or bad in themselves. According to him, and all other *kejawèn* informants, a good or bad action always relates to deeds done unto others.

Infraction of the social rules is not intrinsically bad, and one may think whatever one likes, as long as one visibly conforms to the demands of social life. It is bad when infractions are noted, and one should abstain from such actions because people may see them. 'Conscience' is consciousness of others, of the eyes, comments, and criticism that affect one's position of status respect. A good person is generally described as a person who knows the feeling of shame and who fears the opinion of others. Apparent conformity with the demands of one's group life and one's status are the basis of good conscience; in effect, this means to refrain from actions that would not be tolerated by one's fellows and that would thus threaten one's quiet; even then such actions are not so much bad as plainly stupid.

To hold a different opinion or to act in a different manner when out of eyesight or earshot, are accepted, and often even expected. To cheat, to be corrupt, to frequent prostitutes and the like, when far away, are personal matters that do not concern one's fellows as long as it is done discreetly; such actions merely concern relationships with irrelevant outsiders. Life in the outside world has no connection with one's communal existence, and I have often been amazed by the licentiousness of acquaintances and friends when outside their environment, and hence relieved from the pressure of conformity that is imposed upon them by their group life.

A person out beyond the bounds set by relevant others is considered to be a bag full of emotions and passions that will run wild once given the opportunity. So therefore, it is a good thing to be, and feel, controlled by the members of one's community. Conscious of the formal rules of his social life, he has the compass bearings to sail on; should these rules break down, he may lose both his sense of orientation and of proportion. It is therefore wise to guard one's honour and prestige and to avoid scandal under all circumstances. If a person feels immune to this because of his position of power, he may become a very unscrupulous and threatening character indeed.

Apparently, the claims of society concern the *lair*, that is, one's visible behaviour and outward appearance. These social claims are virtually all-encompassing, but most people appear to feel secure living up to them in remarkable conformity with their demands. Whatever an individual's personal opinions, thoughts or emotions on this matter, as on any other, he is entitled to entertain them privately, as long as he accepts, conforms, and lives up to the public demands of his life in the group. One's role in life is a public one, and it should be shaped by mastering one's impulses and presenting oneself in an elegant, subdued and accomplished manner, the successful role-playing on the social stage being a great source of satisfaction in itself.

This gratification does not come for free, however, but is the outcome of constant efforts to take the desires of others into account in one's own scheme of existence. Socially, one can never really take it easy, always having to stand on tiptoe, as it were, to be cautious and conscious of the impression that one makes on others. Given this need to be constantly on the alert, social life is never relaxing; on the contrary, it often actually creates tensions and problems. The adequate response is to practise the solicitous attitude of *prihatin*, and to have the wisdom to take life seriously. These responses, however, are personal affairs that have little to do with the demands of communal life per se.

CHAPTER 10

A scrutiny of family and gender

In the Philippines, belonging to and deriving a sense of security from the family appear to be the cardinal things in life, those most worth striving after. The family is the wellspring of a meaningful existence, of obligation and fulfilment. Sanctified by popular religiosity and ritual, the household-centred (nuclear) family is inviolable and relatively autonomous; as part of local kin groups, related families are expected to mutually express solidarity and extend support.

However valuable all this is, the family as the dominant social institution is nowadays also a cause for apprehension and a focus of social criticism.

> When we say that we Filipinos value close family ties, what we may be saying actually is that we value closed family ties. For many of us are just that — closed to concerns that do not directly involve our own parents, children, brothers, sisters, grandparents, grandchildren, or close kin. We will move mountains to provide our family with only the best. But how many of us are moved by, much less respond to, the plight of our fellow Filipinos?[1]

Be that as it may, the family constitutes an individual's moral world and the experience of it may have important psychological consequences, and affect his perception of self. Experiencing and seeing himself relationally, for the individual interpersonal relationships, and feeling accepted, become very important. The consequent avoidance of open conflict may be expressed in the apparent acceptance of the

1 From, How valuable, the Philippine value system? *Signal, a primer on social issues,* Experimental edition 1, December 1985.

authority of older family members, submission to parents, and even acting against one's own wishes and ideas. Being pressured into a role, the individual may feel oppressed, while close ties may breed tensions, resentment, anger, and the slow resolution of hidden conflict. Although hurting others should be forgiven in the setting of the family, such slights are not easily forgotten and bad feelings may simmer on.

Relationships with familial near others are primarily relationships of inevitable (inter)dependence, in which people have to adapt and adjust themselves to each other in the belief that the solidarity of the family itself should come first. In contrast with saints and the Holy Mother, and often with grandparents, intrafamily relationships are not necessarily intimate, as illustrated in *The Hazards of Distance*. In this novelette, Linda Ty-Casper tells about the distances that separate family members, even as they try to come close to each other. Still, when very close up, they may feel terribly isolated, or just isolate themselves. Absence of private space may stunt their development, and enhance emotional dependence on family members who have migrated across the oceans (1981:back cover).

Mrs Ty composes fiction, yet the type of family dynamics she describes appears to tally with the ideas of psychiatry-, or psychology-oriented observers who locate the source of mental disturbances or psychological problems in the setting and experience of family life. These ideas also correspond with, for instance, Hollnsteiner's critical description of family culture among lowland Filipinos.[2]

Ramirez appears to be even more negative in her analysis of family life. As she sees it, many a child experiences a deep crisis when it discovers that it is not regarded as a personality, as an entity in itself, but as an instrument of the family's honour and for its support.[3]

> Moreover, he feels his freedom is stifled by parents who openly or subtly persuade him to follow the parents' choice of a profession, of a future partner in life, or of a vocation. This seeming authoritarianism stems from the conviction of parents that as such they know what is best for the child. Understandably, this way of rearing chil-

---

2 Mary R. Hollnsteiner, 1981. *The wife. The husband.* Cordero-Fernando, *op. cit.*:37-59.

3 Mina Ramirez, *Understanding Philippine social realities through the Filipino family.* Metro Manila: Asian Social Institute, 1984:30.

dren makes for a communication gap between parents and children, promoting secre-
cy in the family, while intensifying feelings of isolation. Such feelings of isolation are
resolved at times by taking recourse to intimacy in friendship groups, in over-activity
in organizations, or to an escapist attitude, as projected in rampant elopements... It is
only when children accept this parental attitude that, as in the case of families still
steeped in traditionalism, authoritarianism will be supportive. Otherwise, this authoritarianism may just become a constant irritant, thus nullifying the family as a haven of
peace and security (*ibid.*:30-1).

According to Ramirez, the famous close family ties are primarily
rooted in the mutual support that is indispensable to survival in the
Filipino 'culture of insecurity' (*ibid.* 39-50). This sustenance is largely
economic and "achieves emotional flavour in family gatherings and
reunions or on special occasions like Christmas, birthdays, and wedding
and death anniversaries, where religious rituals play a significant function" (*ibid.*:34).

Close family ties, however, are based primarily on economic interdependence or self-
defense against the threatening pressures of the larger society. Moreover, the infidelity of the Filipino male, the communication gap between husband and wife, and that
between parents and children, demonstrate that close family ties are a myth in many
ways (*ibid.*:34).

I think that Ramirez is somewhat Eurocentric in her emphasis on
the importance of independent personality formation, and may exagger-
ate the economic function of the family. It may be that these are gaining
more importance at present in modernizing, especially urban, environ-
ments. She is certainly right, though, in noting the relation between
'close ties' and 'interdependence' and the function of the family as a
haven in the unruly world of wider society. After all, one's family is the
positive realm in life, it is one's moral anchor, and thus it is worth sacrificing for, even if that entails 'communication gaps', self-denial and self-
effacement.

In spite of the belief in empathy with near others, communication
gaps appear to be real enough. Among the people who matter most to
each other, love is expressed in a direct way, through touching, providing, serving, forgiving, sacrificing, joking, teasing, and the giving of

small presents.[4] Love is not necessarily expressed in a meeting of hearts and minds, in an attempt to explain one's self to the other, which perhaps cannot be expected because to do so requires self-awareness on one's own part, and may in addition lead to confrontation. In the normal course of action this is avoided. "At home we cannot talk about those things, that would be disturbing"; "At home we do everything to keep it peaceful. My father [a prominent member of the Iglesia ni Cristo] knows that I do not care about his church, but we behave as if I am a member"; "When my father broaches the subject of land reform, then please answer in such-and-such a way"; "I got so mad at my brother that I just had to leave the house"; "Sometimes I feel so angered, but there is no way of showing it at home. Yes, we forgive, but we never forget."

> When I was invited to share lunch with his family, attorney Lavasco introduced me to his wife and three adult children, all of them professionals. During the thirty minute event, nobody spoke but the two of us, my interlocutor making it a point to explain family closeness, "It is even written in the law. An unmarried daughter is not permitted to leave home without parental consent before the age of twenty-three. Yes, we are happy to be together, often to the extent that parents will keep their adult children financially dependent just to keep them at home." Yet attorney Lavasco appeared to have a problem that he did not quite understand when he talked about his eldest son, an engineer, who had left home four years before to work in the Middle East. Although he was entitled to regular leave, he had not been back to see his family for well over two years.

Crossing oceans, running away, or just staying mum in order to keep one's opinions and emotions to oneself, each serves to maintain the smooth surface and the pretence that nothing is wrong. These are all common reactions, as are the dissembling and hiding of motives. It leads to Ramirez's 'communication gaps' caused by authoritarianism and

---

4 Small presents serve of course to say, "See, I have been thinking of you". Highly institutionalized is the *pasalubong*, the (mandatory) gift brought by a traveller returning from a trip. For many people, a three day trip to Hong Kong seems to mean three days of shopping to buy presents for all the people they can think of. Some people avoid or postpone returning home because the burden of buying gifts for everybody is either too bothersome or too expensive.

avoidance, and the suffocating closeness that demands relaxation with others within the family or without, with a sister or a brother to whom one feels particularly close, or with a neighbour, or most often with one's close friends. Normally friends, whether male or female, cluster in separate groups, *barkada*, in which they share liquor, adventure, and 'intimacy'; it is the very situation where one can let off steam. Relationships in the *barkada* are more relaxed, more tolerant, and guided by the principle of *pakikisama*, of actively going along with each other as members of a group. The *barkada* is a necessary complement to home and family.

The other way to seek relaxation is in prayer; 'talking with God', a saint, the Holy Mother, or with deceased relatives. When other beings are out of reach, the latter provide courage and consolation. They are the eminently trusted kin in whom one can confide; because of their sacrifices they will understand the problems of their devotees and suppliants. In such emotional encounters, the individual can unburden himself and 'recharge his batteries' to face the vicissitudes of life.

Religious relationships are the best of familial relationships. The love of religious personages is on account of their suffering and sacrifices, that have become exemplary for self-denial as a way to greatness and fulfilment, in which an individual places his family before the self.

According to Ruben, who graduated from college five years ago,

> Since I finished my degree, I work. The money is needed to send my two sisters through college. That is why I am still unmarried. Yet it makes me feel good as a son and brother. My elder brother is already married and lives with his wife and child with our parents — all of us live together; we like the closeness — yet he still depends financially on their resources.

Such self-denial for a noble purpose demonstrates one's sincerity, friendship, worth. It is a way to moral fulfilment, often expressed in migration to the States, in order to send remittances home, or in temporary work in the Middle East to support the family. In the morally vague sphere surrounding the home, it also justifies all sorts of dubious practices as long as they benefit one's family and prove devotion to its well-being.

At the heart of the commitment to these ethical imperatives lies the recognition of obligation to the family as a collectivity. Such obligation, though, tends to become personalized, dyadic, that is to say, between pairs of mutually self-selected individuals. At the centre stand one's obligations to mother and father; these exemplify the morality of the relationships with emotionally important others and spill over into a general sense of obligation toward all those who belong to one's relevant circle of relatives and friends, or whoever else one in actual fact feels indebted to.

These define the horizon of action, and it is by establishing specific relationships that one gets a grip on the world. In other words, there is a need to know somebody to get things done, to feel obliged, to reciprocate, to act; it is by expanding familiar relationships that one's world is enlarged, whether as a patron or a client, a friend or a recommendee. On leaving this personalized sphere for that of anonymity, one is quickly lost and devoid of any moral basis of action beyond personal obligations.

The unknown world is highly unsatisfactory. Consequently, when strangers meet, they immediately begin to check out whether they might be somehow connected through common elements in their backgrounds. Place of origin, school, family name, any of these may provide clues to discover whether one is, for example, the second cousin of the other's brother-in-law, in that way establishing a known point in unfamiliar surroundings, and a way of charting the ensuing relationship. This means projecting the familiar relationships of everyday life, with one's own family at the centre, into the wider world; it is these relationships that provide the model for external actions.

Gender role ascription

It has often been noted that the highly personalized world of 'connections' is an impediment to the development of a wider, institutional sphere based on abstractions such as 'the rule of law' and 'the public interest'.[5] We have also noted that the idealized picture of the familiar interpersonal world is often at odds with the experience and practice of

5 See, for instance, *Building a People, Building a Nation*:4-5 (*op.cit.* p. 60).

everyday life. It is of interest to note that most material that is critical of family life that came my way was written by women.[6] What could possibly be the reason?

It may be assumed that it has much to do with the central position of the mother in the Philippine household, and all the burdens this entails. The role is also that of a kind of ideological pivot that places women apart from men: the purity of women symbolizing the wholeness of the home[7] at the same time that mother as a superego representative is the primary embodiment of conscience. Furthermore, in extending and symbolizing warmth and goodness, the female as a wife and mother should be loving, which is to say, forgiving, should be gentle and compassionate with those who morally depend on her (Lapuz, 1978). Even if we suppose that she is moderately capable of living up to all this, it may be expected that the emphasis on mothering and caring for the family become second nature to her (the *tagasaló* syndrome, Arellano-Carandang, 1987:65-7), while often stimulating a pronounced emotional dependency in men (Lapuz, 1977:61), in which case husbands also tend to become somewhat like sons to their wives.

Of course, the female and male spheres in life are complementary and equivalent, but what often strikes the observer is their separation. The overprotection extended to daughters frequently results in a lack of self-assurance on their part. Then such a woman may seek security in sticking to the culturally prescribed roles that largely define her self-concept. These allow her to be very possessive about her husband and children, in that way expressing her emotional dependency on others, and promoting the 'closed-ness' of the family more than the 'closeness' of its ties; such ties are not 'close', but sticky.

While it is as well to bear this psychological dependency between

6 For instance, M.L. Arellano-Carandang, Mary Hollnsteiner, Lourdes V. Lapuz, Mina Ramirez, Linda Ty-Casper, who have all been referred to. In their novels, Linda Espina-Moore (e.g. *A Lion in the House*) and Lualhati Bautista (e.g. *Dekada '70* and *Bata, Bata... paano Ka Ginawa*) make similar points.

7 In a touching way this point is made by Bienvenido N. Santos in his story "Scent of Apples" when a long-time Pinoy emigrant inquires, "Are our Filipino women the same like they were twenty years ago?" The answer, "They are the same as they were twenty years ago, god-fearing, faithful, modest and nice", serving to reassure him that the world of his background is still whole. In Leonard Casper, *Modern Philippine short stories.* Albuquerque: University of New Mexico Press, 1962:91-2.

family members in mind, people also feel a need to react against the closed-ness, pressures, and oppressiveness of the family. It is the men who have the better opportunities for acting this out. Culture defines their realm as the area outside the home, where they are supposed to earn the money to provide for their families. So they have the privilege of spending a lot of time with others, of leaving the anxieties of home and child care to their wives, of gallivanting, drinking with *barkada* mates, and of getting involved with other women.

This relative freedom of action in the morally vague area outside is expressed in the so-called 'double standard' that allows men to indulge themselves with other females, but that does not allow their own womenfolk to do the same with other males. As pure wives, these women are not supposed to be lovers, but to function as moral mothers (Hollnsteiner, 1981:43,57; Lapuz, 1977:24,102). Erotic adventure is therefore inevitably located in the male area outside the home, and no moral stigma attaches to it.

Pressure to live up to male and female roles is considerable, at the same time that role fulfilment functions as a substitute for self-confidence. Males must be macho and women caring; males go to the cockfight, women to church; men are promiscuous while women are moral mothers; males have an excess of 'face' and are therefore vulnerable, women give in and do the suffering; males hide their insecurity in boastful behaviour and women powder it over with cosmetics; males find emotional realization in authoritarianism and women in the display of grief; often males are compulsively insecure regarding women, and women are supposed to smooth this over by subservient behaviour towards them.

The separation of the male and the female domains seems to be regarded as a sign that the world is all in order as it should be. At most colleges, the co-eds still come in uniform whereas the men are more or less free to dress as they like. When the Ministry of Education proposed to introduce home economics for girls and boys, a newspaper reported,

> conservative Filipino educators find technical training for girls as repulsive as rearing boys for household work. Home economics, they fear, destroys the distinction between a man's work and women's responsibility. Critics have also warned against the 'danger' that young boys may turn 'effeminate' because of home economics.

Complementarity and separation of domains keep the myths about maleness and femaleness alive and make it difficult for both men and women to be emancipated from their prescribed roles.[8] Often people have very strong emotions about these myths, because emancipation from them would reveal a non-individuated ego that seeks its security in dependent subjectivity, in which emotional experience is the measure of things and the right reason for action. In this construction both males and females need their domains as areas of self-validation in the same way that parents need their children's diplomas and graduation pictures, and as 'civic clubs' need the modest monuments they build to make their mark on the world.

While it is true that things are changing, the strength of the family hold over its members is still considerable, and is very probably reinforced by the struggle for economic survival in an impoverished society. That formidable grip appears to have wide-ranging psychological dimensions affecting identity, assurance, and self-realization. The family embodies morality, the right way of life. To that path belong the separation of male and female domains and forceful role ascription.

8 These myths, and the necessity for demystification, are strong themes in, The social construction of the Filipino woman (Delia D. Aguilar, *The feminist challenge*. Metro Manila: Asian Social Institute, 1988:28-48). She observes that whereas the second-rate status of women in the public domain is slowly becoming clear, "elsewhere — in the home to be exact, where the ideological fog permeating family relations is particularly dense — the hallowed theme of woman as mother and wife has so far eluded interrogation" (37). Consequently, "an understanding of the family's position within society remains obscured and, along with it, women's domestic subservience" (48).

CHAPTER 11

Thai and Javanese ideas about the individual

and society

Thai ideas

Cosmological and religious perspectives

Several Buddhist teachings have deeply influenced the Thai conceptualization of 'being human'. Two central concepts are those of rein-
carnation and Karma. Whereas the latter may be empirically understood
as the inevitable progressions of the infinite chains of cause and effect
through which the vast machinery of cosmic justice proceeds, in everyday practice it is taken to mean the present circumstances of one's personal lot (karma) in life. This is believed to be largely predetermined by
one's positive and negative actions in previous existences, though also
to some extent by one's deeds in the present one. In sum, each individual's fate is the outcome of what he has done during the course of
innumerable life-spans; and since no two people share the same moral
history, nobody can be like anybody else. Everybody has to work out,
and through, his own destiny. Liberation comes about through one's
own efforts.

Since both positive and negative acts result in accordant effects,
periods of good fortune may alternate with periods of adversity, a cycle
which reinforces the personal understanding of existential uncertainty.
Yet, since previously accumulated karma may have been 'worked out',
and thus only partly conditions one's experiences in the present, many
people are aware of the need to depend upon themselves in shaping
their present and future.

This self-dependent view of the person and his experience corresponds with the relative absence of the idea that human life is the manifestation of a supreme order to which one must submit oneself. If there
is any order at all, it is the order of contingency and personal action,

that is best expressed in the credo that both meritorious and demeritorious deeds produce accordant consequences. Basically, cosmic law — that is, the Law of Karma centres on personal moral and ethical behaviour, which gives rise to an individual-centred view of the order of life.

This creed of moral independence is balanced by the fact that one is born of parents and is completely dependent on their goodness *(bunkhun)* while growing up. This virtue of the parents places the child under the lasting moral obligation to honour and be grateful to them. To fail to fulfil this basic obligation is to commit the sin of *neerakhun*, or to 'rebuff goodness received'. Such a rebuffal is believed to be an extremely demeritorious act that will result in the immediate experience of bad karma.

Moreover, from an animistic perspective, the person knows that beyond his own moral resources, he can depend on and seek the protection of *saksit* power, which can help him to achieve his aims and enjoy a safe existence. In order to mobilize such supernatural protection, a person should perform a ritual supplication to some spirit for it. While there is a measure of volition in seeking this protection, it also conveniently shifts the burden of self-reliance to dependence on what is more powerful than oneself. This oscillation between perspectives of dependence and independence pervades the relationship between the individual and society.

Social perspective

Thai society organizes itself in a hierarchical fashion in which people occupy differently ranked positions. Most relationships, therefore, are characterized by relative superiority versus inferiority. To the Thai child, the social world appears at first as an aggregate of benevolent superiors. The centre of this sphere is its mother, on whose benevolent and loving care it depends. This dependence on the mother is widely idealized in Thai culture, she being the reliable centre of intimacy, faith and certitude in a basically untrustworthy world.

Yet mother's love does not come free, and as the child is being made to feel that it fully depends on its mother's goodness, it is also taught to reciprocate by the show of obedience. All superiors seem to be entitled to a child's respect as a matter of course, and one of the first things it is taught is to show this respect and to present itself politely. Soon the tot learns that a measure of 'subduedness' and conformity leads to reward and acceptance, and that many people are highly sensitive to the respect owed to their person.

Beyond the circle of benevolent superiors and near others — such as relatives, community members, or classmates — one finds the distant others who represent an awe-inspiring world of hierarchy and unpredictable power. In dealing with such outsiders, it is wise to be respectful, and wary of their motives. In effect, the child has to absorb the lesson that people are to be classified in terms of rank and distance, and its behaviour should be appropriate when dealing with each of these different catagories.

For some people, the hierarchical perception of others tends to become highly stereotyped, automatically equating persons with their rank and status. In a way, this isolates people from each other, and even though the acknowledgement of superior rank does not necessarily imply the recognition of authority over one's person, inferiors will often feel inhibited and restricted in their self-expression when in the presence of such people. Thus many people appear to be keen to guard a measure of autonomy in their social affairs, not easily committing themselves to others, while at the same time pragmatically seeking to promote their own ends.

As popular wisdom has it, "It is best to know how to take care of your own affairs and to stay out of trouble"; the person who is able to do both validates his self-respect. While, of course, it is wise to cultivate good working relationships with one's fellows, it is also shrewd and politic to keep them at some distance. This tendency to stay clear of each other leads to a remarkable tolerance of deviation and a weak measure of social control, a lenience that may reflect respect for the independence and individuality of others. The prime source of interpersonal integration appears to be the recognition of mutual obligations; this principle of reciprocity ties people together in an extended system of personalized, dyadic relationships. Communal integration tends to remain weakly developed; if strong leadership is not forthcoming, members of communities will generally only cooperate on the occasion of religious festivals or ceremonies.

The primary direction of integration among people appears to be vertical. Vertical integration is especially apparent in the patrimonially structured national organizations, for example, the Civil Service and the Brotherhood of Buddhist Monks *(Sangha)*. Yet even in more horizontally structured situations, people tend to interrelate in terms of relative status, social distance and extent of obligation, these social coordinates not only defining the other person but also oneself. Many people tend therefore to identify with their position, and to derive a good deal of satisfaction from recognition of their status.

To protect or advance such recognition, one may need to regularly validate one's status by, for instance, throwing a lavish party, or financing conspicuous religious merit-making. Among Thai men, this quest for recognition is often expressed in typical acts of virile behaviour, such as impressing others by their boldness, womanizing, or big-spending. In identifying with their own vanity, they try to enhance their presentation and may consequently become very vulnerable to questions of 'face', and likely to become stubborn and seek revenge if slighted.

Avoidance and involvement

The 'ethos of relative independence' that was propounded above becomes more meaningful if it is contrasted with the predominantly vertical dimension of hierarchy, and the obligation to pay visible respect to superiors. This suppresses individualism but seems to separate people from each other: it may lead some to almost total identification with their status and the respect owed it, while in others it will stimulate the desire to keep one's distance from other people in order to ensure some room for personal manoeuvre. It also leads to a quest for friends with whom one can share one's frustrations and displeasure at a life in society that often forces one to pose as a mere inferior.

Respect of hierarchy, obligation, and deferential manners are among the first things a child learns as it grows out of infancy. Children soon learn to feel apprehensive about their behaviour in the presence of superiors, and to become sensitive to all forms of criticism. Anxiety about presentation is known as 'shyness' *(aaj)*. Such diffidence is rated positively by elders, and may stimulate the development of the Thai concept of self-mastery. Subsequently, children will learn to keep their emotions to themselves, but also discover that they can get their own way by the show of respectful and obedient behaviour.

To be bashful and shy, or 'to have a thin face', is a positive quality in people who restrain themselves and thus avoid giving offence to others. It is considered important to train children in solicitude and circumspection in facing others, especially strangers and superiors. This attitude should later mature into the more refined one of *kreengcaj*, which reflects awareness and anticipation of the feelings of others. *Kreengcaj* behaviour manifests itself in kindness, self-restraint, tolerance, and the avoidance of interpersonal irritation. The initiation in this lies with the one practising *kreengcaj*; such a person is considerate of others and puts much thought and effort into maintaining a smooth social atmosphere.

The behaviour of some people seems to be the product of an excess of *kreengcaj* that seemingly causes extreme reluctance to draw attention to oneself by actions, resulting in giggling and inertia. Such shyness, inspired by incipient feelings of shame or fear, can hardly be considered as positive 'consideration of the feelings of others'. Similarly, while relating to one's superiors, an avoidance of initiative coupled with an extreme concern to please the boss may lead to acceptance — but smells of sycophancy rather than *kreengcaj*. Even though it is sometimes difficult to draw the line between these two attitudes, it remains true that the *kreengcaj* attitude encourages people in the avoidance of unpleasantness and interpersonal confrontation.

Because of the general vulnerability of 'face', being circumspect about the motives of others is wise, while unconsidered criticism is dangerous. It is better to let the other have his way if one wants to achieve a measure of personal security, and a self-effacing attitude is the safest one to adopt for the relative inferior. Moreover, violence is endemic in Thai society and it is folly to 'build oneself an enemy'. Everybody knows that all are extremely vulnerable to affronts against their 'face' and that revenge for a perceived insult, however unintended, may have extremely unpleasant consequences. Especially with distant others, it pays to be careful. In such cases it is not necessarily *kreengcaj*, but sometimes a feeling of fear *(kreengklua)* that is inspired by the distant other, which motivates the desire for total avoidance.

Often, Thai people seem to be highly aware of living in a dangerous world where one is constantly uncertain about the motives of others. On the one hand, this awareness may be a cause for the idealization of the mother-child relationship that has become the symbol of the only trustworthy and reliable relationship in the world. On the other hand, it may inspire the belief in the wisdom of watching out for oneself while staying out of trouble. Consequently, it is wise to practise non-involvement in the affairs of others, to be tolerant, and to go one's own way if possible. In respect to one's wider social surroundings, one soon learns the wisdom of remaining indifferent *(choej)* and of restraining oneself emotionally, especially when one has no power or influence. Politics, administrative decisions, government programmes or developmental schedules are all basically the affairs of others that one accepts or suffers without involving oneself. Yet, closer to home and in one's direct relationships with others, one may often be more involved than one would like.

However astute holding oneself aloof from others' affairs to avoid trouble may be in theory, in practice it often boils down merely to the mastery of social form, and not to the total eradication of negative emotions. By staying out of others' way and by avoiding undue intimacy, one may try to avoid emotional involvement that might rupture the ideal, smooth surface of social life. To present oneself politely is a good strategy to control situations, and the clichéd 'Thai smile' is one of its manifestations. Although smiling and politeness gives interaction a pleasant façade, it is often a mere self-defensive manipulation of form that keeps people at a distance from each other.

The relative importance of maintaining distance leads to the presumption that many Thai individuals may suffer from the lack of possibilities their society offers for self-expression. They seem not only to avoid emotional confrontation with others, but often also appear to be incapable of confronting their own inner selves. If this is true, then one might guess that the Thai person is highly involved with his presentation, not only as a means of achieving acceptance and status, but even physically, as a body that needs to be presented in the best of order. Often, it appears that outward acceptance spells inner security, and that the distance between one's accepted presentation ('face') and one's emotional self is small; Suntaree Komin refers to this connection as a strong 'ego orientation' (1990:161-4).

For acceptance and the recognition of status, a person may be dependent on others whom he would emotionally prefer to avoid. In many instances, these others are also the source of material security, and may even be superiors who treat one in such a way that ill-feelings arise that must be suppressed. Between these polarities of involvement and avoidance, of dependence and independence, the individual can only hope that the received wisdom of avoiding overt conflict may contribute to feelings of personal peace and satisfaction, and that the quest for fun and pleasure *(sanug)* will provide sufficient release from frustration.

The individual perspective

The orderly fulfilment of one's place in a predominantly hierarchical society defines the person as 'good'. Yet, from the personal perspective, such 'good' or ethical behaviour is that involved in relating dyadically to the persons with whom one has dealings. There appears to be hardly any conception of an overall order of society to which individuals should submit themselves. Thus the Thai concept of ethics is, like the Buddhist one, individual-centred: people are responsible for meeting their personal obligations to status and known others, but they are not answerable for the social order and its 'public' or 'generalized other'.

Society appears to be a stage on which actors willy-nilly have to appear, and often it seems to exist merely for the sake of the performance of the individual actors. This stage is needed for the expression of the self; and thus persons appear to be bound to act on it, though at the same time they have no duties concerning the success of the total show.

The Thai person is socially defined and subject to the acceptance of others. As a consequence, he must find and cultivate his resources in the social world, the commonly accepted validation of the person being defined in terms of his capacity to present himself. For most people, this simply means behaving appropriately and graciously while avoiding giving any offence. Others invest more heavily in their presentation, the successful person often being given to self-admiration and vanity.

The necessity of modifying self-expression to fit in with social surroundings is not to everybody's liking, and many people show a sturdy
tendency to seek another path and go their own way. They try to stand
on their own feet, and seem indifferent to the socially inspired self-
identity with which most people have to content themselves. Such non-
conformists show a good deal of courage and initiative in living as 'outsiders' in society; what they seek is a position in which they can escape
the pressure to live up to the requirements of the hierarchy.

The best alternative that is available in Thai culture is the development of self-mastery and a 'cool heart' *(cajjen)*. This means to refuse to
be carried away by emotions, to avoid conflict, and to maintain one's
dignity by refusing to be ground down by the pressures of social life. It
means mastery of a situation by cultivating a measured distance and
reserve while going one's own way. Even though the *cajjen* attitude
imposes constraints on spontaneous behaviour, it also leads to the satisfaction of solving problems independently. It means a form of social
independence and non-involvement that is immune to criticism and
which is an admired form of personality expression.

Javanese ideas

Cosmological and religious perspectives

The human being is part of the unity of existence, that is, of Life.
Subject to cosmic law, he is limited in experience, purpose, and volition. Life on earth is seen as a mere shadow of that higher truth to
which the individual should submit. With little interest in eschatological
speculations, life so conceived of makes the individual a being with a
(predestined) lot who has to fulfil his course on his way from origin to
destiny.

As a physical manifestation of the great order of Life, the human
being's task is to master his phenomenal existence, such as his body,
drives, and emotions, in order to shape life elegantly. Another task is to
function as a link in the continuity of Life, to marry and have offspring.
In this sense parenthood has a religious significance which places chil-

dren under the obligation to honour and respect their source of life; if they fail in this, they will be subject to unavoidable supernatural punishment *(walat)*.

The human being is, in fact, more than a merely physical expression of the order of Life. In his inner being *(batin)*, he carries a spark of the essence of Life that animates cosmos and earth. Mystically, he is a microcosm in relation to the macrocosm that is Life. It is through his mastery of his phenomenal existence *(lair)* — that includes the passions and power of thought that tie one to the material world — that he frees his energies to develop his inner core and train his intuitive inner feeling *(rasa)* to become attuned to higher truth ('the voice in the quiet'). His outward manifestations are thus of little importance, and the experience of worldly life simply a fact to accept *(nrima)*. This frees a person to realize his true self and deep individuality in isolation. To achieve this, one should strive to attune one's inner feeling to intuitive communication with the secret of Life, ultimately becoming one with its essence.

The mastery of one's outward expressions serves the purpose of self-realization, of enjoying the inner quietness of one's *batin*, that should become the motionless axis around which the outer world revolves. One's inner being is one's integrity and continuity, and thus it is wise to develop it; one's outward, *lair* existence merely serving as a defensive fence behind which the 'true person' lives his own life. Deep down, every person potentially encompasses the universe, which is the reason for the self-centredness that is characteristic of Javanese mystical thought. This bifurcated perception of personhood, that is expressed in two quasi-independent realms, recurs in the practice of everyday life.

Social perspective

To be civilized is to know order, inwardly and outwardly so. When just born, the child is considered *durung jawa*, which is to say, not yet socialized as a Javanese should be. Subjected to its drives and emotions, the child is incapable of orderly conduct and in need of learning self-mastery and the rules of social life. It is the task of its parents to instil these rules. Because the newborn child already carries within itself its own allotted course, the task of parents is not so much the moulding of the character of their children but more one of teaching them self-mastery, good manners, and respect for order. The latter is primarily hierarchically organized, which is reflected in social behaviour and the ranked speech levels of the Javanese language.

Intrafamily relationships serve as the prime model for the organization of society. The relationship to the distant, authoritarian father embodies the hierarchical orientation of social perceptions. In that, people appear to become equated with their rank and status, incorporating, as it were, various bundles of traits and obligations. The emphasis is on well-ordered predictable relationships, in which individuals represent themselves to each other as polite actors who are motivated to keep interaction smooth and free of conflict and disturbance.

On the more horizontal level of communal interaction, life should be characterized by harmonious relationships *(rukun)*. Basically, it is dyadically organized in a structure of mutual obligations that tie individuals together.[1] The acceptance of others is pragmatic: people need each other in life, and should therefore be willing to cooperate and to fulfil one another's expectations. By maintaining orderly relationships, each person enhances his chances of leading a quiet life while assuring his material survival.

The maintenance of orderly relationships has nothing to do with intimacy, but serves as a self-centred strategy to enhance communal and personal continuity. Ritually, this is expressed by the practice of the communal holy meal *(slametan)* which enacts the communality of the participants in their quest for a peaceful *(slamet)* existence in a precarious world. Yet, in the shifting structure of dyadic alliances, each person stands at the centre of his own experiences and the order of communal life is in practice rather weakly integrated.

People appear to be reluctant to commit themselves to each other and avoid undue intimacy. Expectations in marriage are unstable, the divorce rate is very high, while lasting ties of friendship are rare, and indeed are not even visualized as an ideal. In keeping each other at arm's length, people appear to interact as representatives of ranks and

1 Koentjaraningrat (1960) describes this open-ended series of dyads as 'loosely structured'. This descriptive label has often been used to describe similar relationships in Thai society (Evers, 1969).

positions, even in their communal relationships. On the one hand, this is a strategy aimed at keeping relationships orderly and quiet; on the other, it leads to a structure of highly impersonal relationships. In that latter order, people are perceived as the embodiment of the status positions with which they tend to identify in social life. This identification with one's position of respect *(praja)* leads to a high sensitivity to 'face' and a good measure of circumspection in social intercourse. Relationships with others tend to be viewed in personal, that is, particular terms, while public life itself tends to become a kind of independent stage on which one represents oneself as a status that one tries to shape elegantly.

Avoidance and involvement

The pragmatic emphasis on smooth relationships, circumspection concerning the motives of others, dominant authoritarian verticality and identification with one's prestige, combine to give interaction in public a ritual flavour. This style of interaction is supported by a rather effective system of social control, of which the main means of enforcement is a well-developed practice of gossip and backbiting. Often, it seems that people are kept in place by alert eyes and ears, that is, the opinions of others, and the fear of being excluded from the common social process. In that process, one's self-respect strongly depends on the acceptance and respect that others attribute to one's status. The inclination to stop interacting with persons with whom ties are felt to be unsatisfactory, or who are classified as deviant *(ora lumrah)*, is well developed and expressed in avoidance relationships *(jothakan; nengnengan)*. In extreme cases, this avoidance may even lead to the denial of parenthood vis-à-vis intractable children. Anxiety about these sanctions is formulated in the fear of "not being recognized to be a [civilized] human being any longer."

The stress on order and the preoccupation with one's position of respect often give the impression that people are primarily involved with the avoidance of overt conflict and disturbance. In order to live a satisfactory life, one should give in to the others, exercise tolerance, and stick to the rules of propriety. Consequently, it is wise to exercise self-control while going with the flow *(ngèli)*. This wisdom presupposes self-restraint, sensitivity to the opinion of others, a willingness to embrace self-effacement, and humility. This ethos of self-suppression is acquired early during a child's socialization, that seems to aim at self-mastery and the presentation of oneself as a conforming person. One of the first feelings that will be instilled in growing children is a sense of shame *(isin; malu)* that serves to control reactions and behaviour.

This anxiety about presentation leads to a subdued style of inter-action in which people try to present themselves smoothly and politely while not committing themselves to each other. This is wise because all forms of emotional commitment may lead to disappointment and consti-tute potential threats to one's peace. Therefore, one should not get involved unnecessarily and stay out of the way of others.

This received wisdom expresses the general reluctance to involve oneself and a willingness to sacrifice personal wishes and self-expres-sion for the sake of harmonious relationships. Psychologically, this reluctance to disturb the feelings of the other is known as the attitude of *pakéwuh*. This is the positive motive of not being willing to impinge upon the other, combining spontaneous feelings of respect with circum-spection. If social, especially hierarchical, distance increases, however, self-initiated feelings of consideration will give way to the feelings of *sungkan* and *wegah*, which indicate the desire to avoid all dealings. These latter feelings are inspired by antipathy and disquietness; they border on the feeling of fear *(wedi)*.

Feeling thus ill at ease, and not wanting to get engaged with any-one else, one will be given to closing out a disturbing world that threat-ens personal quiet. When commitment is demanded, or overt conflict threatens, one will turn one's back and demonstrate indifference *(mbo-dho)*. Yet people are not, in fact, impervious to whatever happens around them; and may be hurt in their self-respect if challenged. Although a slight to one's self-respect may be answered with a smile, the infringement this represents may result in lifelong grudges and avoidance relationships. To guard self-respect, one is often unforgiving and given to brooding on revenge. Normally, such negative feelings will not be expressed in direct confrontation, but no opportunity of making the perpetrator of the offence lose face will ever be let slip.

It is functional and pragmatic to remain unobtrusive and answer to the expectations of others, because smooth relationships, although partly a purpose in themselves, serve to enhance personal feelings of peacefulness. For the latter, the show of mutual respect is essential and thus one takes part in social life outwardly, while being fully aware of presentation and 'face'. If these remain undisturbed, one enjoys tranquil continuity. Consequently, it is well worthwhile sacrificing the outward expression of one's 'personality requirements', and to hide behind the conformity that serves as the fence concealing the inward life.

The reticent individual

Often the Javanese of Yogyakarta describe themselves as 'closed' *(ditutup)*, by which they mean that they will never reveal their true feelings. While caring for the outward correctness of their behaviour and self-presentation, they tend to be masters of form, at the same time keeping their opinions to themselves. To them, the true measure of all things is their subjective inner feeling *(rasa)*.

Basically, life consists of two realms, the public and outer realm of everyday experiences and the inner realm of subjective feelings. Both these should be in order and mastered to enjoy the experience of personal quietness *(katentreman)*. Life in the outward realm is adverse and vicissitudinous, and can best be mastered by refraining from making any emotional investment in it. Thus it is wise to go with its flow, while containing any anxiety *(pribatin)* about its outcome through self-centred forms of ascetic practice *(tapa; tirakat)*. It is this turning of one's back on society and its demands that permits a withdrawal into the deep self, which is thought to be the true realm of experience. This is often given shape in the widespread practice of *kebatinan*, that is, the cultivation of the inner self which frees the individual from outward pressure while opening up the possibility of entering a self-satisfying realm of inner experiences and free-flowing fantasy *(khayalan; angen-angen)* that is self-validating. Fundamentally, this practice of *kebatinan* fits the Javanese social construction of reality in that it makes the personal ego feel important in spite of adverse experiences.

The exterior life involves suffering, precariousness, and struggle; there the need to give in is often experienced, along with sensations of powerlessness, and the humiliation of losing. Inwardly, however, the idea can be maintained that one is free, which is a secret shared with oneself. It is by this conscious compartmentalization of experience that the individual can attempt to live a private life, irrespective of whatever happens in the public, social world. Internally the person should be self-sufficient and autonomous, denying the importance of the phenomenal world, while developing his *batin* as his quiet and stable inner core. While society may be in control of his presentation *(lair)*, he is, deep down, his own master.

Comparison

There appear to be striking similarities in the relationship between individual and society in Thailand and Java. In both, it appears that the predominant hierarchical order of relationships is felt as a weight upon individuals, who find their security in conformist behaviour that gives public interaction a ritual flavour. As a general rule, persons appear to interact in terms dictated by their relative rank and distance. The requirements of hierarchical order lead, on the one hand, to the common identification of individuals with their position in public life; on the other, these requirements seem to drive a wedge between people, causing them to go their own separate ways.

The quest for a measure of personal autonomy is also expressed in surprisingly similar individual-centred ideas of ethical behaviour: individuals are not responsible for their society or for their fellow man, but merely for themselves and their social self-expression. This naturally leads to a mastery of social form and an admiration for self-restraint. It also results in the experience of social life as a mere stage where one needs to present oneself as a status, and where relationships tend to be characterized by formality, circumspection, a measure of avoidance, suppression of spontaneous behaviour, reluctance to commit oneself, and anxiety about presentation. It would seem that social life in a hierarchical setting restricts individuals to mere role-playing.

The Javanese reaction to this restriction is extremely interesting, not just because of the recognition of an inner, private self, but also because of its elaboration. The acknowledgment of this interior sphere means that people are more than actors or statuses on a social stage, a fact of life that is, however, also recognized in Thai society. In elaborating this fact into a psychology and a conception of man, the Javanese appear to have found a positive way of living with it: the true centre of existence is located in the inner man and this inward self exists in isolation from society. Thais also emphasize the wisdom of maintaining overt form and self-restraint, but they come less close to strategies for radical non-involvement.

Thai social strategies tend to focus on indifference, overt defiance, one-upmanship, gregariousness, or status validation by macho behaviour, and they thus express themselves in the social order. In contrast, the Javanese seem to have found ways in which self-expression takes place apart from social life. In their elaboration of *kebatinan*, whether mystically expressed or not, they pursue an individual-centred expression of the self, irrespective of social demands, in which individual subjectivity is the legitimate and true measure of all things.

PART III
Dynamics of culture

CHAPTER 12

Changing ideas in a changing environment

This third section seeks to analyse the dynamics of culture. To do this, it is necessary briefly to sketch an outline of the dimensions of culture, while also reflecting on the causes and sources of the cultural process.

Culture concerns understanding and attributing meaning to life and experience. It involves 'knowing who you are', and 'having identity', which socially means 'knowing who we are', because culture is the on-going intersubjective negotiation of meaning, or the endless communicative discourse that serves to help to master life and one's participation in it by interpretation. To put it another way, culture means participation in cognitive intersubjectivity.

The sources of culture are in tradition and history, in formal and informal education, in art, religion, science, and other creative interpretations, in political propaganda and critical social thought, in advertising, and in projections into the future, in hopes and ideals. These sources are not all of one kind and should be differentiated. Some concern interpretations that spring directly from the living experience of everyday life, meaning that part of it that is immediately understandable and taken for granted. Other sources concern 'foreign' interpretations that are produced by others elsewhere, such as political propaganda and state ideology, the expertise of specialists, and the ideas that originate from the commercial media which give rise to indoctrination, and mass consumer culture.

The continual turnover in the exchange of all these ideas and interpretations may be called a cultural discourse that provides the references that make communication and identity possible. Some of these references (values, symbols, ideas) show a great measure of stability over time, while others typically belong to certain historical social formations, such as modes of production and power relationships, to which they relate in a dialectical and ever-changing manner, shaping and being shaped by the social process.

The following chapters will seek to identify the most important factors that shape the contemporary cultural discourse. Predictably, some of these factors relate to changes in the system of production, relationships becoming more industrial and businesslike. Especially in the urban environment, contacts with non-familiar others become normal, and during a good part of the day many people function in an anonymous or half-anonymous environment where each looks out for his own interests.

The town is also the area of the most aggressive propagation of consumer culture, and its lifestyles, through the mass media. In combination with the experience of anonymity, this exposure may lead to superficiality, vagueness and indifference, and to political apathy. On the other hand, the urban environment also fosters industrial action, unionism, and frequently a high level of political violence.

Taken altogether, these factors contribute to the genesis of an intricate urban culture that seems to move away very rapidly from all that was familiar and rooted in 'traditions'. Relationships with others tend to open up, become freer and are less prescribed. Additionally, the whole experience of life seems to open up to the outside, to travel and foreign ideas, and even virtually sacrosanct hierarchical relationships come to be questioned.

To cope with the onslaught of mass culture, artists and urban intellectuals may have to work full time to produce a new cultural consciousness, to activate identity feelings, and to disseminate the cultural heritage. Others propagate political ideas; while yet others still are active in promoting both new and reinterpreted, or recycled, creeds in the religious supermarket. In many ways, the raising of consciousness seems to be a growing industry in competition with established political propaganda exhortations and the hawking of consumer culture.

A highly relevant question is whether the family can still be considered to be at the heart of life in Southeast Asia, in the sense that it has been historically the exemplary microcosmos of society, legitimating the latter's hierarchical order and integration. Not only does it appear that life outside is changing rapidly, but these changes may also be having a strong impact on roles in family life and gender relationships as such.

In the introductory chapter to the previous part, it is argued that the family-patronage-dynastic model is the only available moral paradigm for relationships. In other words, there is no competing moral construct to influence the ordering of non-familial relationships, to guide impersonalized relationships with an abstract 'generalized other', in brief, to shape the public world.

What has become available is a morally neutral business model of behaviour and a legal-technical apparatus that is out of joint with the personalized familial style. Over the years, and in pace with the rapid changes in the economy, landlord-patrons have abandoned their client-tenants in the Philippines; their relationships have become purely economical and now lack the elements of familiarity and protection that once characterized the working conditions of the small peasants (Kerkvliet, 1977).

Of course, ideas about democracy, and even the concept of the western welfare state, have also influenced thinking in Southeast Asia, but in spite of all the experimentation with constitutions and political representation, government has remained elitist, acting from the top down, while by and large only serving the interests of those who are best connected in the structure of political patronage. So, in spite of forms and protestations to the contrary, the old, personalized model still functions at the top, in competition or in fusion with the business model, but it now fails to represent the interests of many of those who objectively hold a different class interest.

The cause of the difficulty in grafting on, in localizing, alternative moral paradigms is, of course, their foreign origin in societies that have evolved through an entirely different historical experience. The available exemplar is the dynastic one, the stability of which is sustained by a patrimonial bureaucratic polity. This ideal has remained in place in Thailand and been restored in New Order Indonesia. During President Marcos's New Society, an attempt was made to institute this pattern on a national scale in the Philippines, but it was soon corrupted and subverted; though in a way it does exist, on a diminished scale, in the political organization of the local and provincial levels that revolve around locally powerful political dynasties.

However dynastic the perception and practice of government, the ruling elite have to seek to accommodate contending political forces that do not fit the old model, such as big business and its international connections, the military, and small but very articulate groups of environmentalists, democrats, feminists, and representatives of labour. Others who bring life to the political show are moralists, who press their demand for clean government, or who proclaim and defend human rights.

So, while there is quite some debate going on about how society should be organized in order that it may thrive in this period of modernization and development, the disparities in the ideas of the diverse segments of the population, and among those who participate in the modernization process, have become more visible, while there is hardly any agreement on basic principles or how to give these shape. What's more, those represented in government are political-economic interest groups that are not very receptive to the claims of all those others who would like a share in power, on whatever pretext. In the absence of an egalitarian ethos, and given the lack of popular participation in government, reformers and new political competitors have restricted opportunities for building the sort of power bases that would allow for their serious participation in the political arena.

Some individuals, and even some groups, have meanwhile discovered the relevance of critical social analysis in trying to come to grips with the basic problems, and have set to work to deal with some of the glaring disparities in their societies. In Thailand, such analyses surfaced in the early 1950s in the works of progressive authors; this was concurrent with the writings of Lazaro Francisco, Amado Hernandez, and Edgardo Reyes in the Philippines.[1] In Indonesia, the historical-sociological novels of Pramoedya Ananta Toer appeared somewhat later. In all three countries, the awakening of the students to a sociological approach took place in the later 1960s and early 1970s, when we also witnessed the beginning of the serious discussion of social democratic ideas. But the impact of those ideas on the intellectual climate has remained rather marginal and an elitist concern, and there is hardly any sign yet that these ideas have penetrated where it matters, namely, into the process of political decision-making.

Older and more widespread are the popular ideas of the radical

1 Lazaro Francisco, *Maganda pa ang Daigdig* (1956) and *Daluyong* (1962); Amado V. Hernandez, *Mga Ibong Mandaragit* (1962) and *Luha ng Buwaya* (1963); Edgardo Reyes, *Sa mga Kuko ng Liwanag* (1966).

left, whose Marxist analysis considerably predated the awakening of academe to social questions. It was also this more radical type of analysis that fired the imagination of the socially conscious authors. So, with 'the class enemy' exposed, political decision-making thereafter merely seemed to react to everything that is 'leftist', which in the Philippines still means an all out war against the National Democratic Front/New People's Army (NDF/NPA). By the nineties, though, the militant communist movement seems to have been driven deeply underground in Indonesia, and has almost ceased to exist in Thailand, after a remarkable efflorescence in the 1970s; meanwhile the Philippine movement appears to be disintegrating.

Sociological thinking has not become part of Southeast Asian culture yet, and an indigenous social science still has to develop. So far, psychological, sociological, and even anthropological investigation is still proceeding under the aegis of western academic concepts, and there are only a few social scientists who are as yet aware that this dependence on foreign produced ideas is not only problematic but is also stunting the development of culturally relevant models of analysis. Yet the seeds for the evolution of local forms of social enquiry have been sown.

Whether and when such thought will have an impact on the political process is unpredictable. With traditional politics still going strong, one typically sees a good measure of official interest in value indoctrination and, needless to say, these values connect with the family-patronage-dynastic model. Whether it is religion, such as is taught in school in Thailand and Indonesia, civics and social science in all three countries, or Indonesian Pancasila indoctrination and Philippine Moral Recovery through Values Education, they all aim at creating people who should know their place and execute their duties, irrespective of the problems originating from social structure and institutional order. The message propagated is that it is from people who are morally aware and who fulfil their task that the good order of society flows.

This type of person-centred ethics is the driving force behind many of the fundamentalist or reform-oriented religious movements and sects that have sprouted up all over Southeast Asia. While these movements also constitute a religious reaction against the alienation brought about by modernity and what the Indonesians call 'the excesses of development', they make the individual important in the sense that membership and serious practice emphasize one's moral worth in a corrupt environment. Yet interestingly, though predictably, none of these movements has a social programme aimed at wider society, other perhaps than drawing in converts, and their activities are typically exclusivistic and self-centred.

The political aspirations of some of these movements do not contradict the above observations. The political offshoot of the Thai Santi Asoke sect, The Force of Righteousness, merely wants clean and effective government based on a change of heart among its executives; Islamic fundamentalists and modernists alike strive for the serious practice of Islam and the imposition of the religious Law as the foundations of a good society; and the Philippine Iglesia ni Cristo not only imposes a strict discipline on its millions of members, but also expects them to vote as a block in national elections, depending on where and how the leadership can exact the best deal.

The consequence of this is that both the dominant politics and also the religious reaction that to a large extent thrives on the aversion to those politics pull culturally in the same direction. By their promotion of individual ethical behaviour, both camouflage the structure of the economy and state while at the same time masking the pressing challenges posed to these, and in addition prevent the emergence of a participatory and responsible citizenry, able to articulate its demands and assert them at the political centre.

Also driven by aversion to traditional politics are the 'progressive', consciousness-raising Non-Governmental Organizations (NGOs). In due course, they may be able to activate and organize the mostly rural and deprived groups they typically work among as a means to empower them to exert pressure on the political centre, but so far their activities are generally kept apart from or alongside government and politics. The NGO scene is particularly opaque, because nowadays every group that wants to influence opinion has established NGOs, even the governments themselves! The best thing that can be said is that the contest for the minds and support of the people has spread to the countryside, where we find a whole range of groups generally involved in activities related to 'poverty alleviation', with the ulterior motive of in time earning the loyalty of the target groups concerned.

CHAPTER 13

The Thai opening up to the world

The development of culture, of the ideas people live with, is a steady process, always on the move, and to begin its story from a certain date is arbitrary indeed. But given that the gradual opening up of society to modernity is a crucial theme in explaining current cultural development in Thailand, then the choice of 1855 seems reasonably appropriate. In that year, the Bowring Treaty, which did away with the royal monopolies and opened the country up to foreign trade, was concluded.

King Mongkut, the fourth monarch of the current dynasty, with whom it was negotiated, also exemplifies the trend towards the opening up of the country to foreign ideas. He learned English, held discourses with foreign missionaries on religious subjects, and was interested in science and systematic observation. It was even these latter passions that caused his untimely demise due to malaria caught during a journey to the south to observe a solar eclipse in 1868.

So, while the Bowring Treaty stands at the beginning of Thailand's gradual involvement in the world economic system, it also signals the entry into participation in the world-wide circulation of ideas, of a dawning awareness of events going on elsewhere in the world, and of the first devising of strategies to cope with global political developments, above all the encroachment of the European colonial powers in Southeast Asia. All this comes clearly into focus during the reign of Mongkut's successor, King Chulalongkorn.

When the young heir came to the throne, the country was still basically feudal in its political organization, with local grandees exercising considerable control of the kingdom's peripheral regions. This nobility lorded it over a peasant population that was liable to corvée (statute labour), and in itself divided into freeman and slave classes. Naturally, this aristocracy had no interest in supporting a strong central authority, or the administrative reorganization of the realm.

King Chulalongkorn was a purposeful man who understood the demands of his time, yet it wasn't until 1892 that he finally succeeded in overruling the feudal elite's attempts to block his schemes, thus opening the way for administrative reforms, systematic modernization, and absolute royal control. From this time onwards, a salaried, Bangkok-appointed bureaucracy was instituted, control over the Buddhist monkhood *(Sangha)* established, general education introduced, and a modern communications network built up. In the process, the corvée system was abandoned and the slaves emancipated (Prizzia, 1986).

Inspiration for all this was sought in the administrative models of the powerful colonial states of the region, in modern forms of organization, and in western education. To direct the reforms and advance the country's development, men were needed with modern training, also necessitating the sending abroad of bright young students of common descent. It was these latter foreign-educated commoners in the army and bureaucracy who brought to an end the rather short-lived period of royal absolutism and inaugurated the period of constitutional monarchy in 1932.

So, from the 1850s onwards, we witness a gradual expansion of the economy, with the export of rice becoming the mainstay (Ingram, 1971), along with the immigration of vast numbers of Chinese labourers to build the railways, new canals and other elements of the modern infrastructure, and also to work in the southern tin mines, which increased their output dramatically at this time as well. All of this contributed to the vast changes that were taking place in the thoughts and belief patterns of a significant segment of the urban population. From the acceptance of a hierarchical, feudal order as a naturally given law of society — an idea that can still be encountered among members of the old nobility, and among rural folks in remote areas — a new perception was evolving in urban circles during the period of administrative modernization that introduced the alien concept of nationalism, taking Europe as the source of inspiration. This ferment of new ideas, followed through logically, then led on to the questioning of the legitimacy of absolute royal rights and privileges.

Equipped with such European concepts as socialism, democracy, and constitutionalism, the new men at the helm not only held ideas that are often still a little out of place in Thai society, but also promoted them at the newly established Thammasat University that, then as now, is the bastion of modern social thought. At the same time, Buddhadasa Bhikkhu started to develop and propagate his message of a reformed Buddhism,[1] while modern Thai literary writing in the form of the novel was slowly coming of age.

The following periods of military rule and dictatorship were not particularly favourable to the growth of social thought, but its development was irrepressible, as demonstrated by the novels of Siibuuraphaa and Seenii Sawwaphong, or the concern with poverty and deprivation in the North-east that landed many of the protesters involved in jail. Slowly, new forms of social and political consciousness kept unfolding, although not necessarily overtly, and often in despite of the express wishes of those in power.

Under Marshal Sarit (1957-63), national development became the top priority (Thak, 1979); this was also the period of increasing American involvement in Vietnam, and thus in Thailand, and the beginning of the communist armed struggle in the country, a conflict in which the brilliant intellectual Cit Phuumisak would become one of the first victims. The American presence, especially the excesses of troops during their often wild periods of 'Rest and Recreation', became very visible under Sarit's successors, at the same time that a modern economy was beginning to evolve. In the name of development as a means of fighting communism, vast parts of the countryside were opened up, not only to material but also to ideological modernization, whether official or clandestine. Although the intellectual climate remained repressive, the government in Bangkok had to allow for a modicum of democratic representation, but it suppressed this again in 1971.

Twenty-five years of rule by military marshals came to an end in October 1973, when protracted student demonstrations for a constitution finally escalated to the level of a confrontation with the army and police. The ensuing violence shocked the nation, but ushered in a period of unprecedented freedom during which progressive ideas of all sorts could circulate. Arts, literature, and publishing flourished, while an interestingly diverse press emerged, though at the same time the unbri-

---

1 See his *Handbook for mankind.* Bangkok: Sublime Life Mission, 1969; for elaboration, see Peter A. Jackson, 1988.

dled contentions between opposing political forces resulted in chaos and violence, with the division between the contestants opening up along the lines of progressive versus conservative. It was also a period of anti-American protest, and a fierce nationalism, in which all and sundry claimed to embody the principles and to be striving for the protection of the national symbols of Nation, Religion, and King.

Understanding the intellectual ferment that became visible in the 'democratic period' of 1973-76 is essential if one is to grasp the nature of the forces involved in the further economical, social, and cultural modernization of Thailand. The students 'discovered' the writings of Siibuuraphaa and Seenii Sawwaphong, and began to read the works of the other progressives of the 1950s, plus the socio-historical analyses of Cit Phuumisak (Reynolds, 1987). In doing so, they became aware of poverty and peasants, labour and exploitation, privilege and corruption, and the necessity of critical social analysis. While doing so, these children of the elite and middle classes, on whom the army had trained its guns during the October days, realized that their world of ideas was far divorced from that of their parents' generation, and the dominant ideology in which they had been educated.

The given order of society could no longer simply be taken for granted; politics and questions of state began to become common concerns; Buddhadasa Bhikkhu-inspired Buddhist reform gained in popularity; and the genesis of new Buddhist movements, such as the Santi Asoke moral reform sect and the Thammakai meditation cum self-discipline movement, can roughly be dated to this period of intellectual agitation. It was also a time in which new lifestyles were questioned. With the presence of so many American soldiers, especially those on 'R & R', the public became aware of all sorts of entertainment activities that were neither particularly polite nor 'Thai', at the same time that the nation's political subservience to American interests was also creating widespread aversion and distrust. This confluence of blatant consumerism and alien lifestyles, allied to political dependence, resulted in the emergence of a powerful nationalistic reaction that focused on the country, its interests and culture, as the centre of attention.

In the ensuing debates about nationalism, about what is Thai and what is un-Thai, about what to accept and what to reject, about what is desirable and what should be got rid of, the racial question sometimes

also reared its head. If Americans were to blame for cultural degenera-
tion, why not blame the Chinese also for exploitation, economic ills,
and their lack of nationalism and identification with the country that
had brought them fortune? As attention was brought to bear on this
issue, the realization dawned that it was no longer a real problem. What
some Southeast Asian countries still have not yet succeeded in accom-
plishing had already happened in Thailand, almost without anybody
noticing it: the Chinese, who still in the 1950s were highly visible as a
separate ethnic group, were in the process of disappearing as such, and
had begun to identify themselves as Thais.

Remarkably revealing on this is Botan's novel *Letters from
Thailand* (1969), which tells the story of a Chinese immigrant who
grudgingly witnesses how his children become Sino-Thais. By way of
intermarriage and cultural compatibility, the integration has steadily pro-
ceeded, producing a business establishment and a middle class that is a
proud mixture of the two cultures, and that by and large thinks of itself
as Thai. Notable among this group are many 'reformers', who apparently want to improve upon Thai culture, even though they are only one or
two generations removed from their Chinese origins. They include such
critics of Thai Buddhist practice as Buddhadasa Bhikkhu and the vener-
able Phoothirak of the Santi Asoke sect, and social pundits, such as
Puey Ungphakorn, Boonsanong Punyothayana, and Sulak Sivaraksa, all
of whom made impressive contributions to the discussions of the 1970s
through their vigorous writing and publishing activities.

It is no longer purely Chinese business acumen that explains
Thailand's striking and steady economic progress over the last thirty
years. Apart from the important role of the government in the economy
and its liberal-conservative monetary policy, business and banking have
become respectable in Thai culture. In recent years the Thai and Sino-
Thai business establishment has also grown to be a weighty political
factor. This rapid growth, and the resultant political clout it brings, has
also been accomplished by a further reciprocal interpenetration of the
interests of the state, the bureaucracy, the army, and big business.

The students of the early 1970s discovered and discussed many
ideas that go against the grain of Thai culture, one being 'equality' in
the sense of democracy and accountable government, another being the
right to education, and some have even questioned the morality of hier-

archy by debating the sensitive issue of the authority of the highest in the realm, and by demonstratively refusing to participate in the Homage to Teachers ceremony. Since the moral content of hierarchical relation-ships is firmly grounded in the family, they were bound to fail in propa-gating their anti-hierarchical thinking, but what they did bring about was a more informed debate on the content of democracy and account-ability, and about the right to education.

In the 1970s, the idea of open universities, accessible to every-body, was finally implemented. It has led to an education explosion that is very rapidly creating a broad, relatively educated public that nowa-days makes its demands on the system felt in terms of job and employ-ment opportunities, the calls for the realization of social justice, plus political protests, and a growing ecological movement. These newly educated people cannot in any way be absorbed by the bureaucratic system, as their forerunners were in times when higher education was a privilege of the few. Then, the expanding bureaucracy could absorb the vast majority of the graduates, and a career in government was a com-mon prospect. All that changed at the same time that extra-governmen-tal employment became available in a growing economy that has been shifting over from agriculture and government to tourism, communica-tions, and industry.

It may be revealing to illustrate the magnitude of the demand for education. In 1961, it was estimated that there were 15,000 Thai univer-sity students, not counting some 2,000 studying abroad. Now, in the early nineties, it is thought that some 600,000 people are enrolled at the tertiary level, plus more than 8,000 overseas. In the process, an urban civilization is developing that is no longer in touch with its rural hinter-land, or with the feudal ways of yester-years. That culture is expressed in a lively, informative and critical press, in an impressive amount of book publishing and, of course, in a booming entertainment and fast food industry, in traffic jams, department stores, high-rises, and other demonstrations of consumer culture and economic expansion, such as fashion and design, art galleries and spectacular architecture.

Sometimes it is thought that economic expansion is a precondition for the evolution of a democratic society, but such an expansion may equally well serve conspicuous consumption, mass cultural entertain-ment, and a self-centred materialism that distracts attention away from democratic and critical social thinking. Compared to the 1970s, the level of political awareness in Thai society does not seem to have grown. There has been, of course, the stunning electoral success of Bangkok Governor Chamlong Srimuang's party, The Force of Righteousness, that is closely associated with the Santi Asoke sect, but it is difficult to see what else that political triumph means beyond a general (urban) distaste for traditional politics, and the craving for a clean, efficient government. Apart from these, it is hard to imagine what implications the party programme might have in terms of societal reorganization.

Technocracy and the expanding economy seem to have led to political indifference, at least among the general public, and to extra-governmental protests and activities, for instance, of environmentalists, or social welfare activities of Non-Governmental Organizations (NGOs), which have multiplied dramatically in recent years. The agendas of such groups seem to be confined to dealing with symptoms rather than examining the system that produces them, and they normally fall short in ideological or theoretical sophistication. That is, they do not seem to have developed a sociological picture of society, where things are inter-connected, but instead loosely blame 'capitalist development' for all social ills. In their analysis, since capitalism feeds on greed, then the moral reconstruction of the individual is the target to aim at. Consequently, moral development programs prosper in the urban environment, as is demonstrated by the burgeoning of the various Buddhist reform movements, the NGO scene, and Chamlong's Force of Righteousness.

The high level of political awareness of the 1970s was expressed in student radicalism, by the students' efforts to connect with life in the countryside and to conscienticize the rural population, by a massive production of 'social realist' literature, and the composition of hundreds of 'songs for life', such as those performed by the travelling student group Caravan. This has changed. At present, most students seem to prepare themselves for a career in society rather than for changing it, and if they are politically active, they tend to protest corruption or the abuse of 'democracy'; if they are active at the grass roots' level, they are typically engaged in NGO activities which, more often than not, try to learn from the experience of life in the countryside rather than to impose urban political views on the villagers.

In parallel with Thailand's economic development, an urban working class culture seems to be in the making. While a huge proportion of the urban work force still consists of migratory labour that maintains a close relationship with the countryside and its culture, for a gradually expanding number of people the city has become home, and factory or harbour the 'natural' places of work. Unionism, labour action, and a good measure of class consciousness have become part of their prospect. Instead of the elitist Caravan of the 1970s, it is the more earthy Carabao Thai-rock group that expresses their thoughts and aspirations.

Other urban subcultures that are springing up as by-products of a booming modern sector, and the money that it generates, are the condominium yuppie lifestyle, and an emerging youth culture. Such subcultures only partly generate their own idiom, and give rise to a culture industry that produces the items, symbols, and entertainment that a certain public is said to need. In the urban environment, this may range from luxury apartments and flashy cars to modern forms of fast food, audience specific types of music with their song books, movies, star cults, and scores of magazines that tell people how to live and what to want. The amount of social criticism contained in these approximates to zero.

So, during the period under consideration, we have witnessed enormous changes in Thai life. From a dual structure of society, the estate of the noble rulers and that of the peasantry, Thai society has gradually developed a considerable degree of diversification and social differentiation. This is especially apparent in the modern urban environment. Its culture sets the pace for the rest of the country, sending the population at large messages about how life can and should be lived, of what things to aspire to.

The cultural influence of modern Bangkok is sustained by the administrative reforms of the late nineteenth century and the ensuing, and still ongoing, rather uniform penetration of society by the state. As this went on, the previously autonomous peripheral regions were integrated with the centre, and by now regional cultural differences are declining at an accelerating pace. Recently, it was discovered that local differences may stimulate tourism so, since a few years back, every province boasts a cultural office to promote the 'characteristic' features of the area. This, of course, does not detract from the fact that, leaving aside hill tribes and southern Moslems, a very recognizable, nation-wide modern Thai culture is developing, meshed together by an increasingly extensive system of communications, whether by road or rail, by broadcast media or the press, a centralized system of school education, and by the effective diffusion of nationalism and its symbols.

While this national integration may be described as an internal opening up of the country as a by-product of centralized administration, the development of communications, and an expanding economy,[2] the country is also unfolding more and more to influences from abroad, not only by responding to impulses from the world economy, but also by taking in quantities of new ideas, new technology, new ways of doing things, and new consumption patterns. It also absorbs, temporarily, some six million foreign tourists a year and, less temporarily, a very large number of expatriate workers, mostly employed in the cosmopolitan Bangkok metropolis. Simultaneously, more and more Thais have been gaining first hand experience of foreign countries, not only through tourism and study on the part of the more well-to-do, but also through massive labour migration to Singapore, Japan, the Middle East, Europe and the United States. Thais have now spread out pretty well everywhere, and they bring their experiences back home with them when they return.

This opening up to the world has been a most spectacular movement, especially over the last thirty years. As recently as the fifties, it was almost impossible to find English speakers outside two or three elite university campuses; tourists were uncommon; social scientific knowledge about the country was in its infancy; Thai-speaking foreigners were rarities; the press was subdued and inward looking. Which is to say that while not exactly complacent, Thai society still gave an impression of cultural self-sufficiency, providing its own idiom and content for its national discourse, while only occasionally being disturbed by new ideas voiced by the few who had studied abroad for years. Naturally, the rather repressive regimes of the military marshals did their

2 For an exhaustive survey of Thai and foreign interpretations of the development of the Thai economy and its social formations, see C.J. Reynolds and Hong Lysa, Marxism in Thai historical studies, *Journal of Asian Studies* XLIII/1 (November 1983).

best to keep things just the way they were.

Probably the most powerful single factor that led to the opening up of society was America's massive involvement in Vietnam, soon followed by the consequences of economic growth and the education explosion. In the 1970s, international tourism reached Southeast Asia in a big way, and labour migration began in earnest. All this affected the world of ideas, first among students, but then for many others, too. The resulting discourse was one in which a developing quality press played and continues to play a highly significant role. But while all this was going on, the rapid and continuous growth of consumer culture, with its fetish called lifestyles, was also observable.

Now the question that has arisen is whether this opening up, internally and to the external world, is threatening to deform Thai culture and its style, whether these will be 'modernized' in the process of the globalization of culture to the point of becoming a mere caricature of their time-hallowed image. Although there are Thai social critics who warn that Thai society is on its way to losing its own identity, while prescribing, for instance, the serious practice of Buddhism as an antidote to alien influences, most Thais are rather confident, as they always have been, that future developments will be adapted to the Thai way of life rather than that this way will suffer from its contact with foreign elements.

This cultural self-confidence is perhaps typically Thai, along with a good measure of skill in pragmatic adaptation. They still like a well-regulated style of life, just as before, which not only involves a bent for aestheticism, but also the appreciation of harmonious social order, in which is implicit respect for interpersonal relationships and hierarchy, and the ensuing rights and obligations; all this is also expressed in pleasant manners, and the proverbial smile. Of course, many people in Bangkok have stopped smiling, but generally they are polite and expect other people to be polite in return, and the expectation that society should be orderly remains.

Sometimes the Thai predilection for order and a decorous style of life is violated by their encounters with western tourists. For instance, until the new airport terminal was finished, the first thing tourists saw, while waiting to get their passports stamped, was a sign displaying a long list of presentational requirements, specifying how foreigners should dress and look if they did not want to be treated as 'hippies' — the implication being that the latter would find themselves at the end of every queue: no to shorts and singlets, no to open sandals and long hair, and so forth. It did not deter the tourists from coming to the immigration officials in attire that seemed more suited for a holiday at the beach than for a visit to the national capital. Naturally, they are not allowed to enter the royal palace that way, but I have never seen anybody ordered out of a government office for not respecting the Thai dress code. So in the Thai way, if one cannot win by admonition, one should either get tough or find a compromise. It is, perhaps, noteworthy that these regulations are no longer posted up in the new arrival hall.

Tourism, and thus being exposed to the view and judgment of alien others, has on occasion highlighted both Thai concerns about order and decorum and also their sense of pragmatism. The opening of a new road from Chiangmai to Chiangrai incidentally brought the shrine of a powerful female spirit to the attention of all passers-by, including foreigners. This irritated the local District Officer, because the offering that this particular spirit prefers in return for her granting favours is a replica of a penis, and those phalluses soon accumulate in remarkable piles in front of such shrines. The D.O. had a sign put up; "Please offer flowers only". Of course, no local devotee would be so foolish as to risk the spirit's wrath by making unwanted offerings like this. Later, when the Bangkok Hilton Hotel, honouring the terms of agreement reached when purchasing the land, kept a similar shrine in its compound, and even made it a tourist attraction, the northern District Officer's sign was taken down.

New possibilities for expressing Thai aestheticism are made available by the tourist trade too, such as in the production of beautiful and well-crafted souvenirs with very inventive designs. They are also offered by the increasing prosperity of many in the countryside, who invest in renewing rustic local temples or in constructing new ones. The building boom in glittering religious structures is highly visible as these showy edifices embody the villagers' pride and satisfy their taste for vivid and elaborate decorations. It also makes clear that in rural Thailand religion is alive and well, that people continue to invest in merit, and that the traditional way of seeking some education for the rural poor by (temporarily) entering the monkhood, is still valid: the ratio of monks and novices to population has changed only very slightly over the past twenty-five years.[3]

Religious interest remains inspired by the same old spirit and is directed to blessing and protection. The trade in amulets is as lively as ever, and the guardian spirit shrines erected in front of the new business buildings in Bangkok seem to vie against each other in size and ostentation. And it is not only in the areas of religion and aestheticism that the Thais remain very Thai indeed. There is a growing interest in their own history, not just for the sake of the nostalgia that is expressed in the many 'coffee-table books', but also at the deeper and more serious level of an interest in the elements that go to make up their own identity, which some feel is under challenge in the modern world — the recently established National Identity Board in the Prime Minister's Office being a good example.

Materialism has made rapid inroads in Thailand, of late at an almost explosive rate. Inevitably, such a change has brought new problems in its train. The rape of nature has led to erosion and serious hydrological problems. Bangkok's traffic appears close to gridlock jams, and one wonders what further urbanization is going to bring. There seems to be no end in sight to the building boom with office and apartment blocks rising higher and higher all the time. While the need for decentralization is a common topic these days, it remains to be seen whether the powers-that-be will ever consent to this innovation, since it runs counter to their own interests — all the reins of power can run through their hands only for as long as Bangkok reigns supreme. The determined centralization of authority is a policy that has been followed by every government since 1892, one side-effect of which has been the conversion of a green tropical city into a concrete jungle that can only function by the use of air-conditioning. In short, there is no lack of manifestations of 'modernity' and unrestricted economic development, all of which are affecting the quality of life.

In spite of all this, the Thais also remain impressively their own.

3 During the Buddhist Lent *(phansaa)* of 1966, there were approximately 24,000 temples accommodating 175,500 monks and 87,000 novices. This makes 1 monk to every 34 adult Buddhist males in a total population of 32 million. In the same period during 1986, approximately 33,000 temples housed 285,000 monks and 145,000 novices, making 1 monk to every 35 adult Buddhist males in a total population of 53 million.

pers vs. gov

Whatever the changes and problems, they seem to cope in a self-assured way that may strike outsiders as surprisingly nonchalant in relation to the scale of societal problems. Perhaps this is related to the dichotomization of life's experience into an area that really matters and that concerns one's immediate personal relationships, and public life that is thought to be a matter of state and government, far away entities that are beyond the reach and control of individual citizens. Consequently, public control is still weakly developed, a fact that increasingly gives big business the opportunities to manipulate the political process, in transactions largely obscured from public view.

The consumer culture is not exactly helpful to any who might be eager to foster the growth of the checks and balances of public control and civic-mindedness. Politics is something to watch, a spectator sport that may be exciting, but it still has to go a long way if it is to evolve to the stage where party programmes, platform politics, and the representation of the public interest in its all diversity are included in its dimensions. Politically, the main contemporary goal seems to be more and more economic expansion, with the resulting goodies to be shared out among those who are part of the 'modern sector'. But the pursuit of this objective has also created a vast gap between urban affluence and rural poverty that is reminiscent of the old, two-estates structure of society, in which some had all the privilege and control over resources, while the others were allowed to suffer and to serve. Meanwhile, though, society has grown in complexity and in possibilities for individual advancement. It is these opportunities for social mobility and material progress rather than political reform that preoccupy the minds of most.

171

CHAPTER 14

Contemporary cultural dynamics in Java

Changing social relationships

Background

The core institution of Javanese culture is the nuclear family. There the child is given the elementary samples of social life and taught how to behave. It learns the most basic of all values, namely, good order, and a whole set of behavioural strategies to maintain it. This order consists of a system of hierarchical relationships among unequal moral positions, each of which holds its own set of prerogatives and obligations.

The system of relationships should be *laras*, harmonious, which comes about when everybody knows his position, is careful about respecting the position of others, and faithful in his duties. Patience, humbleness, acceptance, politeness, avoidance, and withdrawal all help to keep it that way but, since friction is unavoidable in human relationships and avoidance and withdrawal impracticable in family life, one is taught the value of *rukun*, of glossing over differences, of compromising, of living in friendship, of reconciling oneself to the will of others. One could say that *rukun* is the way to harmonious relations among people who are near to each other, not necessarily intimate, but close enough to have to live with each other.

These family-centred values serve as the pattern for the conduct of life in the wider society, in one's immediate community. There is an emphasis on *rukun*, this being essential to surviving, to living together, to sharing, borrowing, lending, and such like. In other words, it lubricates the wheels of the system of interlocking obligations that are inherent in working relationships. While communal relationships also have a hierarchical dimension, formal hierarchy applies especially to one's relationships with society beyond one's community, with unknown persons, with government and its functionaries, and all other persons entitled to

173

honour. That system of ranking is neither strange nor vague, but on the contrary, as the order of the sultanate, it is fully legitimate, accepted, and known. In the old days, it even had sacred dimensions and, as in the family, emphasis was placed on the faithful and selfless fulfilment of the duties corresponding to one's position, so making the world a beautifully ordered place.

Dynamics

These days it appears that the order of life is changing. Society has expanded, and so have individual horizons. The encompassing codification of the sultanates have faded into the past. A mastery of the intricate levels of the Javanese language is not taught any more and it has to compete with Indonesian, the national, more egalitarian language of school education. The classics of Javanese culture, especially its *kejawèn* heritage, are threatened by the indifference and ignorance of a young generation that is oriented to the world outside, and an eager consumer of Indonesian and imported mass-cultural goods.

Formal education and the expanding systems of communication now provide greater opportunities for social and geographical mobility, and have increased the distance between home and work, while sweeping away the traditions of communal social control. Economic opportunities have produced a more diversified society, giving rise to a minuscule class of very rich and often politically influential people, a sizeable middle class, both in towns and in the countryside, with considerable purchasing power, and a vast mass of poor and very poor people who are left behind by the process of development, and who are suffering from the effects of modernization. While many other relevant changes are also influencing the cultural process, the above-mentioned will suffice to show what is happening to the system of social relationships, especially as articulated by the hierarchy, *rukun*, and *laras* values.

To begin with the macro-order of society, we may note that it is no longer limited to a personal cultural horizon. Where formerly the area of social participation roughly coincided with the area of cultural intimacy — for instance, a *pesantrèn* education preparing people for life in the Islamic community *(ummat)*, or *kejawèn* beliefs being a good guide to life in the sultanates — we now find a vague Indonesian order of society centring on far away Jakarta. That new order cuts across ethnic and cultural lines, uses a new language, and prepares children in school for a life in that wider and still ill-defined order.

It is not only by way of the schools that New Order Indonesia has penetrated the lives of its people. Government and administration also descend from Jakarta to regulate their lives, to tell them what is good and what is reprehensible, to propagate its Pancasila state ideology,[1] and with the powerful instruments of state, the centre tries to mould society into the image of its policies. Although, for many, Indonesia still remains culturally distant and vague, it is definitely a force to be reckoned with. It lacks, though, the charismatic, sacred legitimation of the old sultanates, as it is not a well-ordered place where one has clear ideas of duty and obligation.

But then again, what the vague social order of Indonesia does offer is a field of opportunity and mobility, for rich and poor alike. Concurrent with its economic development and the rapid increase in the circulation of money, social relationships have tended to be monetarized and social positions commercialized. Its status symbols are fast becoming consumeristic, mass cultural, and alien to local ethnic traditions. For all those who aspire to mobility, there is now a chance to get on in life by acting in this field.

The innate contradiction in this Indonesian field of opportunity and mobility is that it fails to promote participation in nation-building. Governmental and administrative practice is from the top down, political participation is discouraged, elections are mere legitimation rituals, the population is expected to be depoliticized between elections, social criticism is a dangerous activity, and culturally only a few things are on offer to identify with, such as Indonesian movies, Indonesian pop music, comic strips and pulp literature, political rhetoric, and censored newspapers.

All this makes for an indifference to social concerns that is scarcely counterbalanced by the generally poor teaching of national history at

---

1 The Pancasila is the ideological basis of the Indonesian state. Its five principles are: 1) Belief in 'God' *(ke-Tuhanan Yang Mahaesa)*, 2) Humanism, 3) National consciousness, 4) Sovereignty of the people, 5) Social justice.

school, the weary slogans of the 'generation of '45', and nowadays the Pancasila courses. Interestingly though, these latter emphasize trust in the government and obedience to its authority (= to know and fulfil one's place) for the well-being and development of the nation, while recognizing that the prosperity of the whole sprouts from the inner order, or the strong and developed *batin*, of the individuals that compose it.

It is worthy of note that this political cum ethical notion of good citizenship, with its loci in the inner order of the individual and obedience to the state, is very *kejawèn* and agrees with the *kebatinan* teachings. After all, the Javanese cultural locus is the inner order of the individual, the fulfilment of social obligation merely being instrumental to personal well-being and development.

This also corresponds with Nakamura's analysis of the Muhammadiyah (modern Muslim) ideology. According to him, it is a doctrine for individual conduct based on Islam, which is to say that it is an ethical theory for individuals that lacks specific programmes for social reform, or any political strategy to achieve them. An ideal society is one in which everybody is a good Muslim and behaves as such (1983:176-7). This teaching expresses the view that society is a mere aggregate of individuals, and as such it is a-sociological. Yet it appears to have deep cultural roots, and it may be expected that it will reinforce the *kejawèn* conceptual bifurcation of life into an inner individual and outer social realm; in this way it may impede any whole-hearted participation in national processes.

We may therefore conclude that the extension of hierarchy up to a distant apex in Jakarta has weakened its acceptance and legitimation, yet, despite that, it may still intervene powerfully in each person's social and individual life. It seems to belong to an order that is far from *laras*, while its vagueness and forcefulness may stimulate self-centredness, both in its negative and positive *kejawèn* connotations; it may also ferment a resurgence of ethnic cultural identity and participation in religious life.

Focusing on community life, it must be noted that geographically circumscribed ties have become far less compelling then they once were. For many people the relevant source of income and ties of association are outside their community of residence, and those, especially, who have money are now free to choose whether they want to be part of the local networks or not. For instance, formerly, if one wanted a job done, one was expected to ask a neighbour or a poor relative for help. That aid, or favour, would then have to be returned at some future time. Thus people were linked to each other by innumerable dyadic ties of give-and-take. Nowadays, however, the better-off people will often prefer to hire labour or pay for the things they need, in that way freeing themselves from the network of mutual obligations. But this cuts adrift the poor, who, as a result, now have few opportunities to oblige their social superiors; consequently the disadvantaged are more marginalized than ever and, in their struggle for survival, they have become more dependent on each other, or on migration to the big city.

Of course, the ethic of neighbourly life is still *rukun*, but in substance it does not amount to much any more. Communal *slametan* have also become infrequent, with most celebrations and activities now centring around Independence Day. One is still expected to show interest on the occasion of a death in the neighbourhood, but the authority of neighbourly relationships is a thing of the past. People greet each other, and avoid open conflict, but they are mostly concerned with the world outside, or the demands of family life.

Whether the family is still the training ground it once was for life in the social order is debatable. The inside and outside orders are far from congruent these days, and the anonymity of external associational ties may even be compensated for by tighter and more intimate internal relationships, since neither the local community nor wider society appear to be 'natural' extensions of the family any more.

Life in the modern nuclear family is different from what it was in former days. Its inner hierarchy receives far less emphasis, which is often evident from the choice of language in which children address their parents. Where it was formerly the rule to address elders in High Javanese *(krama)*, there is now a strong tendency to use Low Javanese *(ngoko)*, or to speak Indonesian, even with the fathers. This often conforms to the desire expressed by fathers to abandon their formerly almost ritual position, and to come closer to the other members of the family, to share in their intimacy and warmth.

Children are much freer vis-à-vis their parents these days, and more subject to the discipline of formal education. This education clearly elevates a number of other authority figures in competition with the knowledge and the prestige of parents. Another trend is the growing consciousness of parents that they are not automatically entitled to respect because of their position, but that they have to earn this from their children by attempting to see life from the latters' perspective, too.

The modern family tends to be less authoritarian, to place less value on hierarchical position and ritual relationships, and to emphasize mutual understanding and communication, intimacy and trust.[2] It is the most solid source of identity formation in a world that is increasingly vague and morally less compelling, yet it may be expected that the integrity of family life will need to be defended against the greater freedom of movement of the young, school learning, and the fascination with the gadgets of consumer society. All these provide fertile ground for the growth of a youth counter-culture, generation conflict, and the puberty protest so familiar in western society.

Another apparent trend is the strengthening of the bonds of blood relationships. This should not be understood only as a predictable reaction against the increasing insecurity of ties in the world outside, but also as an attempt to defend and keep what one has. Especially among upwardly mobile middle-class families, a tendency has been noted to formalize family relationships by organizing themselves into *trah* that trace their descent from a common apical ancestor. While this was formerly a means by which the nobility safeguarded the exclusiveness of their descent, it has now, among commoners at least, little to do with the impeccability of pedigree but more with creating and defending an exclusive opportunity structure for its members (Sairin, 1982).

Cultural change in Yogyakarta

For a long time, the Central Javanese sultanates have demonstrated the capacity for creative and versatile reaction to the disturbing penetration of first colonial, then Indonesian, and finally cosmopolitan and mass-cultural influences. From the beginning of this century, Yogyakarta has been the most prominent centre of proto-nationalistic and emanci-

---

2 See for instance, Hardjowirogo, M., *Adat-istiadat Jawa*. Bandung: Patma, 1980.

patory movements. Examples are the Budi Utomo association of native colonial administrators, the Muhammadiyah with its emphasis on religious reform, and the Taman Siswa with its synthesis of Javanese and Western educational goals. At the same time, the prince-mystic Ki Ageng Suryomentaram formulated his influential secular *kebatinan* doctrine of self-realization. In the thirties, the ruling sultan even opened a part of his 'sacred' palace to commoners, while entrusting his sons to the care of Dutch families in order to ensure their modern education.

After the Japanese occupation, Yogyakarta became the temporary capital of the Indonesian Republic, and the first centre of university education. With Independence, however, the town reverted to its role of a quiet court city, where a remarkable efflorescence of Javanese *kebatinan* mysticism unfolded. Originally, its main thrust was the endeavour to give Javanese meaning to the displacements occurring in the transformation to modern life, but later, in concomitance with the high degree of politicization of Indonesian life at that time, many mystical movements began to flourish in opposition to militant Islam. Taken all together, the development of *kebatinan* can be seen as a Javanese quest to maintain identity in face of the Indonesianization of national life and Moslem political intransigence (Mulder, 1980).

At present, the following experiences are having a marked effect on life in Yogyakarta. First of all, a greater degree of openness to the outside world through which Indonesia is becoming more important than Java itself; second, a decrease in social pressure and control due to increased social mobility and anonymity; third, greatly improved chances for access to welfare and income, and thus more opportunities for personal freedom, independence and consumption; fourth, the compulsory school education in a national curriculum; and fifth, the gradual disappearance of the court as a cultural centre and the demise of the old status structure of society.

Erosion of the old order

The previously dominant culture of the court and the aristocracy lost its vital centre when the former sultan decided to live in far away Jakarta, after which his palace became a mere tourist attraction. As a result, the ranked social relationships lost their compulsion and legitimation. Simultaneously, all kinds of behavioural codes lost their function and became relics of the past. These entailed the extreme elaboration of good manners, the obligation to speak High Javanese to superiors (an obligation that can now easily be circumvented by speaking Indonesian), the pressure to hide behind one's public mask and image, and even the practice of mysticism and the cultivation of the inner self.

Slowly, social relationships are opening up, becoming more spontaneous and relaxed. Such liaisons are stimulated by modern schooling and compulsory education that foster an orientation to a wider sphere than the once tightly ordered worlds of community and family. The importance of status has also been reduced by the emergence of a wider, looser and less personal system of associations.

Along with these tendencies has come a loss of knowledge of the classical Javanese culture, and a diminishing interest in participating in organized 'denominational' mystical *kebatinan* groups. In school, teaching is in Indonesian, and even at home the child does not learn to master the various levels of Javanese any more. Consequently, all kinds of mixtures of muddy Indonesian and bastardized Javanese are arising that amply illustrate a new openness, accompanied by the much diminished importance of the refinement of the older Javanese culture.

Mass culture

If we add to these intra-cultural developments some other factors that threaten Javanese cultural integrity, such as tourism, social and geographical mobility, a rising standard of living and increasing social-economic polarization, then it would appear that ideal conditions have been created for the development of a modern mass culture characterized by social indifference, consumerism, and political apathy.

The relatively affluent are content to demonstrate their newly acquired status symbols. Their children sport blue jeans, dance at discos, and ride Japanese motorcycles. All watch national television, while to many watching *wayang* shadow plays has become a symbol of a non-progressive past. The influx of sloppily dressed Western tourists has given rise to extensive home industries producing cheaply made artifacts, to the detriment of the former refinement in the arts and crafts. Additionally, the national centre, Jakarta, is far away, and it might seem as though Yogyakarta, instead of being the living centre of the old and new Javanese culture, is now fated to the obscure role of a languishing provincial town.

Creative reaction

It appears, however, that more is happening. The loss of a living past and the unconvincing attempts to create an Indonesian identity seem to have stimulated the quest for new expressions of Javaneseness. A good example is furnished by the Indonesian literature written by ethnic Javanese authors. Toward the end of the 1960s, Javanese authors seem to have begun to deviate from the mainstream developments in Indonesian literature, by writing a new kind of writing that is mystically inspired, and often constructed along the lines of the *wayang* shadow theatre plays. In these writings, life is depicted as an inescapable course that one should accept, any deviation from this bringing death and disaster. At the same time, some classical Javanese literature began to be translated and printed in Indonesian.

These literary activities in the Indonesian language demonstrate a growing, conscious interest in things Javanese, and an attempt to find ways to connect the past to the living present. But it was a long time before the political taboo on regional studies was lifted. In the multiethnic Indonesian state, with a strong unitary, nationalist ideology, the issues posed by regionalism and diverse cultural identities were understandably matters of concern to the fathers of the Republic and their immediate successors, who wished to discourage too great an interest in them. Then, in the 1980s, Indonesia appeared to have reached a point of stability at which academic institutes could be established for the study of the rich cultural heritage of the regions, and so, finally, Javanese cultural studies can officially be conducted in Yogyakarta again.

While study and literature are preoccupations of the educated public, the developments in *kethoprak* theatre appear to have their basis in popular culture. *Kethoprak* is a twentieth century theatrical development that is immensely popular and free from the trappings of upper class rigidity; it is spontaneous and lively. These days, this dramatic form appears to be upwardly mobile, accepted as it is by the newly educated classes, while its themes are developing in a socially critical way. The more established forms of the Javanese expressive arts, such as shadow theatre, dance, and *gamelan* music, are also experiencing a real renaissance. Inspired by classical forms, it is perhaps experimentation that counts most, and while it is too early to predict where all this is leading to, it is certain that Javanese culture is undergoing a process of rejuvenation, while deriving its inspiration more from popular models than from the almost extinct dinosaur of court-culture (Mulder, 1992).

It is intriguing to speculate about the possibly parallel developments in political culture. Such thoughts and ideologies are concealed beneath the surface in a climate of political repression. Officially, public participation in this field is undesirable and the people are considered to constitute a 'floating mass' under the guidance of the 'enlightened' political leadership. In this way, the exercise of power appears to be very similar to that in olden days, when 'inspired' kings held a divine mandate, and all political decision-making centred on the palace. Sultans and their court counsellors were exponents of an established and legitimate order that was beyond question; a similar theory seems to hold true nowadays, and it is wise to conform publicly to the reigning political orthodoxy. Just as in former days, so also at present, a means of dealing with the strait jacket of public life can be found in the development of the deep self, by the practice of *kebatinan*, because deep down, each individual is his own centre of truth and satisfaction. In spite of the classical Roman 'bread and circuses' aspect of modern mass culture, the old compartmentalization between a public and a private realm of personal expression still holds. For many, the retreat into the self remains a very satisfactory way of compensating for the exigencies of public life.

Even though current political culture appears to be stagnant and uninspiring, other segments of Javanese culture are demonstrating a considerable vitality, especially in the Central-Javanese court towns of Yogyakarta and Surakarta. This vitality, and the creative power evident in the reinterpretation of cultural elements, may very well be related to the widely accepted alternative of retreating into one's deep self in the face of political adversity, the exigencies of public life, and mass cultural indifference. On the other hand, the weight of the tendencies toward indifference, uncertainty, non-participation and materialism, in an environment that is rapidly losing the last vestiges of its former integrative order, should not be underestimated.

What we are witnessing in Yogyakarta is something like a contest between the creative forces involved in the renewal of Javanese cultural consciousness versus the inertia brought about by the loss of identity due to a vanishing history and cultural heritage, and also by Indonesianization, plus the dulling of the senses by mass culture. The outcome of this tussle will decide whether Yogyakarta is to remain the proud centre of Javanese culture, or to lapse into ordinariness and provincialism.

The Islamicization process

Most students of Javanese society are familiar with the dichotomy between faithfully practising and nominal Muslims (*santri* versus *abangan*). As a formulation claimed to describe social reality, it still guides the thinking of many scholars, as if life in Java were static and not subject to change. Nowadays, there are good reasons to doubt the heuristic value of the *santri-abangan* cleavage. This fission, elaborated in Geertz's *The Religion of Java*, can now be seen to have belonged to a former structure of society, that has vanished rapidly over the past twenty years. At present, at least as it appears at the level of the urban educated middle classes, the two mainstreams in Javanese culture seem to converge. Moreover, and this is often insufficiently appreciated, all Javanese, whatever their degree of Islamicization, share in Javanese culture. That culture is not necessarily religiously expressed, and contains a common vision of man, society, and the ethical conduct of life.

At first sight, an observer is struck by the vast differences between *kejawèn* and orthodox Middle-Eastern religious conceptualization. In the latter thinking, the centre of the universe is God, and the course of history is His Volition; man is a mere creature who should live attuned and subjected to the will of God, since if not, he is damned and incapable of a just life. In other words, a transcendent God is the measure of all things, and man a mere servant who derives satisfaction and legitimation from following the rules and religious obligations set by God. In this creed, therefore, man wants to discover and know God's will: hence the importance of the Koran, the Hadith, the Shari'a, and the religious scholars *(ulama; kiai)*, who interpret and hand down the rules to go by.

Yet a second look is warranted. As in any place where a high or universal religion reaches new converts, it undergoes a process of localization. So, also, Islam in Java was moulded into a Javanese image. Furthermore, the Islam that reached Java had travelled a long way, and en route taken on the mystical and esoteric traits of Sufism, which fitted Javanese thinking and religiosity. Then again, a basically syncretist and tolerant mentality provides fertile ground for new religious inputs. Thus, step by step, Islam was able to establish itself even at the *kejawèn* courts of the Javanese rulers, who appropriated some of its titles and symbols, until nowadays almost all Javanese will acknowledge themselves as Muslims, while blending Islamic thought and practice with older Javanese elements.

In recent history, a typical cultural conflict emerged, first as an inner Islamic struggle, then gradually also along the line of *abangan* versus pious *putihan ('santri')* Islam, finally culminating in the political power struggle that marked the period from the preparation for Independence to the fall of Sukarno (roughly 1945-1966). The origins of this cultural conflict date back to the late 19th century, when the influence of orthodox and reformist Islam first made itself felt in Indonesia. This influence roused and stimulated conscienticization and emancipation movements among Javanese Muslims. In other words, a (religious) 'way of life' began to be questioned, and conscious choices needed to be made to establish a self-assured identity. In that conscienticization process, debate developed about a Javanese versus an Arabian way of doing things, a traditional *(kolot)* versus a modern practice, Muslim reformism versus traditionalism, secular (colonial or national) state versus a Muslim society, and finally about the lifestyles and practices of committed versus non-committed Muslims.

This quest for identity also led to a split between those who practice their religion faithfully and those who are not interested in the formal practice of religion. This cultural cleavage became aggravated when it acquired political dimensions, giving rise to disparate cultural communities, intolerance and intense ideological struggle. It was at that time that Clifford Geertz did the research for his monumental *The Religion of Java*.

For many years now, the New Order government has been trying to defuse the conflict, first, by a rather effective policy of depoliticization of the religious issue while supporting (national) policies of interreligious tolerance, and further, by making religious (Islamic) education compulsory in all schools, by building religious infrastructure (institutes for higher Islamic education, mosques, prayer houses), and by fostering a unifying national Pancasila ideology that transcends the religious diversity. These policies seem to have been remarkably successful.

At the same time, the divergent Islamic communities have entered the modern world. If self-proclaimed righteousness once legitimized their isolation (and reputation for backwardness), now they have become emancipated in terms of modern education, leaving the *kolot* image behind, while opening themselves up to the life of the nation — rather than orienting themselves almost exclusively toward Mecca — and by developing an openness towards and tolerance for others.

The combination of government policy and emancipation is resulting in a rapid acceptance of Islam by people who would not willingly have identified with it some fifteen or twenty years ago, when the *santri-abangan* conflict was still in the open as an emotional issue. Especially among members of the middle classes, acceptance of Islam is spreading rapidly now; first of all, because it no longer implies a political choice; then secondly, due to the emancipation of large segments of the Islamic community; and thirdly, as a result of the religious instruction their children receive in school.

Among these people, there is a trend away from Javanism, especially from its hierarchical orientation, from its rituals and esotericism, and the practice of mysticism. To them, the congregational religions (especially Islam, but also Catholicism and Protestantism) seem timely and attractive in providing an identity and a mental grasp on life. By contrast to the practice of mysticism as an individual endeavour that is time-consuming and self-centred, the congregational Middle-Eastern religions seem to offer a truth that is independent of the self, a book as revelation, and a theology that is reasoned and systematic, all of which is very similar to university learning, and eminently modern. In their contemporary lives, there is less room for mystical speculation and more interest in organized religion.

Congregationalism may also attract members of the lower classes to join in Islamic practice. Often dispossessed, and almost excluded from community life, their sense of belonging to a moral community may boost their identity feelings and self-respect. Among these same classes, however, a new and strong interest in the coarser expressions of Javanese mysticism, such as magic, healing and invulnerability cults, has been noted. It may also be expected that the religious banner will occasionally still be raised for basically political purposes, especially in times of declining economic opportunities, when feelings of powerlessness and oppression grow strong.

On the whole, a weakening of both the *kejawèn* tradition and Islamic isolationism may be expected, and thus a weakening of the opposed cultural identities. Both ways of life essentially belong to a past period, namely, the order of the sultanates with its dominant *kejawèn* tradition. That order was of a politically stratified (two) class society, in which commoners (and Muslims) were expected to accept the social hierarchy and their lowly place in it. This has now vanished. These days, education has emancipated the commoners, while giving rise to a mixed, educated middle class that is giving shape to a new Javanese-Indonesian culture. Consequently, the *abangan-putihan* opposition will no longer be the stress line along which conflicts are expressed, which is as it should be. After all, *abangan* and *putihan*, although contrasting, belong together, as in the *sang Merah Putih*, that is, the noble Red and White Indonesian flag.[3]

---

3 This is a pun. In Javanese, the root *abang* means red, *putih* white.

CHAPTER 15

The cultural process of lowland Christian

Filipino society

The cultural process

It would be foolish to deny the influence of four centuries of colonialism, and intensive contact with the western world, in shaping Philippine society and culture. Almost everything one can think of, such as settlement patterns, agricultural practice, food preparation, land transportation, artistic production, and religious expression, was deeply affected by the contact with Spain and the subsequent exposure to the West. And yet, when in the Philippines, the evidence is clear that one is very much in a particular Southeast Asian country.

While international fast food — an imitation of something that probably never existed — is pretty much the same the world over, and also one of the outstanding features of Philippine consumer culture, that same mass culture of jeans and coke, of pizzas and pop, also has a distinct Filipino flavour. So, if even the most trivial commercial and mass produced things can acquire a Filipino quality — perhaps merely by details such as the insistence on speaking English by the attendants of a McDonald's — how much more Philippinized must other cultural items be that are closer to the heart and soul.

However mixed-up the symbolic language of the Philippines appears to the outsider, that same idiom holds the highest degree of integrity for the insider, whose expectations it expresses. What we see is Philippine culture in action; plazas and churches, fast food and flag-raising, constitutions and oath-taking, all being statements about Philippine society past and present.

In their quest for nationhood and identity, some 'nationalists' are still searching for the pre-Spanish Filipino — running up into the hills, collecting folklore — in the hope of discovering a pristine and colonially uncontaminated original identity. Perhaps they had better concentrate on the deep characteristics of present day Philippine culture if they want to find out about the past. This is not meant to minimise or understate in any way the cultural havoc that has been wrought, but it does honour the obdurately persistent elements and patterns of culture that give the Philippines that characteristic Filipino identity.

Comparatively little is known about pre-Spanish history; and so a great deal of conjecture and conjuring up of the past fill the pages of many a school-book. And even if the data are straight, the facts alone may not explain much, because culture is a process, meaning that it is forever in flux. Yet despite that, Pigafetta's observation that Filipinos drink a lot and hold their liquor well is still valid for the present.[1] Considered anthropologically, therefore, the St. Miguel slogan about the special quality of companionship when drinking *(ibá ang may pinagsamahan)* may actually be hinting at cultural continuity.

While at first blush this seems trivial and superficial, such facts become more interesting when they acquire depth. Was drinking, in public at least, also then the prerogative of men, was it also then the gregarious companionship that was important, and could one also then be killed for refusing a drink, that is, refusing the other's company? Was drinking, then as now, an expression of manliness? Was society, then as now, setting a remarkable valuation on macho behaviour?

By raising the historical question of localization, while combining it with contemporary observations, one will find Philippine content and the Filipino quality of life hidden behind foreign inspired epiphenomena. Yet there is no denying that Philippine society also suffers from a historical affliction called colonial mentality, and though it is fashionable to blame Spanish and friar oppression as being the root cause, it may more accurately be argued that the Americans were at fault.

If there is a Spanish root to colonial mentality, it must be looked for in a different area. While centuries of oppression, contempt, and discrimination seemingly explain *Indolencia*[2] and inferiority feelings,

1 Pigafetta was the 'Italian' chronicler of Magellan's circumnavigation of the globe. They were the first Europeans to visit the Philippines (1521).

2 Reference is to a well-known essay by José Rizal, La indolencia de los Filipinos (*La Solidaridad*, 1889), in which the author argues that, if Filipinos are considered to be indolent, this is the fruit of their colonial exploitation rather than an innate trait.

the same 'causes' also explain the rise of nationality and nationalism, critical awareness and protest, and the thinking that inspired Propaganda, Revolution, and Republic. In response to economic opportunity, European education, and exposure to modern western ideas, a self-confident class had arisen that aspired to participate in European culture, and whose *ilustrados* were firmly rooted in western intellectual tradition.[3] A few of these realized their dilemma, namely, that of being native to the Philippines, but of thinking in terms of a western 'great tradition' that had no roots in their country. Hence their colonial mentality, and their subsequent search for origin and identity in the early Spanish sources,[4] or in local folklore.[5]

Had the politically elitist leading class of the Malolos Republic had its way, the implanted hispanicization would have moulded itself into the Philippine image, and there was certainly no contradiction between an authoritarian style of leadership and local family and political customs. Moreover, an elite culture with its western trappings had coalesced slowly in the long colonial period, and seemed to fit the environment. Culturally, therefore, the break with Spain was not a watershed event but a mere change of government in a continuing history.

The real rupture is the cultural break with the past occasioned by the advent of the Americans, a rending that took some twenty to thirty years to accomplish, of course, but that culminated in a new generation without history, one that was spiritually 'without fathers and grandfa-

3 *Ilustrados* are the sons of the native gentry and incipient bourgeoisie educated in Europe. In the 1880s in Spain, they pleaded for the equality of the Philippines in its relation to the Peninsula, while protesting the obscurantism and economic, cultural, and political dominance of the Spanish friars (clergy); this effort became known as the Propaganda, which in its turn gave birth to the emancipatory and nationalistic ideas that fired the Revolution against Spain (1896-8).

4 *Sucesos de las Islas Filipinas por el Dr. Antonio de Morga*, anotada por José Rizal, Paris 1890. *Sucesos* was first published in Mexico, 1607.

5 Isabelo de los Reyes, Sr., may be considered to be the first native folklorist. Later, in the early period of the American occupation, he founded the first labour union, the Union Obrera Democratica de Filipinas (1902); in the same year, he was instrumental in establishing the Philippine Independent Church that broke away from the Roman Catholic Church, not only for reasons of nationalism, but especially in protest against its conservatism, and the continuing dominance of the friars. This church is also known as the Aglipayan Church, after its first supreme bishop, Fr. Gregorio Aglipay.

thers'. Where the Spaniards succeeded in awakening and uniting the people and bringing a nation into being, the Americans doused the enthusiasm by fostering a generation of privileged politicos who lacked any great plan or vision.

Although elections and political prize-fighting became the favourite national pastime, reminiscent both of the fiesta and the cock-fight, the original cry for 'immediate independence' ceased to have any relevance once the Commonwealth was in place; since then ideologies and platforms have largely been absent from Philippine politics. It is concerned solely with privilege, power, and pelf, centring on persons, not on programmes, all of which is consistent with the old patterns of authoritarian, elitist leadership that saw 'public affairs' as the private matters of 'men of prowess'. It is the contests among the latter that make politics a spectator sport for the masses, and an expression of what the NDF likes to call the semi-feudal, semi-colonial mode of production.

So what exactly does the break with the past consist of, if the Americans were unable in their 'efforts to prepare for Independence' to affect basic patterns of production, leadership and politics? By means of their educational policy, that involved shipping over boat-loads of teachers and new ideas, the Filipinos were mentally recolonized by means of a eulogistic monologue that not only extolled American culture, its standards, history, and idea of progress, but that also savagely criticized and degraded the Spanish colonial past. As regards the results of these measures, it is fair to speak of a rupture in cultural reproduction, of relegating the past to insignificance, of interrupting the discourse that created the nation in the face of Spanish oppression, of erasing or at least gravely distorting the collective memory, of aborting whatever might have grown into a distinct Filipino civilization.

Americanism substituted the future for the past. The Philippines became a country without history, future-fixated and progress-directed, while simultaneously lacking any clear goal; its people became a nation in limbo, oriented outward to, and protected by, Mother America, who shielded her ward from all cosmopolitan ideas that were displeasing to her. This was 'progress' without any progressive, nation-building ideas, 'progress' in the absence of a national discourse, 'progress' in terms of borrowed, expedient ideas.

Those the Americans imposed were above all concepts of politics and government concerning the ordering of the public sphere. In the Philippine context, these ideas were completely divorced from their original consensual, moral content. As a historical, colonial imposition, they stood for a technical order of impersonal control, the rule of law. While this may have been in America's own best interests, this preparation for self-rule and independence was rife with internal contradictions. How was it possible to prepare for 'early independence' while suppressing nationalism? How was creating a civil public sphere, a commonwealth, conceivable, while not allowing public participation, when discouraging public debate on the meaning and function of the nation as a moral body politic filling that public sphere? With the destruction of history and nationalism, the culture of politics focused merely on power and competing personalities. In the process, the Philippines also became a nation of lawyers.

The American ideas did not fit any pre-existing reality, and so could not find roots. They descended on Asia from 'God's own country', and were held to be superior in every way. What the Americans were able to accomplish was to impress a notion of their superiority, and for a long time American ideas about almost anything under the sun were held to be authoritative, worthy of admiration and emulation. By measuring their own condition against this yardstick, certain Filipinos became greatly daunted by inferiority feelings, thus contributing to an undeniable measure of cultural dependency and insecurity, a cultural 'bi-nationalism' that denigrates the local and imitates the foreign model. In this manner, the 'colonial mentality' became instituted.

It was thus a fantastically distorted culture that most members of the political class and the educated public inherited by the time independence was granted to a country that lay in ruins; and that not merely in a literal way. Whatever decency was still in place after the devastation of the war was soon corrupted by making collaboration a non-issue, by backpay and war surplus profiteering, by the rape of democratic representation and tampering with the constitution. In as far as a stable bureaucracy had existed as the backbone of the state, it was thoroughly subverted by patronage politics (Corpuz, 1989 II:570-1), the interests of political dynasties replacing those of the common weal.

As a result of the American presence, the better educated stratum of society came to suffer, wittingly or not, from various forms of cultural alienation. Because of their education and urbanity, they naturally viewed themselves as living at a great remove from the ordinary Filipino people; through their Americanization they largely ignored and forgot about their origin, history and national roots; as a result of their intellectual and artistic dependency, many were sooner or later forced to recognize their provincialism vis-à-vis the western heritage; by measuring themselves against the standards of a foreign 'great tradition' they were constantly reminded of the flaws in their society; from their own involvement in Philippine everyday life, they experienced the incompatibility between a private moral sphere and 'official' public life. Uprooted in more than one sense, most clung harder still to the American heritage, though at the same time some began to doubt the value of cultural dependency, while protesting the non-creative sterility of the 'colonial mentality'.[6]

The best known personalities who stand at the beginning of the 'Second Propaganda' in the 1950s are the politicians Recto and Tañada, the historian Agoncillo, and the social activist author Amado V. Hernandez. Their nationalism was not widely understood, and was felt as threatening by most, yet it provided the basis for the democratic awakening of the 1960s. Only then did students and intellectuals begin to look anew at their own condition, to be interested in history, to scrutinize the still colonially influenced school education, to search for vision in progressive thought, to discover Marx and Marxist analysis, to become socially and politically aware, and to ask disturbing questions about the status quo, about social justice, Philippine identity and nationhood. Awareness grew of the dysfunctionality of the political system, the colonial-feudal mode of production, of the awesome gap

---

6 The irrelevance of American standards to Philippine life has often been argued, for instance, by O. D. Corpuz in, The cultural foundations of Filipino politics (1960) (J.V. Abueva and R.P. de Guzman (eds), *Foundations and dynamics of Filipino government and politics*. Manila: Bookmark, 1969:6-18). He reasons that in Filipino politics, nepotism is ethically normal, and that party loyalty is subject to family based interests, and therefore, "We do [should] not judge ourselves by the irrelevant idiosyncrasies, eccentricities, and even wishes, of alien nations". In a comparable way, Lumbera argues that Filipino literature should be judged by Filipino standards and by its relevance for life in the Philippines. (Bienvenido Lumbera, *Revaluation*. Metro Manila, 1984:91-101).

between the elite and the people, and the whole train of associated issues. Protest against the existing order of society, and the behaviour of its traditional politicians, ranged from the founding of the New People's Army (NPA) in 1969 through the First Quarter Storm[7] and on to the declaration of Martial Law in 1972.

From the late 1960s onwards, elements of progressive ideological thinking and social analysis began to filter into public thought and perception. For some, this process was greatly stimulated by the imposition of Martial Law in September 1972, while others retreated from their ideological positions at that time. Most ideologically based movements and organizations that exist today, as also the phenomenal growth of the NDF, can be traced back to the period of Marcos's dictatorship, but Martial Law also created a generation of 'martial law babies', meaning those who had their schooling during those years. The contemporary Education Development Plan claimed to be 'reform directed at problems of national identity', and succeeded in cultivating a generation of students who are highly outward directed, uninterested in any questions of nation and/or ideology, and almost devoid of historical or cultural perspective (Doronila, 1986). In brief, they are a perfect generation of television watchers with little, if any, political awareness.

It was only for a short period after February 1986 that moral issues, such as national reconciliation, human rights, good government, social justice, and constitutionalism, were allowed to interfere with political expediency, and soon these were drowned in the usual rhetoric of traditional politicians, reducing the public sphere to an area of moral obscurity. While this seemed on the surface to suit the culture of the mass media and the interests of political dynasts down to the ground, it also had the opposite effect of stimulating the vitality of all kinds of cause-orientation, bringing together people who reflected on moral issues, from feminism to land reform, from cultural dependency to national self-assertion, from patriotism to justice with peace, from anti-militarization to political reform, from debt repudiation to environmental issues, from unionism to child prostitution, from poverty to moral recovery, and all the other brave causes.

---

7 The vehement, protracted students' and social activists' protests of the first few months of 1970 became known as the First Quarter Storm.

This is not the place to describe these educated middle stratum- and lower class-based movements, their ways of organizing, and their political aspirations, though we will return to them later (chapter 16). The point here is that many people have started thinking, that their debates now essentially address public issues, such as the order of public life, of the common interest, which are the type of thoughts that originally arose during the Propaganda, and that were effectively suppressed by the Americans and their elite supporters, whose peddling of 'early' or 'immediate independence' and 'democratic government' could hardly camouflage the fact that the politics they practised were, and are, those of power and personal advantage, and not about the common interest, about *res publica*.

This was, however, only to be expected. By its very nature, colonial government cannot enjoy a high degree of legitimation in the eyes of those who fall under its sway. The new, neo-colonial, rulers who took over in 1946 did not boost their legitimacy by morally exemplary action, and perhaps with the short exceptions of President Magsaysay (1953-57) and President Aquino during her first year in office (1986), we should realize that Philippine society has had no tradition of a legitimate, a morally-backed, state, and that the public sphere has not evolved to become a moral order. State and the public world belong to the domain of amoral power, existing in separation from the religious and non-expediential norms that belong to the private realm of the family.[8]

Now, a hundred years after the original Propaganda, a culture of the public world seems to be arising that centres on moral issues, on the legitimacy of the state in terms of nationalism, social justice, and popular political representation. This culture is being developed by committed members of the urban middle classes who, in one way or another, are dissatisfied with elite politics and cultural dependency.

Due to the great variety of points of departure, and their often fuzzy theoretical positions, for a long time the various groups of intellectuals developing critical social thought had difficulty in coming together, or in taking each other seriously. In line with the fractious

8 For elaboration, see Niels Mulder, 'This God-forsaken country': Filipino images of the nation. Tønnesson and Antlöv, 1996.

character of the Philippine social process, they existed separately, and preferred denouncing each other to engaging in serious debate. Nowadays, though, it seems that the perception is taking hold that the various strains of critical thought sprout from a common experience and history, that the issues concerned are basically connected, and consequently, a willingness to discuss and coalesce is emerging. This could be the beginning of the growth of a national discourse[9] that is inward, Philippines oriented, a disquisition expressive of intellectual self-confidence, and most of all, one that transcends the immediacy of politics.

Whether the 'objective conditions' for such an internally oriented debate are in place, I do not know, but the moral bankruptcy of traditional politics and militarization is increasingly evident to most (David, 1991). An important development is the urge to listen to the voices of the dispossessed, in other words, to treat ordinary people in a decent manner, and to address their poverty as a serious national problem. This reaching out to them by NGOs not only illustrates the relative impotence of government but is an important cultural, a nation-building, event, in which the matter of social justice prevails over nationalism.

Yet nationalistic questions remain important and divisive. Contentions over a national language, the school curriculum, interpretations of history, centralism versus regionalism, are all still very emotional, and potentially obstructive to the growth of a national discourse, unless they are dealt with in a moral-rational way. On the other hand, the media may be having a positive influence in relating the various parts of the country to one another, in involving people in each others' lives. In this regard, the national school system also has great potential, and while it is gratifying to see a gradual decolonialization of the materials for the teaching of social studies (including history, geography, economics, culture, civics, and national identity)[10], one sometimes despairs at the snail's pace of curricular change, and the low priority given to cultural engineering and growth.

From the English language press during the 1980s, especially since

9 National discourse: the continual negotiation and interpretation of those major ideas that express and create national identity and community by a nation's intelligentsia, based on historical consciousness, a shared canon of culture and common experience, and which transcend politics.

10 See Mulder, 1996,b: chapters 3,4 and 6.

195

August 1983 and then February 1986, it is clear that there is now a tremendous amount of interest in the potential for the rule of law and constitutionalism, in the relationship with the USA, in peace, and so it is now evident that the obstacles are gradually being identified. These days the ruling elite and traditional politics are more and more often recognized as the enemy within, who are to be blamed for all the ills that beset the country. Another thing of note is the debate about the meaning and connotations, and the very frequent occurrence, of the word Filipino in the newspapers — whether or not in the perspective of moral recovery — indicating a growing tendency towards becoming more inward and self-directed, more self-dependent and less colonial-minded.

Whether all this is enough for the emergence of a civil culture of the public sphere, and the restructuring of the country's institutions, must, for the time being, remain moot, partly because of the near absence of national leadership. According to some, it is states that make nations, but what we see in the Philippines is a cultural process from below that propagates the concept of the nation. Where this process collides with the vested interests of the elite that dominates the state, one cannot but expect that it will fight back. The threatening possibility of factions in the army mounting a coup d'état does not augur well for cultural growth, either. Although again, sometimes having a clear target, such as opposition to a junta, may stimulate awareness.

There are more subtle problems, though, that blur cultural bearings. Overzealous (Tagalog) nationalism and anti-Americanism collide with the sense of history and cosmopolitanism of many intellectuals, who are outward oriented and consider themselves citizens of the world. While this attitude is perhaps most characteristic among members of the English-speaking educated public, these people and their style also set the example for a middle class that is not interested in innovation, and that is alienated from a native base, while lacking a 'great tradition' of its own.

Openness to the outside world, and the emigration perspective, are very symptomatic of contemporary Philippine culture, and may partly explain the seemingly irresistible advance of mass and consumer culture with its foreign produced fads and fancies. This not only brings in apples and American B-movies but also an abundance of English language television programmes, with their outlandish role models and glorification of violence. The free enterprise, fully-commercialized broadcast media may dull the sensibilities, stifle creativity and depoliticize their audiences, in spite of all the private conscientization efforts to the contrary.

Similar results may be effected by the many holier-than-thou, and other rightist, religious sects that are actively and successfully recruiting among all segments of the society. Consumer culture, the mass media, and religious zealotry are not really conducive to the creation of a viable, civil public world, and may, taken together with the amount of energy invested in the struggle for survival and the emotions devoted to the prevailing culture of the family, offer a tremendous challenge to the ideologues and intellectuals — despite all their coalitions — in their efforts to create a just national community.

Overview

The depth, persistence, and elaboration of certain originally Spanish cultural forms in Philippine life can be explained by the fact that they chimed in with what was available in the local cultures. In that way, Spanish Catholicism to a large extent could be appropriated, and then develop as the symbolic expression of the family, and reinforce the position of the mother as the moral anchor in life. It also justified authoritarianism and the cult of manliness. Other notions that belonged to the original package, such as sin or the legitimate state, did not find roots, and so have survived only in a stunted condition that is marginal to the cultural process.

Spanish forms grew to become part of the national expression of the Philippines, transcending and unifying the different local cultures. Towards the end of the Spanish period, a hispanicized leading class, whose intellectuals thought in European ways, was in place. A few of them recognized that their dilemma came from their not being rooted in a native 'great tradition'. This predicament, however, was no impediment to the growth of a national discourse and the discovery of nationhood.

By denigrating Spanish culture and introducing that of their own, by avoiding the image of oppressor and bestowing political power upon the economic and intellectual elites, by their vaunting of American superiority and progressiveness ('modernity'), by promising early independence yet discouraging a nationalistic shaping of the public sphere, the Americans destroyed nationalism, thus alienating educated Filipinos from themselves, and making it possible to institute cultural dependency and a colonial mentality. Once a native history and identity had been driven out, cultural production became largely sterile, imitative, and superficial.

So, whereas the Spanish heritage was largely absorbed and subsequently reworked in their own image, the second colonization engendered attitudes of dependence, mendicancy, imitation, alienation, and self-doubt, thus destroying (national) self-confidence. When the Americans went, they left a neo-colonial client state behind them, with no other culture of the public world than that embodied in the rhetoric of rapacious, dynastic politicians. In sum, the growth of a national discourse was arrested for almost a hundred years, and it was not until the late 1960s that a vision of the nation once more began to emerge.

Marcos's oppression and arbitrariness were incidentally instrumental in promoting social and self-awareness, which gave birth to the multitude of associations striving after emancipation, justice, peace, moral recovery, educational reform, national pride, decency, human rights, and so forth. But the repression of those years was also responsible for bringing about an outward orientation and social indifference, plus the logic of familism with its concentration on economic survival. Nowadays, the subsequent cultural ferment can be seen as an important stage in the development of a culture of the common weal. To be successful in this, matters of nationalism should be far less important than issues of social justice; they are not always so. The development of that culture through the emergence of a national discourse is held back by the powerful forces of disengaging mass culture, religious zealotry, familism, and a persistent outward orientation. A factor that also may retard such a growth is the near absence of cultural leadership by the state. Nationalism and a national discourse simply seem to be surfacing from below, often in reaction against whatever emanates from the political centre.

CHAPTER 16

The development of political culture

After the Aquino assassination in August 1983, protests against Marcos and his political establishment regularly emanated from Makati, the country's main business district. Street demonstrations supported, and even initiated, by businessmen are a rather unusual occurrence, but the people in Makati had good reasons. Economically, the country was on the way down, a decline that was exacerbated by the continuous pillage of the economy by the privileged business friends, or cronies, of the president.

Dissent by businessmen, and many other representatives of the urban middle classes, continued until the popular demonstrations against Marcos and his armed forces on the EDSA boulevard sent the *Apô* (Old Man) packing in a hurry, while simultaneously catapulting Corazon Aquino into power. Because of the role of respected members of the middle classes in all this, the connection between business, economic growth, and the establishment of a viable democracy is frequently discussed in the Philippines.

The ascent to power of the tycoon Chatichai Choonhavan in Thailand in 1988 was also hailed by many as a victory for democracy, because Chatichai was a popularly elected prime minister and his cabinet consisted in the main of civilian businessmen. What's more, the Thai economy was booming and continued to grow rapidly thereafter. But are there any good reasons to suppose that there is a causal connection between business, economic development, and democracy?

The belief that there is such a connection may be inspired by reflections on the western experience, and most especially on the role of the bourgeoisie in its emancipation from dynastic control and the subsequent growth of a civil society, in which democratic processes came to control government and state. We should, perhaps, question if this model does not sound simply too good to be true. It may also be asked whether a 'civil society' ever existed in which a real participatory democracy prevailed. Seen from a class viewpoint, this can never have been in the interests of a capitalist bourgeoisie.

The evolution of rather democratic structures of state and society in western history is an extremely complex story that is intricately linked to the development of certain modes of production in Western Europe and the United States of America. It has also given rise to big government, big business, and the welfare state. In the process, politics has not become very transparent, and popular, democratic control over big business is tenuous indeed; while many voter-citizens and influential ideas play out their roles on the political stage, the manipulative force of big business interests is quite clear to every critical observer.

There is no necessary connection identifiable between business, its growth, and democracy. What counts in the political process everywhere, and very clearly so in Southeast Asia, is belonging to the in-group of political decision-makers. And what goes on inside the backrooms of the halls of power remains rather murky and obscure to the public. It is not a public affair in spite of the trappings of democracy. No, business is not going to make the world a more democratic place, even now when it has obviously penetrated the Southeast Asian bastions of politics. Businessmen are now among the 'ins', but not all who are in business are in, nor is it always the same people who are influential, as the experience of the Marcos cronies illustrates.

The fact that entrepreneurs and managers protest or get elected is no reason to suppose that society is on its way to evolving into a civil society or a welfare state. The emancipation of the subject from the dynast may also lead to dictatorship, or the imposition by force of a state guided by communist ideals. This, at least, was the model promulgated in the Soviet Union, among others. In Southeast Asia, we find an emergent educated public — probably the most essential ingredient for a civil society — that is still too small to produce much of a politically effective public opinion. Yet its members often desire emancipation from a dynastic or neo-colonial order of state, where a few hold all the privilege. They aspire to the rule of impersonal law and ethics in political, in 'public', affairs. Because they write in and to the newspapers, and are active on the NGO scene, their voices can often be heard. Their political influence is weak, however, even though they may write the Constitution, as happened in the Philippines in 1986, or become advisers to the government, such as in Indonesia.

In time, with education becoming available on an impressive scale, popular opinion will come to be a more important factor, but it is still debatable whether it will result in a politically enlightened public. For this is also a time when the economy, and 'development at all cost', dominate the thinking of politicians and government alike, while issues of staying afloat, mobility, and raising one's standard of living preoccupy most individuals. For the majority, it is the stark matter of survival that counts, but for a considerable minority, their anxieties concern status considerations, leading to increased consumption.

Consumer culture in a semi-anonymous environment does not make for responsible citizenship or the growth of democracy. The education invested serves individuals accumulative skills, rather than fostering the desire to participate in national affairs. Thus, as long as the government legitimizes itself by stimulating economic expansion and the opportunity for individual advancement of the educated segment of the public, its members will be more interested in their private affairs than in creating politically relevant public opinion and debate. One of the reasons why there is relatively more debate going on in the Philippines than in Thailand or Indonesia may be precisely the combination of education and a long stagnant economy.

So, while it would be going too far to say that public opinion is entirely irrelevant in Southeast Asian politics, in order to grasp the nature of the political process there, the observer should not let himself be deceived by the democratic window-dressing. The relevant questions to ask about political development are: Who is in power? Who are the 'ins'? Which are the groups, institutions, or establishments that can effectively manipulate the political process and the state? But the observer should also bear in mind that the 'ins' are changing; new interests get 'in', older interests may decline in importance, sometimes unexpected moralists get in and gain access to the levers of power, perhaps even in the name of democracy or democratization.

The 'ins'

When Thai royal absolutism was replaced by constitutional government in 1932, those who led the revolt to achieve emancipation from royal prerogatives were mostly the foreign-educated elements in the military and bureaucracy. The centralized bureaucratic polity that had been organized toward the end of the nineteenth century was firmly in place, and continued to expand and dominate society in conjunction with the military establishment (Riggs, 1966). The tendency toward centralization of state control continued unabated and, in cooperation with the largely Chinese commercial class, the state claimed a prominent role in the economy.

Since then, other groups have come to the fore who demand a say in the polity. During the unruly and nationalistic open society of 1973-76, demands for social justice, popular participation in the political process, and accountability of government were forcefully expressed. Naturally, the initiative was with university students, supported by broad popular movements. At the same time, and on up into the present, the business community has been pressing for a share in power, and even succeeded in dominating the political process from 1988 to February 1991. Then the military, bureaucracy, and technocrats reasserted themselves, a move that was initially well received by the population and disenfranchized competitors, and also, importantly, not opposed by the King.

The present picture of Thai society is more complicated than in 1932, or even 1973. Business (commerce, industry, banking, services) has grown explosively and is, directly or indirectly, well represented in the power establishment. The business class appears to be rather self-serving, has strong international connections, and is less inspired by nationalism than by economic motives. Business, the state and its bureaucracy, however, seem to need each other and are not natural antagonists.

As the main contenders in the Thai political arena at present, we find the bureaucratic, the military, and the commercial establishments, all sharing many common interests (Chai-anan and Suchit, 1985). Along with these, the monarch at the apex also performs an important function, one that is simultaneously political and moral. In its moral-charismatic aspect — the ruler symbolizing the nation — the king's role is to bridge the gap between the power elite at the centre and the populace at large.

A more recent element in Thai politics is the emergence of a political party that bases itself on moral issues and popular consensus. This party is The Force of Righteousness *(Phalang Tham)* that has brought Brigadier-General Chamlong Srimuang to the governorship of the Thai metropolis. Nicknamed 'Mr Clean' or 'Holy Monk', due to his prominence in the unorthodox religious (moral revival) movement Santi Asoke, the population overwhelmingly voted him into power, much to the displeasure of the traditional political establishment, who subsequently tried to obstruct Chamlong's policies, and even moved against the Santi Asoke independent monkhood. None of this discouraged the electorate from renewing Chamlong's mandate in 1989 with a landslide victory, not only because of his moral stature, but also due to his energetic tackling of urban problems. So far, the *Phalang Tham* party is still unique in Southeast Asia; though its theme — rather than programme — that the wellsprings of an orderly society are located in individual ethical behaviour, is more traditional than progressive.

In Indonesia, the people who led the nationalist movement against the Dutch government (Van Niel, 1960) were professionals, and when they had emancipated themselves from the colonial bond, they still needed the old civil service to maintain a measure of law and order. This colonial civil service has been described as a patrimonial bureaucracy and the backbone of a bureaucratic polity (Sutherland, 1979), and it was able to reassert itself fully when order was imposed after the unruly years of early independence, during which civil political parties, local elites, religious groups, and factions of the army competed for a share in power. After the military became the decisive force in Indonesian politics, a set-up emerged that was very similar to the Thai situation up until 1973.

In these circumstances, the focus of power is the capital. It is there that power increasingly concentrates. Centralized control over the bureaucracy and the army as the instruments of government penetration in, and domination of, the provinces make Indonesia a typical patrimonial-bureaucratic polity. The state also plays a prominent role in the economy, while largely accommodating the interests of the Chinese-dominated big business establishments, the so-called conglomerates, to the detriment of those of a fledgling native entrepreneurial class that can only slowly develop (Robison, 1986).

Throughout this, and in spite of election rituals, the incumbent president has styled himself more and more after the Javanese sultans of old, initiating a kind of monarchical control that legitimates the claim to constituting the exemplary centre of the realm, which thus also justifies the attempt to exercise moral control of the population (Anderson, 1983). This is evident in the weakening of the political parties, the obligation to identify oneself as professing a religion, and the massive propagation of a Javanized Pancasila ideology that stresses the values of hierarchy, leadership, duty, and obedience. While there is ample reason to talk about an army-dominated government, we should also bear in mind that it is patterned after an authoritative and respected Javanese model that leaves little room for an autonomous citizenry, moral protest, or movements pressing for social justice. Over time, the public sphere has acquired the characteristics of a dynastic realm, much like in the old sultanates, or in the former colonial order under a governor-general (Mulder, 1995,b).

At first sight, the Philippine situation appears to be vastly different. Lacking in native royal traditions, it would appear to be a republic ruled by a boisterous democratic process that ought to give a fair chance to the development of a civil society, in which the state functions as the guardian of a civil order — and in which state and society could fuse, creating a true nation-state led by a native bourgeoisie.

Upon taking a closer look, however, the picture changes. Even though the Revolution against Spain may be seen as resulting in the emancipation of the gentry and educated class from the colonial master, still these same people were later co-opted by the American colonial government. In this sequence of events, they acquired political position and power first, which they could then use profitably to enhance their hold on the economy. Hence, the long colonial period produced a small oligarchy dominating the Philippine political economy. When political independence was finally granted to this ruling elite, it did not signify a break with the colonial past. As the new, neo-colonial, masters they legitimately succeeded the Americans, to whom they remained closely allied. In their hands, politics is an instrument for regulating intra-elite competition, and the source of pervasive patronage, which naturally led at an early date to a politicization of the civil service that became almost entirely subservient to political expediency.

While there are strong centralizing tendencies in the Philippine polity, it remains fractious and somewhat brittle by nature, because it is essentially locally, provincially and regionally based. The members of the oligarchy who manoeuvre at the national level represent the dynastic interests of their families, clans and territories. Wherever they have their base, they regard it as more or less their private bailiwick that needs defending against all-comers. Treating their territories pretty much as fiefs, their thinking is dynastic, and when nationally oriented, it is merely to fight for a better deal for their own private interests.

Under such circumstances, it is small wonder that the oligarchy has no interest in promoting nationalism, a civil society, the rule of law, or a sense of the common weal. The elite's interests are best served by the absence of such ideological notions because they equate their own interests with those of all. So, whatever passes for party programmes is always subservient to the 'respectable' expediency of 'free enterprise', 'liberty', the rights of private property, and (non-participatory) democracy.[1]

Thus, while it appears from a distance that a civilian and rather bourgeois establishment is in control, close-up it becomes apparent that this is more feudal than civil in character, and more internationally dependent/neo-colonial than autonomous, with the passive acquiescence of the people serving the elite's best interest. Stemming from this, politics remain opaque and political debate about programmes negligible, while, at the same time, sociological analysis is branded as 'oppositionist'. If things are not as they should be, causes for this must be sought in individual moral decay, to be remedied by an endless string of Values Education and Moral Recovery programmes that originate from the Department of Education, Culture and Sports, the Senate, or any of the many active civic societies, sects and churches.

The significant differences that set the Philippine situation apart from that of the other polities discussed are the absence of a royal tradition and a charismatic exemplary centre; the near absence of nationalism from above and the lack of a nationalistic doctrine; the way the political elite came to power by inheritance; the absence of a bureaucratic polity or a civil service that functions as the backbone of the

---

1 For a comprehensive account of the evolution of the Filipino political system and its culture see Wurfel, 1988, ominously subtitled "development and decay".

nation-state; a fair number of territorially based political dynasties; and the clear primacy of private landed and business interests over national interests. State power is thus emasculated and organizationally weak. While the military has traditionally been under civilian control, it now seems to be headed for a more weighty political role, and the influence of the army in current political affairs must be deemed considerable.

For Thailand, we noted that the dynastic prerogative of absolute monarchy had to cede power, and that Thai politics evolved into a contest between the bureaucracy, the military, the business establishment, and a more recent idealistic civilian political stream. Relative to these, the role of the monarch has been steadily increasing in importance over the past twenty years. In Indonesia, it appears as if a new dynastic order is in the making. That order relies heavily on the military and the bureaucracy, in conjunction with the foreign and Indonesian-Chinese business establishment. In the Philippines, the main contenders are political dynasties, local and foreign business interests, and probably the army.

In comparing the three polities, we note that the business class plays an important role in them all, which corresponds with the state's emphasis on economic development as the pre-eminent means of achieving national progress. This conjunction of interests fuels the materialistic appetites of those who benefit from development, while aggravating the gap in living standards between themselves and those who are left behind at the mere subsistence level. In both Thailand and Indonesia, the state is patterned after the dynastic model that also entitles it to extend moral guidance to the population; the backbone of the state is its centrally controlled bureaucracy, which provides continuity and stability. The Philippines lacks this model on a national scale, so the organization of effective state power is rather weak. It is accurate, though, to speak of a set of regionally organized dynastic systems under locally dominant political clans, who do not run their territories bureaucratically, but through patronage and their 'political machines'. This latter pattern of organization makes the Philippines a far more volatile place than its neighbours. In all three we note the politically important role of military officers (Djiwandono and Yong, 1988).

The political centre stage is hidden from public view, and its actors do not feel accountable to a population, whom they expect to be apolitical. Yet, sometimes, groups do muster around issues of gross exploitation, and may demonstrate for better wages and conditions of work, or in favour of land reform, or against foreclosure and the arrogance of old landlords or new agribusiness. Organized by the militant left, such mobilization is perennial in the Philippines, but also surfaces spontaneously time and again in the other countries. Other, moral, forms of political organization typically organize vertically, cutting across class lines — Bangkok Governor Chamlong's Force of Righteousness being a perfect example. Engaged in by members of the educated urban middle classes, this type of activism protests corruption, arbitrariness, the power of business, the destruction of the environment, the absence of social justice, or human rights abuses. For the time being, to what extent these various forms of mobilization and protest against established political practice will be effective in penetrating to, or influencing, the political centre stage remains to be seen.

Alternative thinking

Among members of the urban middle classes, different ideas about the order of wider society have taken root, and these people may share an interest in instituting the rule of law, administrative predictability, political accountability, and government inspired by a vision of the common welfare. In other words, among members of this class the idea of a civil society regulating a common *res publica* is developing.

These issues are typically discussed by academicians, students, and professionals who are in contact with the global world of ideas, but often this intelligentsia has difficulty in relating their ideas to the specific situation of their own society. Despite this, their arguments may prove persuasive to other members of that broad and largely powerless middle stratum, like the *petite bourgeoisie*, and sometimes even to higher levels, such as disenfranchised big business, and other opponents of the regime.

Depending on the measure of press freedom that governments allow, the debates are typically conducted in the press, as is currently the case in the Philippines and Thailand, or reach the incipient citizenry by more devious routes. No government, however, is able to block these ideas out entirely, thus effectively mentally isolating its population in an increasingly open, media-dominated world. And so, discussions are taking place, protests being expressed — and awareness generated.

The earliest urban demonstrations against the actual social set-up were grounded in the emergence of nationalistic, anti-dynastic, and labour movements, but such events did not then, and still do not now, automatically imply in themselves the birth of a civil culture of the public world. One of this nature consists of elaborated and interlinked formations and configurations that for comprehension's sake require sociological analysis: this involves consciousness of structure, of history, of institutions, and the concept of legitimacy in order, first of all, to be able to identify the root causes of the political economy's problems and the obstacles confronting it. Only after this has been accomplished is it possible to begin to devise means of tackling them. Consequently, a modern public world can only come into existence through the efforts of an educated public that is sophisticated enough to reason all this through, and determined enough to bring about its own emancipation from the status quo.

So far, such theoretical and ideological consciousness is only at the nascent stage in Southeast Asia. All concerns are still gut issues. The fact that such topics are now being aired, though, and some thinking about solutions is taking place, is new in itself. The recognition of problems, and the expression of people's concerns about them, are the first steps in the creation of a relevant public opinion. Discussing difficulties raises consciousness and, in the process, society at large is elevated from the domain of the taken-for-granted everyday life into a realm of challenge and responsibility; one that concerned citizens desire to bring under their own control.

Toward a civil culture of the public world?

Historically, the most important contribution toward the development of the present public debate on society and its problems, on social justice and the common weal, has been made by progressive intellectuals and socialist parties. This political left is marginal in the three societies under discussion. In Indonesia, anything critical is anathema to the

authorities, and even Pancasila-based student protest (1978) is vigorous-
ly suppressed. Censorship keeps the press sterile, and issues of social
justice are side-stepped. Given such heavy-handedness, it is difficult to
observe the rapid spreading of the ideas that are vital to a modern civil
culture of the public sphere.

The political left is unobtrusive in Thailand, not because of censorship, but since it seems to have run its turbulent course between the
mid-sixties and the early eighties. At present, it is hardly stirring as a
political organization, and the *Phalang Tham* party, plus religious
activism, may be enough to keep progressive intellectuals or labour
removed from the centre of politics.

By far the most active underground political organization in
Southeast Asia is the NDF/NPA in the Philippines, still waging an intense
ideological and armed campaign to promote its vision of a national
democratic, or Marxist, future. In addition to these, one finds the legitimate, social democratic left organized in some small parties and trade
unions, but these have so far failed to make any dent in the political
establishment by achieving democratic representation. Still, there is
quite a lot of open discussion going on, and the idea that politics
should be more participatory, and less of an oligarchic monopoly, is
spreading rapidly among the educated, newspaper-reading public.

It would be a mistake to expect the initial stages in the evolution
of a civil culture of the public sphere to be evident in the explicitly
political realm. Civic action already exists alongside the political and
administrative sphere of the state, and is typically organized in all sorts
of NGOs, in ecological activism, feminism, anti-corruption campaigns,
and other such cause-orientations or issues. While these are conspicuous in all three countries, and complemented by such courageous
human rights activists as the members of the *Lembaga Bantuan Hukum*
(Legal Aid Institute) in Indonesia, NGOs are so prominent in the
Philippines as to warrant a short discussion.

The Philippines may easily count the most NGOs per head of population in the world, and they are spread out all over the country. Work
that in many countries is thought to be a government activity is typically
tackled by them, and such NGO activities may be seen as a middleclass
response to governmental neglect. As such, it breathes a civic spirit, yet,
since it is equally typically issues-oriented, it does not address the prob-

lems of society within an encompassing ideological frame, and those involved generally concentrate on symptoms rather than causes.

Closest to working within broader frames is the liberation-theology-inspired Basic Christian Communities (BCC) movement, that originated among liberal elements in the Roman Catholic Church, and which has community organization and conscientization at the core of its activities. However, the philosophies guiding these church activists — mainly in the countryside — most often do not connect well with local perceptions, which creates a fair amount of confusion. And secondly, it is difficult to analyse the BCC activities from a single point of view, since the priorities in one community may be widely different from the next, ranging from simple evangelization to the organizing of protest against local landlords, which, especially in the latter case, may trigger a lot of rural violence.

Since the BCC movement is largely a rural affair addressing the problems of the poor and disorganized, it remains somewhat removed from the concerns of the urban intelligentsia. It is they who are behind the plenitude of cause-oriented associations that most often try to act as political ginger groups, a fine example being the Congress for People's Agrarian Reform (CPAR), that temporarily even succeeded in getting a pro-farmer Secretary of Agrarian Reform appointed. This was, alas, too good to last. Another interesting feature of CPAR is that it has succeeded in extending its organization down to the grass roots level.

Because many people in the Philippines believe that the landlord-dominated conditions in the countryside are the basic cause of poverty — and many other kinds of social ills — support for (radical) land reform is broad, even including that from segments of the business community, and industrial entrepreneurs. The same may be said about the foreign debt issue, which many hold to be strangling any possibility for development. Thus, the Freedom from Debt Coalition also enjoys wide support. Infringements of sovereignty, neocolonial exploitation, and American meddling in Philippine affairs are also seen as issues that obstruct social and economic progress, and since, until 1992, the American military bases provided a highly symbolic target for all concerned about these, the Democratic Anti-Bases Movement, the ABAKADA, coalesced around this quarry.

The founding rally of ABAKADA in 1989 is illustrative of how cause-orientation can bring opposed political opinion together, in that it does not depend on an ideological or theoretical commitment. In this case, the antagonists Renato Constantino, a Marxist nationalist historian, and the opportunist political wizard Juan Ponce Enrile, appeared together on the platform, each presumably thinking of the other, "He's standing up here for the same right cause for all the wrong reasons".

Apart from being anti-bases, for agrarian reform, or against debt, the number of causes around which groups crystallize is bewildering, as is also the number of coalitions — variously called aggrupation, alliance, block, congress, network — plus also religious associations and people's organizations. These, again, may come together under the umbrella of the Caucus of Development NGO networks (CODE-NGO), or else the People's Caucus. This latter organized a Conference on National Unity, Survival and Reconstruction, when groups convened ranging from the National Organization of Businesspersons Advocating Sovereignty and Economic Stability (NO BASES) to the Community of Fasters for Justice and Peace, and from the Communist Party of the Philippines to the Philippine Alliance for Human Rights Advocates. The point to note is the proliferation of serious discussions among members of varying political persuasions, who now sit down together to find out how and where they agree, rather than practising mutual avoidance and treating each other as ideological enemies. This in itself is a rather recent development.

Taken all together, one thus sees the flowering of a counter-culture protesting the political status quo. So far, only very few of its representatives have penetrated the bastions of power, but along with the feverish activities of networking, coalition building and conferences, tactics are being thought up not only to fight for causes where government has failed, but also to enter politics and take on the traditional politicians *(trapos)* from within the establishment. The basic elements of the reasoning about political participation, people's empowerment, and development cum social justice matured during the long Marcos period, when there was a clear target to protest and unite against. In the post-Marcos period, the traditional, dynastic politicians with their vested interests are increasingly being identified as the source of all the ills of society, as the enemy within. It is only now that really national networks have begun to emerge, and it is instructive to remember that, for instance, the NDF only achieved a national structure in 1990.[2]

Only very recently have national frameworks of thinking begun to evolve, and they are developing in opposition to the attitudes of the traditional ruling class. It is the emancipatory thinking of conscious, responsible citizens who want to have a say in political affairs, and who have often started to view their causes in the context of the national and international political economy. The overriding concerns seem to be the imparting of a moral, consensual element to the exercise of power, the fight against poverty and its causes, the establishment of credible democratic processes, the promotion of social justice and the rule of law; in sum, the creation of a civil culture of the public world with the involvement of a responsible participatory citizenship.

As of now, participatory citizenship that is able to influence the political centre does not yet exist, and it will encounter formidable obstacles in its realization, such as the power of inertia inherent in the present organization of the political economy, and a well-entrenched political elite that will not easily be dislodged. What has come about so far is the growth of alternative thinking about politics, an emerging vision of how the future should be. This new social reality seems firmly ensconced.

Comparative note

While similar citizen-based thinking and social movements can also be observed in Indonesia and Thailand, what is going on in the Philippines offers a particularly lively spectacle. Whether this means that participatory politics is going to be instituted in the Philippines ahead of Indonesia and Thailand is a moot point, however. The latter two may even have a comparative advantage in having a tradition of a transcending culture of the realm, epitomized in kingship, a national discourse that is founded on a sense of history, a treasured collective memory, and a common culture. In contrast, the Philippines has no established tradition of legitimate government, let alone an exemplary

---

2 See to this the issue 18/4 (1990) of *Liberation*, the official publication of the National Democratic Front of the Philippines.

charismatic centre, and a national discourse is incipient at best; the consciousness of both legitimation and national culture seems to have grown from below, and so far lacks central leadership and institutions.

Yet a weak organization of the state may give citizens a better chance to transform it than if the state presents itself as a powerful executive. But then again, the Philippine political elite seems to be well organized and capable of defending its own particular interests — as indeed do the powerholders in Indonesia and Thailand. All three groups are guided by the same (dependent) capitalist notions of development, in which the approach to modernity is basically technocratic. Such an approach fits the amoral business model and normally bulldozes flat any demands for popular representation and deliberation. As far as the powers-that-be are concerned, their nation's subjects should be just that: depoliticized, obedient and passively acquiescent.

Once more though, in these latter matters, the Philippines appears to have advanced further than the others. Labour seems to be better organized, and large segments of the rural population are highly politicized and aware of the causes of their sufferings. Militarization and an active NPA keep the issues afire, at the same time that BCC and NGO activities have a high mobilizing and consciousness-raising potential. Moreover, the sense of being bored, or disgusted, with the current political situation is pervasive.

Such feelings, though, are not necessarily a stimulant to seeking positive change. They may also promote cynicism, escapism, sectarianism, indifference, consumerism, or just dogged individualism and a sheer survival orientation in an impoverished environment. Whether Thailand and Indonesia, with their more successful performance in developmental and national areas, have produced better 'objective conditions' for developing a civil culture of the public world and participatory citizenship remains to be seen. It is not at all clear yet whether these are ideas whose time has come.

The main trend still seems to be toward a media-dominated consumer society, at least for those who have entered the modern sector. The life of the others can only be described as an endless, yet persistent, struggle for survival. With economic concerns overriding in the minds of most, the demand for participatory politics seems likely to remain subdued, while the civil culture of the public world will concern itself more with moral protest and cause-oriented civic action than with effective political reform. This, at least, is the probability, for some time to come, though sometimes in history, momentous shifts appear to come about swiftly after a long period of gestation that is only traceable with the benefit of hindsight.

CHAPTER 17

Transformations of democracy and human rights

What is democracy for?

The democratic process can be regarded as an instrument by means of which civil society tries to control and regulate the public world as a common interest. Related institutions are constitutions, the rule of law, and human rights. The ideas implicit in these institutions, and in democracy, sprouted from the historical experience of the West and, especially since the Enlightenment, have become part of its culture.

By the public world I mean society in the sociological sense of *Gesellschaft*, that is, the wider society beyond family and community, where people are mutually anonymous and where they transact in a businesslike way. This wider society is largely dominated by the independent subsystems of state and economy, and animated by the public opinion and participation of its citizens. It is brought to life by the discourse going on in civil society, a discourse that makes it public, and of the public.

Sometimes, with reference to Southeast Asia, people have commented on 'village democracy', but even if the presumed deliberative and elective processes ever existed, they were meant to regulate community life, which is very different from a public world. Besides, I doubt whether the idea of a public world is felicitous in the case of Southeast Asia. There, a public world has never existed, the recent introduction of ideas about democracy and human rights notwithstanding. What existed, at best, was the theatre state, visible to all, yet monopolized by the political centre. In this case it is preferable to talk about the external world of society.

The image of the external world

There are two main images of the external world beyond community, the primordial one representing nature — the surrounding wilderness in opposition to settled life and civilization. It is nobody's and everybody's land, a field of opportunity to be appropriated as the need arises, but none of one's responsibility, really. It is a shared resource, but not a common possession. This image is still important to understand behaviour in and vis-à-vis the external world, both in its natural and social aspects.

The second image is that of the dynastic realm, of a ruler uniting a diversity of local communities under his sway, claiming rights over all the land and its inhabitants. What is not held by community members or groups is considered to be 'of' the king, the boss, the cacique, the government, or the governor-general. It is their 'private' space which they regulate and for which they are responsible; it is not 'of' the public, the people, or the nation; hence it is not the public good.

This dynastic, pyramidal image of the external world as belonging to a paramount chief, who is seen as a superpatron to whom persons relate in a patrimonial fashion, is reminiscent of the order of the family, that is, a place where moral inequality comes naturally. In a way, the family's arrangements and ideology are projected into the external world; they explain the ideal order of society and serve to construct its image.

The cardinal elements of this image are hierarchy, moral obligation, shared well-being, mutual dependence, and the recognition that individual members' identities are primarily defined by the group to which they belong; personhood is membership. This relational image makes for a very personalized conception of social life that, in combination with hierarchy, leads, by its own logic, to the idea of ethics as the ethics of place. If everybody behaves according to his (temporary) station in life, fulfilling its obligations, the family, community, and ultimately the external world of society, will be in desirable order.

Apart from the role of individual moral awareness, keeping society in good order is definitely the task of the government, culminating in a personalized leader, a 'man of prowess' capable of dominating the external world. He enforces desirable order, and what is good for him, as a father, should be good for all. It is, therefore, loyalty to him, and the collectivity he stands for, that is far more important than law as a means of maintaining good order. Consequently, the seeking of patronage defines political action, in the same way as the group — nation, state, region, country, people — sees and defines itself in moral rather than in legal terms; society is a moral construct.

Trust in hierarchy and loyalty to leadership are basically moral acts that agree with the highly personalized image of social life, in which the unknown areas of the external world are somewhat alarming and definitely awe-inspiring. In a way, it is like nature, filled with mysterious forces and spirits, but also a field of opportunity; socially it is the arena of competition for power and position of the grandees and bosses, often rather violent, where an unobtrusive little man may also appropriate an occasional prize.

Localization

The external world as depicted above provides the matrix in which foreign ideas and practices concerning it need to be localized. The theory of localization holds that, in order to live, foreign elements need to be grafted on to a local stem; they will feed on local sap in order to develop and flourish. In other words, they will not spontaneously fit in with the new environment, but need to fuse with it, in the process acquiring local content and meaning. The new local environment will redefine their characteristics, but at the same time that it will itself be changed somewhat by the adoption of, or exposure to, these new elements.

Because an idea generally comes in a package of related ideas, we normally find that some of them readily secure a local stem, and then evolve into the image of the receiving culture, while others fail to connect and to develop local meaning. For instance, Southeast Asian religion is future-oriented and preoccupied with seeking blessing and auspiciousness, potency and efficaciousness, in the here and now. As a result, sources of the latter could easily be appropriated, and saints, statues of Buddha, graves, and sacred texts could feed and flourish on native lifeblood. Conversely, ideas about sin, salvation, and moral autonomy, although 'physically' present, remained peripheral to culture and practice (chapters 1 and 4).

Premises of democracy and human rights

In their 'new world order', the Americans apparently push to conduct 'free and fair elections' as a sign that democratic government prevails. Yet, democracy is part of a complex set of ideas; some of its related procedures are easily adopted at the same time as its spirit and participatory practices fail to acquire local meaning. To understand what became of the western ideas involved, we should be conscious of them in the first place.

The ideas of democracy and human rights stem from an environment that grounds morality in equality: individual people matter, they have a right to their opinion, are morally autonomous, and equal before the law; they have the right, and the duty, to be informed and to partake in the public discourse. Practically, this highlights the role and function of a free press, and implies the freedoms of expression and association, and the right to vote.

As a means of regulating wider society, democracy involves the people, thus making that society a public world. It sees that world in a sociological manner — as an abstract structure of institutions and power relationships, of conflicting interests and ideas, that are subsequently discussed in a frank fashion and that can be influenced by policy decisions and the implementation of law. Society is neither static, nor merely subject to contingent forces, but governable and constructable, most often in the name of the public interest or common good.

Transformations

It should be clear that the premises of democracy do not quite agree with the Southeast Asian image of the external world, and that their localization may therefore lead to interesting transformations and surprising outcomes. The picture that it yields is, of course, not a static one, and the ideas and practices surrounding democracy and human rights are perennially evolving in pace with the globalization of the world community, and very strongly so under the influence of the many tens of thousands of local intellectuals familiar with the West through many years of study there. The following stock-taking, therefore, is nothing more than a summary overview of present political culture in Java, Thailand and the Philippines.

What we find in all these countries is 'procedural' democracy, meaning that certain, ostensibly democratic institutions — such as constitutions, parliament, elections and laws — are in place. The question, though, is how they are animated and substantiated. Constitutions without the spirit of constitutionalism are modern documents that show the world that the country is 'civilized', yet they neither appear to refer to a moral consensus of the populace, nor are they exactly awe-inspiring. Thailand, with sixteen constitutions in sixty years, offers an excellent example of the 'patience of paper' and the tenuous connexion of basic laws with the ordering of the external world. And then, parliaments: what and who do they represent? Granted, some politicians have indeed been elected; others have been appointed, and the military is heavily represented in all of them. Yet, do they represent the people who elected them? Or the district that voted them into power? Or the entity that appointed them? Do they stand for a programme or an ideology? And do the decisions and laws they issue really regulate life in wider society?

The democratic institutions of Thailand and the Philippines are dominated by strong figures and their interest groups ('parties'), and often have a recognizable provincial basis. In a very personal and confrontational manner they work for the interests, of themselves and their factions, apparently equating their affairs with 'public affairs'. They offer a very competitive and often violent spectacle, are normally able to buy, or otherwise manipulate, the vote, and still excite the people enough to trigger off considerable election violence. Yet, in reality, they offer no plans or programmes, though elected strongmen will see to it that money and projects to improve infrastructure are directed to their districts or provinces of origin. And so the people of Suphanburi are rightfully proud of their Banharn Silpa-archa, who now even presides over the country's affairs.

The focus of the political process is with such godfathers (*chaopor*, Chai-anan, 1991:78-80) or caciques (Anderson, 1988) who, in cases where they become powerful presidents (Soeharto; Marcos) may even dominate whole countries, while sharing the benefits of their sway with their political, military and business cronies. In their rhetoric they pose as fathers who preside over the family that is the nation-state, an institutional position that in Thailand is the prerogative of the king. They embody the dynastic image of the external world.

Popular culture surrounding the political process highlights the theatrical aspects of the nation-state. It is national events that stand out in the press, featuring the confrontations between prominent politicians representing themselves. Sarcastically referred to as 'the clowns' in Thailand, and as grandstanding *trapos* ('rags', but also 'traditional politicians') in the Philippines, they provide a public show reminiscent of the cockfight to which the people figure as kibitzers and audience. According to the Filipinos, politics is their favourite pastime, and although the Indonesian population is supposed to 'float' *(massa mengambang)*, that is, to be politically disinterested in between elections, once every five years the government allows for the venting of emotion during the 'democratic feast' *(pesta demokrasi)* of the election campaign. Less confrontational but no less spectacular are the representations of politics as a national emblem in the electronic media, such as presidential appearances, royal ceremonies, national celebrations, ritual discussion of and newscasts about political events, endless screening of national symbols — in short, the ingredients 'civil religion' is made of. Politics is spectacle.

Politics is about power, about laying claims to the external world; a contest for privilege and of setting the law. To understand the exercise of power it is important to know how it is perceived. Power is an attribute of strong men, of 'men of prowess' who can impose their will on an unruly, an unlawful external world, enforcing their order there. In the modern context, that order is subject to the expedience of state and economy, that is, independent systems of power (and competition) in and by themselves. There power operates in an area that is beyond the moral, consensual rules of the inner world of family and community, in an area that is 'anonymous' and businesslike. Such power is morally neutral. Of a politician, or a person in a privileged position, it is expected that he uses this power, for his own purposes, his benefit, and in the interest of those who depend upon him. As a result, the idea of corruption sits uneasily in the Southeast Asian context. The external world, like the forest, is there to be exploited; it is a shared resource, not the public good.

The moral model that is projected into the external world of nation-state-country-people-realm is that of the integral, cohesive family that subsumes its members, who are supposed to identify with and serve it. That model is strongly hierarchical and emphasizes conscious-ness of place, role and obligation: it is these that seemingly define per-sonhood. This is not only apparent from the teaching of civics in school, but also surfaces in the dogma that the family is the basic build-ing block of society, and in the propagation of — nowadays often west-ern, middle-class — family values as the redeemer of good society. While the image of the nation-state as family is ubiquitous, the reifica-tion of values as causes of desirable order is most tangibly expressed in the Indonesian state philosophy of *kekeluargaan* ('familism'). People who are deviating, because of their excess of 'individualism', 'liberal-ism', or demonstrative disrespect for order, should be, and are, brought to heel. As a result, people who assert their opinion, their (constitution-al) 'rights', oppose their exploitation, or protest political arbitrariness are often confronted with the might of the state. The state, the collectivity, is supreme; individuals submit; political and official violence are endemic.

Protesting people do not know or accept their place and role, their insolence perhaps even being based on the idea that they are as good as their leaders, that they are 'equals' in a moral sense and so can assert their causes. Such assumptions are more than threatening of the order that has hierarchy as its backbone: they are immoral. The point here is that the threat to order, or good society, is seen to originate from individual people who do not know how to behave (*kurang ajar*, I) and do not accept their place. This is illustrated in school-books and the press, which highlight the problems of having many poor people who go without schooling — and thus are not taught manners — who squat on valuable property, who do not like to work, but gamble and get drunk, tend to crime and prostitute themselves. Individual poor peo-ple are the source of problems; the issue is seldom discussed as a struc-tural question, namely, that of institutionalized poverty.

Official political culture is therefore preoccupied with teaching morality. If everybody knows his manners and how to conduct himself, the external world of wider society will be in good order. The Thais devote seventy-five per cent of primary school time to the teaching of how to be a good and tractable subject; in Indonesia, the Pancasila Moral Education course is obligatory fare throughout primary and secondary education, and grown-ups are showered with the noble insights of the P4 programme; the Philippine school texts bulge with moralism, and to set the country on a desirable course again, an official *Moral Recovery Program* has been launched (1993).

The emphasis on individual morality and the reification of values as causes, together with the imagining of abstract society as an integral, functionally integrated, hierarchical family, all hint, on the one hand, at the old dynastic model of social order and, on the other, at the absence of a sociological view of and approach to society. It is not abstract structures, institutions and relationships that feature in (official) social thinking, but personal bonds, society being perceived as composed of subjective sets of moral obligations inhering in relationships.

This dominant discourse is reflected in most of the press, and not just because of censorship and repression (which is the case in Indonesia). Social affairs are moral issues and the avid reporting about politics highlights the confrontations and exploits of individual politicos. Apparently, most newspaper reportage is a commentary on the behaviour of the national family members, and although some incisive treatment of economic and financial matters can readily be found, structural social analysis is very scarce indeed. As a result, the press, however critical of individual politicians, hardly offers a modern discourse about democracy and its public affairs and, in a situation where the abuse of justice is common, human rights issues are only commented upon when they are as spectacular as East Timor, the Khmer Rouge, urban massacres, or the cancelling of aid relationships between Indonesia and the Netherlands.

Discussion

Political culture — thinking about power and society — is part of the social imagination that is only slightly affected by the recent, twentieth century, supply of western ideas about regulating the external world. Like the community, the external world of wider society is seen in hierarchical, and thus moralistic, terms and is, therefore, thought to respond to individual conduct and values education. Seen from such a familial, moral point of view, the modern outside world of politics and economy appears to be in moral decay; it constitutes a field of opportunity, too.

This perception is pervasive, and most western-trained Southeast Asian social scientists soon revert to moralistic analyses and recommendations when they address the problems of their own society, thus not only demonstrating their personal and emotional involvement, but also revealing the way in which they fundamentally see society. This is very apparent in Thai and Philippine newspaper commentary (Mulder, 1996,b), and the near-absence in public discourse of a more sociologically or ideologically-oriented debate, where abstract social forces are thought to move social history and where — social or national — democracy is thought to be the best means to rein them in.

As a result it hardly comes as a surprise that local conceptions about the ordering of the external world easily prevail, and so we see a continuity of the ideas about and practices related to hierarchical order, its positional ethics, leadership, privilege, patronage, and personalism. Yet the introduction of elections and 'representative' bodies has brought a new element to the regulation of intra-elite competition that, by its own logic, allows for the voicing of 'dissident' opinions and the articulation of new groupings, especially economic interests, in the political centre. This means that politics gets more diversified, rather because of the diversification of sources of power than because of democratization. The latter would more substantially be the case if political power were ceded to 'popular', 'participatory' influences, but present power-holders are not ceding more than elections and nominal representation; they remain 'traditional politicians'.

A weird element — not introduced because of democracy, but rather because of the idea that politics is about regulating the public world, and very much used as offensive political ammunition — is the idea of corruption, meaning that the external world should not be exploited for personal gain, because it constitutes the public interest. This idea is so baffling that it lames all Anti-Corruption Commissions and Presidential Commissions for Good Government at the outset. All the vernaculars express the idea of corruption by the European word, because nobody had apparently conceived of the practice before, and how could one if the external world is seen as a field of opportunity?

Yet, it cannot be denied that a certain basic ingredient of democracy and human rights is being promoted by the expansion of modern mass society, namely, the fact of equality. In the new urban environment most people are unknown to each other, and anonymity means equality. Social order, with its relative positioning of actors, only arises when people interact in other than a businesslike manner. So, because mass society does not require the personalized elements of loyalty and solidarity, it generates an equality that may affect the experience and conceptualization of personhood. Persons, after all, find that they have more free space to move around in and develop themselves.

Whether factual equality and relative freedom will translate into the ideological demand for equality remains a moot point. While some may argue that the proliferation of NGOs and other ginger groups, environmentalist and feminist demands, and so on, are indicative of the development of a new political culture centring on participatory citizenship, others may point to the non-modern tendency towards moral particularism that expresses itself in such reactions against the anonymization of social life as familism, dogged individualism, religious revival and sectarianism, 'civic' club membership, and place-of-origin and ethnicity-based association. These latter manifestations of 'civil society' are parochial, that is, inward-directed, and befit the current evolution to an urban mass society that is indifferent to politics as long as the economy expands. In such an atmosphere, state and economy are not to be subdued by the weak demands for democratization and respect for human rights as expressed at the fringe of society.

The main argument here, though, is that the idea of moral equality, fundamental to democracy, human rights and the rule of law, does not connect well with the Southeast Asian social imagination. Social order depends on hierarchy, and respect for it is the ethical imperative; by its own logic it sees society as a moral construct. Because it does not take distance, society-in-the-abstract remains difficult to imagine, and to run it, that is, the external world, on the basis of equality is literally a far-fetched idea. Because of the absence of a practicable moral model of the external world, the expedient logic of state and economy will define how political affairs are run, and make for a 'traditional' political culture that involves the population as subjects at best. Legality exists on paper, but equality before the law is very weakly developed; the concept of human rights, let alone respect for them, is only vaguely understood, although people understand the idea of personal dignity — and respect for it — very well; (critical) sociological analysis is almost non-existent, and a public world, with its morally autonomous citizens, is not in the offing, other than in the visibility of small segments of civil society who push for democracy and human rights. For the time being such activists are ill-understood.

The timeliness of political indifference

The activists referred to are basically the heirs of a culture of the public world that was developing among the generations of idealists who strove for social reconstruction and national independence, for democracy and human rights, roughly, between the late colonial era and the first three decades of independence (±1920-1975). These days, though, such ideas belong to the past and disagree with the culture of the public world that is evolving among members of the new urban middle classes, the bulk of whom are without a tradition of critical thinking about and participation in the public world. They are the product of a period of very rapid urbanization and equally rapid changes in the economic opportunity structure of the past thirty years. They differ qualitatively from the more exclusive middle group that studied when going to university was still a privilege, and whose members indulged in the luxury of thinking about democratization and social reconstruction. Most of the new people are upwardly mobile, mass-educated, and oriented more towards professional advancement than to ideological musing. Besides, they acquired their skills during the period, beginning with the 1970s, of the systematic propagation of lifestyles and consumption. They grew up with television rather than with books.

Theirs is a culture of cynicism and indifference regarding the 'public' world of politics and the economy. Although they would like to see 'law-and-order' prevail, they tend to be socially inattentive; while suffering from the urban disorder they experience, they have no great ideas of how to improve it. This drives them to a stronger identification with family, friends, and other particularistic associations that emphasize individual worth.

Their individual-centred choices are given in the drive for self-improvement and careerism, and in the lifestyle phenomenon that, at the centre of consumer culture, enables people to accumulate the status symbols they need in order to assert their identity. These self-centred orientations lead away from ideological or theoretical attempts to come to grips with their public environment which, as a result, remains vague. As in the early days, they believe that personal ethical conduct is the wellspring of good society, while wider society appears as a field of opportunity where the individual carries little or no responsibility. It is everybody's and nobody's place, where people compete for scarce resources and where power is the most desirable commodity. As a result, only minimum demands on the public spheres of politics and the economy appear to be evolving, and so it seems that there is a general deficit of enthusiasm and idealism to promote 'substantial' democracy and human rights. In the contemporary Southeast Asian context democracy remains procedural rather than substantial, at the same time that 'the duties of the subject' are better understood than 'citizens' rights'.

Conclusion

CHAPTER 18

The common cultural construction of social life

The cultures of the Southeast Asian littoral along its inner, mediterranean sea (South-China Sea cum Gulf of Thailand and Java Sea) not only distinguish themselves from those of neighbouring India and China, but show an impressive number of shared principles that lend the area its cultural uniqueness. So, while there can be no denying the variation of observable, epiphenomenal appearances of these principles, it is intended here to demonstrate the similarities in the fundamental ways of thinking that inform everyday life. This conclusion will, therefore, consolidate the thinking about supernature, social relationships, the public world of wider society, gender, personhood, ethics, and leadership. This common heritage of the coastal local, or little, traditions raises questions about the position of the distinct, imported great traditions in social life, and proves the relevance of the idea of localization (chapters 1, 4 and 17) as a point of departure for cultural analysis.

Here, only scant attention will be drawn to the characteristic structural features of the inner seaboard, such as bilateral descent, matrifocal nuclear families, actor-centred social networks, and the near absence of overarching institutions such as clan or caste (altogether sometimes referred to as 'loose structure'). Neither shall we engage in speculation about the 'causes' of the remarkable unity of the fundamental ways of thinking, such as a common physical environment, or the intensity of long-standing maritime intercourse (Reid, 1988). Also, the contrasting social features of inner and outer Southeast Asia, elaborated as the centrist versus the exchange archipelago for the insular part (Atkinson and Errington, 1990), fall beyond the present consideration. Here, we should concentrate on the question, "How do people imagine their social life?", while drawing conclusions about its common 'logic'.

The concept of order

Perhaps because of the rapid changes in the economy, the arrogance of politicians, the unpredictability of justice, or just the confrontation with the havoc of the urban environment, its chaotic traffic and poor services, people in Bangkok, Manila, and Jakarta agree that they live in a time of disorder, that public life is hard to control. So gaudy are the *nouveaux riches*, so flagrant the corruption, so callous the powerful, so brazen the youth, so poor the delivery of justice, so power-hungry the politicians, so profiteering the businessmen that the past appears as an oasis of calm and order. Those were the good days of monarchical rule, when people still knew their place, when the Americans ran the government 'like heaven', and to which many Indonesians still refer as *zaman normal*, the normal times when the Dutch pursued their policy of *rust en orde* (quiet and order). Those days were not necessarily just, but at least they were predictable and, compared with the hectic present of migration and mobility, of urbanization and even globalization, life was surveyable and its pace unexciting.

With the countries being run conspicuously according to economic and political expediency, it seems as if the opposite of normal times has descended on the scene, a situation known to the Javanese as *zaman édan*, 'crazy times', when the clarity of order has given way to unruly dynamism and a suspension of norms. It is a period when deserving people will suffer, when there is a loss of good manners, when people do not know shame any longer, when they forget their religion, when the lazy ones get rich, when the liar gets prosperous, when normality declines, when hard work is not rewarded, when the law is unjust, when people cannot trust each other; in short, an age in which fools profit from their folly and the wise suffer for their wisdom (Anderson, 1990).

This representation demonstrates that disorder is a morally decayed condition and that order is, in itself, a moral concept expressing that deserving people will be rewarded if they keep to their place. Respect for such order is moral conduct per se and, if Javanese-Indonesian, Tagalog-Filipino, and Thai notions are a guide to go by, such behaviour can be learnt. *Kekurangajaran* (I, J) translates as lack of respect, rudeness, and even as wicked conduct, while *kulang sa pinag-aralan* (TF) connotes brusqueness, being rough in manner or speech, and lack of respect for others — yet the literal meaning of these words is being uneducated, falling short in knowledge. From the Thai Buddhist point of view, ignorance is one of the three root causes of all evil, the want of knowledge, or awareness, leading to heedlessness and immorality. And so knowledge of the rules and consciousness of social place equate, according to the title of a traditional Thai school text, with *The Treasure of the Gentleman.*

In the three countries, values or moral education is a very important subject of the school curriculum. The teaching emphasizes respect for and submission to morally superior people, first of all parents and teachers, but also all those superior in age and rank, up to the king and his servants, or the president and his officials. All such people occupy positions that should be respected. In this image, hierarchy is the backbone and thus the support of moral order.

The core characteristic of hierarchy is relative super- and subordination, or the basic inequality of individual people. Some are senior, others junior; some are officers, others soldiers; there are leaders and followers, patrons and dependents, parents and children, and what is good and moral for one, is not necessarily praiseworthy or expected of the other. Superiors have to lead, to teach, to protect, to be responsible; inferiors follow, accept, are grateful, and extend honour, while awareness of relative position is — and should always be — expressed in manners and choice of words. Not to observe that code is rough and disrespectful indeed, a demonstration of not knowing one's place, of not knowing manners, and so, of being morally stunted.

People who are morally aware will behave according to their station in life, respecting the relative honour and dignity of their fellow men. Doing so is to demonstrate respect for good order; it is the act of letting reputation prevail over individual drives and emotions. It is, therefore, not only accommodation to hierarchy but also to the group. This notion of how people and things should be in their right place, is well expressed in the Javanese-Indonesian *keselarasan* that both translates as harmony and conformity, and also in the Thai desire that they should be *riabrǫj*, in 'calm composition' and thus in pleasing order. In the same way literature about the Philippines endlessly elaborates the importance of smooth interpersonal relationships and the necessity of *pakikisama*, of getting along well with each other while letting group prevail over individual. The Indonesian moral education course summarizes the mainstay of good order; it is getting along with each other as in a family. This family principle, *kekeluargaan*, should guide the organization of wider society, which seems to equate with the nation and the state, too.

The nuclear family is seen as a small, self-containing moral world to which one feels committed and obliged, and from which people derive their personal and social identity. It is supposed to be the cohesive kernel of life, in which people identify with each other and whose shared interests transcend the personal. As a result, people are thought to avoid confrontation and to compromise with each other while subordinating their ego-drives to solidarity. They should consider their family as the firm moral basis in life and jealously guard its reputation.

The pivot of family life is the mother, who becomes the epitome of morality. She symbolizes the moral basis of family and society, meaning that transgressions against her spell fundamental disorder. And so Thai treatises may state that people who do not honour their mother — and thus disrespect the harmony of their family — cannot be expected to respect the king — and thus the order of society. Similarly, there is significance in a Javanese politician's mother proclaiming on a newspaper's front page that her son has always honoured and been submissive to her, and thus must be a moral man.[1]

Yet, there is more to order than its moral basis; order is moral in itself, and to maintain it is good. So, even if persuasion, pressure, or power are necessary to enforce conformity, unanimity, and the appearance of harmony, this act of maintaining order is what is expected of a leader, a patron, a father, a boss. Disorder in his ranks is a stain on his prestige. Disorder is simply distasteful, threatening of reputation. And thus unruly or wayward individuals have to be brought to heel, not so much to punish as to reabsorb them; after all, they are expected to submit to the transcending interest of the encompassing group.

---

1 This happened in late February 1992 at the time that the secular leader of the Nahdatul Ulama, Abdurrachman Wahid, had called for a controversial, or confrontational, mass meeting of his followers, and who was, as a result, put in a negative light by the government. The newspaper was *Bernas*.

This idea of a leader being responsible for the order among potentially unruly individuals demonstrates the idea that the group, or society, is a moral construct, and also hints at the purely personal nature of hierarchical society.[2] Its order is not in impersonal law, but in the individual knowledge of moral behaviour, in loyalty to the group and superiors, and respect for hierarchy, while good, or ethical conduct is that which befits one's station in life, which causes no dissonance, which confirms, or instates, smoothness. The very notion of order implies an aesthetical conception of ethics, such as the Javanese express in the idea of *alus*, meaning refined, cultured, sensitive, and thus of nice and pleasing manners, or such as the Tagalogs express with *mabait*, meaning both gentle and virtuous, and thus of courteous conduct and tractable disposition, or as in the Thai notion of *khon dii*, literally good people, but meaning one who is morally polished while following the rules of polite and considerate intercourse.

Order, therefore, is a social concept and rests in people who are morally aware, who know the rules of good association, and who confirm it by their complaisant behaviour, avoiding friction and confrontation. This may require patience and indirectness, also some inner discipline and effort, but the moral man understands why it is good to fulfil the obligations and expectations surrounding his reputation and position. In doing so, he will make the social world a better place or, as the Javanese have it, he will 'adorn the world' (*mamayu hayuning buwana*). This idea of order is both moral and aesthetic, while connecting morality with awareness, or wisdom, too. It merges 'the good, the true, and the beautiful', a phrase that sounded pathetic from the mouth of Imelda Marcos, but that expresses the Southeast Asian idea well. To be morally good is to behave according to station and place; truth is the awareness of what creates harmony, in opposition to what is false, dissonant, and unwise; this results in the beauty of a smooth arrangement, a 'calm composition' expressed in affable manners and the absence of stir. As an ethics of place, it should be noted that this thinking highlights the role and duty of the individual as the wellspring of good — or bad — social order; as long as he conforms to the requirements of social harmony, society cannot be but a well ordered place.

2 For elaboration of the ideas surrounding leadership, see Antlöv and Cederroth, 1994.

The life-world: society as personal experience

1. The moral inner core

In the absence of overarching structuring principles — such as castes, clans, or lineages — the characteristic bilateral, and often multi-generational, nuclear family assumes extraordinary importance. According to the teaching of ethics in the Thai grade school, the family is the basic social institution; in the words of the Philippine Civil Code, it is the foundation of the nation; in Indonesia it is thought to exemplify the moral principles on which social life should be based. Generally, it is thought that if the family is in good order, so will society be. The state, therefore, endeavours to safeguard and strengthen the integrity of the family, in Thailand by the official promotion of western middle-class family values, alongside a campaign to curb male marital infidelity; in the Philippines by declaring the family to be 'an institution that public policy cherishes and protects'; while in Indonesia the state even introduced legislation to regulate the nuptial behaviour of its soldiers and functionaries (Mulder, 1995,b:87).

Individual households are part of far-flung networks of related families, and relatives are often known to each other as far as the third degree. The way they stick together, however, is primarily based on dyadic, face-to-face relationships that pair persons on an individual basis, and bonds are characterized by a fair degree of voluntariness. Yet, there is a sense of obligation, too; ritually and emotionally, for instance, on the occasions of Songkraan, Christmas, and Lebaran; economically, in taking in and supporting the children of needy or isolated relatives for the sake of their education, or by sending money. But, whatever their obligations, families, and even close relatives such as brothers and sisters, are not subject to any corporate organization; inheritance is divided and, normally, equally shared; their belonging together is primarily ritual, with an important identity function.

In accord with what is officially stated, most people under discussion here will agree with the idea that the family is extraordinarily important in social and personal life. Yet, the resulting family-centredness is sometimes questioned in terms of whether it is beneficial for the development of the public sphere of nation or state when people appear to be living for their families and close relatives only, while being reluctant to sacrifice for the public interest (chapter 10). Officially, however, the moral, solidary family remains ideologically firmly entrenched as the exemplar of desirable national order.

The mother

If order is moral, then the nuclear family — centring on parents and their progeny — should exemplify it. The Philippine Constitution even refers to 'the sanctity of family life'. Order and sanctity do not come for free, and while a father's authority may help to enforce order, its day-to-day maintenance appears to be the mother's responsibility. She is the focus of the home and its affairs, eulogized in most Thai literary writing (chapters 5 and 7), and in the Tagalog idea that she is the 'light of the house'. The Javanese know that 'heaven is located beneath the soles of her feet'.

As the epitome of the moral order, the symbolic position of the mother has a deeper foundation than the fact that she cares for the family and functions as the heart of the home. Her morally exalted position derives primarily from the belief that she sacrifices herself, that in giving birth she puts herself in jeopardy, and that her child grows because of her selfless love, dedication, and even suffering. She is the person upon whom the child can rely unconditionally, a permanent and self-effacing source of protection and care (chapters 7 and 8).

It is this idealized qualitiy of being a source of goodness, even at the cost of self-sacrifice, that places her children — the recipients of her goodness — under a debt of gratitude (*nii bunkhun*, Th; *utang-na-loób*, TF; *utang budi*, I; *utang kabecikan*, J) and the moral obligation of honouring, of loving their mother. She has given them life and nurture; they depended on her for their early teaching, and so for the opportunity of becoming moral men. Practically, part of that teaching was the indoctrination with the idea of the impeccability of the mother, of the respect and thankfulness due to her, and so, of the values of obedience and tractability. As a result, she imprints herself deeply on the emotional life of her children and easily becomes their foremost superego representative. For them, conscience becomes consciousness of her. While this is, naturally, not uncommon as far as young children are concerned, it appears to be a continuous fact of life in Southeast Asia, lasting at least into middle age. The mother remains the touchstone of conscience, or, in other words, a good part of a person's conscience remains dependent on her.

This is supported by the idea that the most reprehensible conduct is to go against the mother, to be disrespectful of her, and thus to show ingratitude, denying the goodness received and one's moral obligation. Such conduct places a person beyond the pale of civilized life; worse still, it is an offence to the moral order; it is sin. Practically, this is thought to be substantiated in concrete feelings of guilt and unavoidable supernatural retribution (*karma* immediately retributed, Th; *mabusong*, TF; *walat*, J).

Speaking in the abstract, it is probably not too far-fetched to talk about the cult of goodness. Concretely, this means that the mother figure assumes cultic, religious proportions. Being the first one to be responsible for the good order, for the wholesomeness, of the family, this quasi-religious position is no sinecure, but obliges and demands a lot of hard work. She has to care for her household as a business, holding the purse strings while seeking the extra money needed to keep it going, at the same time educating her children.

The double identity of woman as mother, namely, to be the living symbol of the moral hierarchy, and to be the active, reliable centre of the family — to be the home-maker — equates the idea of having a family, of having home and household with fulfilment, thus strengthening the family ideology. To this manner of thinking, people should be close together, firstly, emotionally, but also practically and physically, while being supportive of each other. They derive their identity from being a cohesive group, identifying with each other, so to speak.

Personhood

According to the Philippine psychologist Bulatao (chapter 4), the practice of life in the moral inner world may have far-reaching psychological consequences and partly define the image of man, of what it means to be a person. Intensive togetherness leads to the tendency to see oneself as part of a 'closed' group that spells an important part of a person's self-experience. Defining oneself in regard to others makes for, what he calls, a relatively low degree of 'individuation', which he further describes as 'vague ego boundaries', others being part of, or shading off into, an individual's identity definition. The most important of these others is easily the mother, then the other family members or, in peer groups, one's friends. The normal self-experience appears to be relational; this means that it is concretely known persons who matter, and so their acceptance becomes crucial to a satisfactory experience of the self. Because of this, at least within the relevant groups, conflicts should be solved and, preferably, avoided, by a willingness to give in for the pleasure of enjoying solidarity (chapter 8). This makes for the relatively low assertiveness that goes with a relatively low degree of individuation, while fostering the security of conformity and respect for order — at least, in the inner core of life that is so important for one's identity.

By identifying, sympathizing and empathizing with each other, people only rarely experience themselves as the main agent in their biography; they live reacting to others and to circumstances, and are given to explain their fallibility by blaming others, by having to live up to status and reputation, by being tricked into situations, or by the pressures of group solidarity. In brief, people seem to be most concerned with their reputation and their being accepted by their fellows. They are acutely aware of mutual dependences, and it is safe to say that their conscience rests in relationships with concretely known people, in their opinions and feelings. Conscience as such seems to be consciousness of others (chapter 9).

The idea of a relatively low degree of individuation seems to be a very plausible thesis that, in the Philippines, has been supported by research and further psychological interpretation (chapter 4); it seems to affect women even more than men. So, a lowly individuated mother will tend to find her identity and security in her role, implying not only that caring for others becomes a second nature, but also that she will be very possessive of her husband and children. It is role fulfilment as such that becomes exceedingly important, in other words, it is living up to expectations and conformity with norms that matters, with little interference from the deep self and with little need for frank communication.

The role pattern of the wife in marriage is a given, and it emphasizes mothering more than anything else. While this implies the preparation of her daughters to follow after her later in life, it also includes the indulging of husband and sons who may grow extremely dependent on female attention and care, which contributes to the formation of an, often vulnerable, male ego whose identification with status easily leads to anxiety about it. As a result, he tries to compensate for outside frustrations by the relaxation in the home environment, where he must be pampered and respected, thus frequently transferring the burden of mother-dependence to the wife. Often she may refer to him as 'my eldest son' or, in Java, as 'the old baby'. In terms of individuation, we may surmise that the male identification with status, and thus with the opinion of others, reinforces the relatively undifferentiated experience of the self; willy-nilly, one is, partly at least, defined by others.

In terms of personhood, these observations seem to lead to the idea of people who derive their identity to a good extent from others, while scoring relatively low in autonomy and high in dependence and identity. They experience themselves as parts of groups and relationships that define their obligations, conscience, and decisions.

2. The wider, known social environment

The moral inner core that is symbolized by the female as mother, is surrounded by a known outer world. Symbolically, it is male territory; it is about politics, public affairs, business, but most of all, about social hierarchy, about status. In that area the father, as its head, represents the prestige of the family. This domain outside the home is rather mercurial, susceptible to competition for power, resources and, most visibly, honour.

In many ways the arrangements in the known world outside the home appear to be similar to those within; they are personal, relational, hierarchical, and carry obligation. Yet, since it is also a competitive area where people vie with each other for prestige and power, where prowess is admired, and where the most successful become the patrons of others, it is qualitatively different from the 'stable' inner core. In order to make it work, the exercise of power often seems to accomplish much; it becomes more effective still if a moral element is attached. Again, this shows a great similarity with the inner world; in the latter's moral hierarchy, beneficiaries incur a debt of gratitude that creates obligation for life. In the hierarchy of power, protection, patronage and prestige, favours given also oblige, and those debts of gratitude tie people to each other, often in rather predictable ways; it functions as the cement that keeps the known, the personal world together.

Reneging on such obligations is despicable, is denying goodness received, but is not — as in the case of going against parents — felt to be sinful. Rather, this abomination of good and civil behaviour heaps shame upon the offender. Yet it may very well be that the claim one imagines having on the other has expired, has lost its vitality. The principles of pragmatism, competition, and expediency, after all, share the world beyond the home with that of obligation. Claims, therefore, need to be kept alive; they can be reciprocated, repaid, and may oscillate, too.

All this makes the moral content of the male territory outside the home considerably less compelling than that of the inner core. The overriding positive value of this outer territory is status, which enforces a presentational and competitive style of life in which power is most admired, whether as political efficaciousness, reputed inner resources, or money, and where those who hold power are seen as 'men of prowess', as leaders and lords. To be on top of a local pecking order is most satisfactory; yet, to remain there is not always easy, and the struggle to maintain position may be fought by all means, fair and foul.

Because of the concern with hierarchy and the emphasis on status, there is a tendency to outsmart one another, to demonstrate superiority, perhaps sometimes to be somewhat arrogant, and this may cause feelings of irritation, slight and injury in others, stimulating vindictiveness, grudges, and the desire to rectify the balance. In being, the men vie with each other for recognition, for the demonstration of influence and potency, and set a prize on their virility (*citcaj nakleeng*, Th; *pagkalalaki*, TF; *kelakilakian*, I). Because he has to operate in a competitive sphere, the male is far more vulnerable than the female. Early in life he has already learned to identify with status, which is a much more volatile substance than role. So, with the female's and mother's role offering a solid pivot of identification, status places a person more at the mercy of others. It needs to be validated all the time, to be defended, and demonstrated. As a result, the male develops a sensitivity to honour and to slight, to everything affecting 'face'.

The identification with status, honour, and manliness may lead to generosity, to the conspicuous spending of money, to demonstrations of male irresponsibility and daring, or to gambling for high stakes. However this may be, they are also easily hurt by whatever is perceived as criticism, which may then activate the desire for revenge. Yet, since people know of their mutual vulnerability, they will also try to avoid irritating each other, playing things in an indirect manner, or making it appear as a mere joke. In general, they are given to cultivate a smoothness in interaction, not giving cause for upset, holding conflict and confrontation at bay — at least among those with whom transactions are frequent, that is, in the known personal world. It is better to be considerate of, or to avoid, the other than to provoke him, and so friendly appearances should keep the lid on the volatile mixture of male identifications.

Keeping the known world surrounding the home in order is, of course, good, and requires clear hierarchical relationships and compelling leadership. If everybody knows his place, and behaves accordingly, the community will be good to belong to. Yet, a good measure of rivalry appears naturally to belong to community life, too. Then, moral constraints may give way to the rules of the political game that is about power pure and simple, and so the personally known world soon loses its compelling moral content, while shading off into the still further, impersonal and institutional world of amoral anonymity, of big business and big politics.

Gender

It has often been observed that women in the region under discussion are no less appreciated than men. They share in the same humanity, complementing each other. There is no preference for male children, with many parents seeing daughters as the more reliable ones to depend upon in old age, while the ranking of children is on the basis of their relative ages. Be that as it may, the symbolic value of men and women appears to be starkly differentiated, the male apparently standing for status and the known world surrounding the home, the female for morality and the home itself. However, this is not to say that men or women are practically confined to the domains they symbolize and that these are exclusive preserves: there are women generals, village heads, politicians, professors, and many are reputed for their business acumen. There are also men who fulfil tasks classified as female, yet women seem to have the greater freedom in 'border crossing', and they are, as we shall see, free to pursue any type of career in the modern 'public' world.

In spite of rapid change, the pressure in the life-world to live up to female role and male status is still considerable, while, at the same time, role and status fulfilment function as substitutes for self-confidence. Besides, in spite of their achievements and demonstrated responsibility, the prestige of women is largely defined by the status of their men. As a result of this, plus the complementariness and separation of domains, the myths about maleness and femininity are firmly kept alive; a fact to which the current state propagation of the wholesome, undifferentiated family as the basic unit of society, and the current wave of religious consciousness-raising and revival, certainly contribute. As a result, the view that the sexes are naturally given, and that each has its specific tasks and duties, remains well ensconced, and although a gendered view of the male-female dichotomy is, in itself, nothing more than a symbolic construction of the known world, it also has considerable compelling force in ordering its praxis.

Religious representation of the life-world

In its moral aspects, the 'religious' representations of personally known society are in the symbolic value of parents as the living representatives of the moral hierarchy (chapters 2, 3 and 4). It is against them that sin is committed, in the sense that infraction of their well-being results in unavoidable, automatic supernatural retribution, in the same way as it is thought that the wayward child will suffer from feelings of guilt. Parents are also held to be the necessary sources of blessing, a quality that becomes particularly apparent in honouring them after death, when they can still extend help, protection and consolation. It would be a gross exaggeration to think of this as ancestor worship; people honour and relate to those who were personally known in life; they know that such personages — parents, grandparents — care.

What life in society demands is respect for its order, and that is how a moral way of life is understood. Sometimes that esteem may be formulated in almost religious terms, such as when the Javanese say: "The person who honours his parents, his elder brother, his teacher and the king, honours 'God'." Yet the crux of the matter is respect for the hierarchical order of society. This begins at home, where it is exemplified in the morally unequal relationships of obligation between exalted parents and dependent child. By extension, the measure in which a person is thought to be moral depends on his way of handling the obligations inherent in his relationships with others. This way of thinking makes morality more of a social than a religious matter.

The focus of Southeast Asian religion is neither on morality nor on salvation nor liberation (chapter 1). Corresponding to the fascination with power and prestige in social life, religious practice is concerned with individual potency, with protective blessing, and with safety from danger and misfortune. In short, it is a relationship with 'sacred' power, potency, or energy (*sasksit*, Th; *bisâ*, TF; *kasektèn*, J). Such power is located in the nature/supernature in which human life is embedded. In other words, this power — however concentrated and whether manifested in deities, saints, spirits, exceptional personalities, the recently deceased, or potent objects, such as heirlooms, amulets, or graves — is very much part of the human situation and everyday life.

Implicit in this view is the conviction that power is near, tangible, accessible. It can be supplicated and manipulated, which is to say that humans know the attributes of the various manifestations of power, and how to deal with them. Whether this nearness, tangibility, and accessibility of power demonstrates itself in the Filipino intimacy with Jesus, His Mother, and the saints; in the Javanese mystical attuning of the self to that which is greater than man; or in magical manipulation and mediumship, the point is that a relation to supernatural power is taken for granted.

This does not mean that all people have the same relation, are capable of, or interested in, close relations with such power and its manifestations. Generally, men are thought to be superior in such things to women, but individual differences are very considerable. Those who are so inclined may seek to enhance their potency in nature, to tap its power, so to speak, in the practice of asceticism and meditation. Others are ritual specialists who manipulate and cajole power to ensure protection and auspicious continuity. Others still relate to power magically for curative or malign purposes. Mediumship is widespread and its practitioners mediate between the invisible and the concrete world; they may give predictions or transmit messages. Most people recognize a direct relationship between health and invisible power; they will rely on the expertise of specialists and on the efficacy of amulets, prayer, ritual, offerings, and mild forms of ascetic practice to achieve their purposes.

The line between life and death is as fluid as the line between the visible and the invisible. These are not really separate realms but interpenetrate each other, religious manifestations being pervasive and present to the senses — at least to intuition or the sixth sense. The latter phenomenon is most developed in the Philippines and on Java, where it leads to trust in and acceptance of a 'divine' plan and purpose, but it is not uncommon in Thai meditational practice either, or in the more general fascination with things mysterious, such as encounters with spirits, including those of people who have recently died.

Life is experienced as a whole, with religious phenomena and 'sacred' energy being an indwelling, an immanent part. The 'religious' is directed to achieving palpable results here in this world, here among the living, and is therefore concerned with the present and the near future. As a pervasive phenomenon, it invalidates such distinctions as sacred versus profane. Perhaps the best way to put it is that the most important locus of religion is the individual person, and that religion concerns feelings, potency and efficaciousness, and intimacy with invisible powers.

In summary, the religious symbols of the local-traditional world in which social life is a personal experience can be analyzed as representing, on the one hand, the moral inner core and, on the other, the surrounding and more volatile 'male' area with its preoccupations with power, potency and patronage. In the latter area people seek sacred objects and inspired guidance to depend on. The related — and variform - practices aim at blessed and auspicious continuity.

The image of wider society

The primary image of that vast social space beyond the personally known world is that of the state, personified in king, president, and government; it appears as their private space, as their possession, or at least as their responsibility. It is a territory that is not well-known to ordinary subjects, somewhat awe-inspiring because apparently filled with the power and influence of those who call the shots in politics and, increasingly, in the economy. The best thing little people can do is to attach themselves to such bosses who seemingly know their way around in that vast world, to seek their patronage, thus personalizing access to 'public' space without it becoming any of their business.

Wider society appears as a rather unruly place, a realm where might is right and where the rules are set by those who hold actual power. In a way its image is like nature's: uncharted territory to be appropriated by all who can lay, and maintain, claim to it; it is a field of opportunity where people hunt for a prize. In that area people are unknown to each other, being anonymous actors in unruly, and often very dangerous and violent, space. Being unknown to each other implies equality, which also means that the familiar coordinates of the personal world, such as hierarchy, gratitude, obligation, and so forth, are lost and do not offer the security of orientation. As a result, the place appears in flux and disorder; it is the area where amoral power rules.

Historically, the state tried to force its authority upon the 'loosely structured' population it claimed as its subjects, often by incorporating structures of obligation and 'patronage'. This strategy proposes that the instruments of the state and local power-holders be seen as patrons, that is, fathers. It is founded on the moral model of the family, which in this situation is mobilized to provide the moral model for wider society. Much as, historically and ideologically, that may be, the resulting order of the state has long been infiltrated and subverted by economic influence and power, and the public world of wider society appears to be increasingly anonymous, competitive, and confrontational. It is a sphere far divorced from the life-world and one that not only stimulates feelings of powerlessness and exclusion on the side of the ordinary subjects, but that also appears to them as an area where ethics have been suspended, that is disorderly and in moral decay.

This perception is validated by official, religious, and other moralists who complain about the 'liberalism', 'individualism', and 'irresponsibility' of the individual nationals who all seem to pursue their personal aims in life irrespective of the 'public interest', and so the state seeks recourse to moral education in order to discipline the individual people, while making them aware of role and obligation. If everybody behaves accordingly, state, nation, society, public life, the country — the concepts are typically not differentiated — must be in desirable, that is, orderly shape. The interesting communality of such values education is the (old) idea that the family and community values of the personal world have regulatory power in 'anonymous', 'public' society.

Religious representation of and reaction to wider society

The perception of wider, anonymous, public society as an area of opportunity where amoral power reigns supreme, revitalizes the local-traditional, 'animistic' quest for power, potency, and protection. Amulets and mantras are not on their way out; many types of spiritual advisors mediate between 'sacred' power or the future, and businessmen and politicians; all sorts of people seek miracle cures and winning lottery numbers. As an endemic phenomenon centring on shamans, charismatic monks, and all sorts of mystics, visionaries, and miracle men and women, these practices have often been described. Most interesting is the current flourishing of cults among members of the Southeast Asian middle classes. Next to the new devotion to the Chinese goddess Kuan Yin, the cult of the Fifth Reign (King Chulalongkorn) has spread like wildfire throughout the Thai kingdom; its practice is thought to result in material blessings. In the Philippines, the cult of the Santo Niño (the Jesus Child) has grown explosively over the past thirty years; this devotion is thought to be protective, but is also reputed to bring in health, business, and money. In Java, *keramat* (holy places) show a steady popularity, and devotions there are also thought to result in the goodies desired.

More spectacular are the larger sects that seem to operate under the auspices of the established world religions and that yet have little to do with reform or renewal. The fast-growing middle class-based Thammakai Buddhist movement is rather esoteric, and stresses the acquisition of individual potency. Also, the charismatic movements within Philippine Catholicism, particularly El Shaddai, emphasize the power, blessing and healing energy that emanate from the All-Powerful while forgetting the other aspects of the Christian message, such as sin, the need for redemption and the sacraments. At the same time similarly oriented Islamic and mystical groups enjoy a perennial popularity in Java, Islam Jamaah being an irrepressible example.

Next to these, one finds the reform and/or revival-oriented movements that are solidly part of the great religions. They stress a moral way of life and oppose the 'animistic', magical, esoteric, and power-focused 'accretions' that lend colour to Southeast Asian religious practice. Santi Asoke, the Catholic Cursillo movement, and the modern Muhammadiyah can serve as respective examples, although they do not among themselves contain the moral appeal of reformism and revivalism. Such 'modern' religious enthusiasm is widespread indeed, and surfaces in all kinds of religious study clubs, serious and regular attendance at major rituals and services, retreats and revival weekends. Its appeal to a moral way of life is in full harmony with the old familial ethics of place: if everybody is a moral man, society will be a moral, a well ordered domain, and so it is not necessary to raise any question about structural reform or social engineering. It is safe to observe, though, that the old view of morality is re-establishing itself in face of anonymization, migration, urbanization, globalization, and the fading perspectives of social (re)constructability; it is re-establishing itself in face of perceived disorder. With its origin in the small group and its emphasis on individual morality, this implies that the impact of modernity strongly promotes the attitude of moral particularism, at least in regard to wider society.

Basic classification

Social life is imagined in three areas that connect and shade off into each other; from the best order to political confrontation; from a known, intimate world to a vast, anonymous one; from connectedness and identity to becoming one among 'the others'; from structured group to aggregate of individuals; from the life-world of family and community to *Gesellschaft* or impersonal, institutional society. The inner area is the home, the family; its symbol is the female as mother; psychologically, individuation is low, its identity and conscience functions high; it is the moral core of life. The known world outside the home is about prestige and prowess, hierarchical — such as the inner core — yet with the focus not on morality per se, but on dignity and presentation. Because this involves a measure of competition, it is far more turbulent than the inner core, yet carries obligations. Symbolically, it is male territory. This area then shades off into the unknown, the impersonal area of existence where one is seemingly on one's own and where attachments are tenuous, pragmatic, and expedient. It is a morally neutral area beyond the security of the life-world where conflicts are fought head-on, and not solved by way of compromise and reabsorbtion. It is neither male nor female, and there is no law of the land or of culture that prevents women from competing there; it is public but not of the public; it is the area of politics and business; it is symbolized by 'the powerful' and, to have power, to be able to set the rules in wider society, is greatly admired.

This image of social life highlights its personal, experiential nature, with ethics grounded in concrete relationships. Good order derives from moral awareness, and its basic example seems to be located in the familial ethics of solidarity and relative place. Moving away from the private sphere, life seems to be increasingly devoid of moral guidelines, and no value-laden model for the public sphere of business and politics emerges. According to some, morality there has decayed, and so disorder must logically be expected.

The hostile, the threatening image of the unknown, 'public' world that reduces ordinary people to anonymity, by itself reinforces the desirability of and identification with the inner world, especially of the family, but also with cults, sects, and religion, and often with ethnic associations and civic clubs. In this way, personal or primary relationships are strengthened, because these, of all things, should be relied upon for psychological, social, and economic security. It is, therefore, clear that the confrontation with the expansion of the modern public world of wider society strongly promotes 'individualism' and moral particularism there, so reinforcing the basic classification that is further potently invigorated by its symbolic anchoring in ideas about femininity and masculinity, in moral ideas and religious representations.

Epilogue

In spite of the region having disparate great traditions that also imply important national and individually perceived identity functions, we find, along the Southeast Asian inner littoral, an amazing unity of basic ideas about how life on the ground is and should be lived. It was and is in this local-traditional milieu that the imported worlds of ideas had to be localized, giving rise to Thai Buddhism, Filipino Catholicism, and Javanese Islam that all have a remarkable orientation to life in the here and now, and its future. Local religiosity directs attention to auspiciousness, potency, blessing, and continuity; religion is a power-station and as such in harmony with older, 'animistic' practices and representations.

As in the family, social relationships are seen in a pyramidical fashion and normally emphasize relative super- and subordination, and resolute leadership. This hierarchical view is potently enforced by its moral dimension, expressed in the ideology surrounding the parents, the 'cult' of the mother, the locus of conscience in relationships, and the ideas of obligation and debt-of-gratitude. The cardinal importance of the latter two as the cement of the social edifice also highlights the personal, relational, and experiential nature of the social imagination: society is concrete relationships to known people; it is these together with primordial social embeddedness that define the ideas surrounding personhood and the ethics of place.

This actor-centred image of social life, befitting family and community, is then projected to get a grip on the anonymous, impersonal, institutional society surrounding the known world, an endeavour that is currently supported by the state and religious reform and revival. It must be surmised, though, that such moralizing thinking will show a poor fit with wider society, with *Gesellschaft*, and that the latter, as an area beyond familial morality will increasingly be subjected to the rules of political power play and economic expediency, reinforcing the old and familiar Southeast Asian idea of the wider environment as a disorderly field of opportunity where the individual carries little or no responsibility.

Bibliography

Anderson, Benedict R., Old state, new society. Indonesia's New Order in comparative historical perspective. *Journal of Asian Studies* 43 (1983).

Anderson, Benedict R., Cacique Democracy. *New Left Review* 169 (1988).

Anderson, Benedict R., The idea of power in Javanese culture. B. R. Anderson, *Language and power: exploring political cultures in Indonesia.* Ithaca (etc.): Cornell University Press, 1990.

Antlöv, Hans and Sven Cederroth (eds), *Leadership on Java. Gentle hints, authoritarian rule.* Richmond, Surrey: Curzon Press, 1994.

Arellano-Carandang, M.L., *Filipino children under stress.* Quezon City: Ateneo de Manila University Press, 1987.

Atkinson, Jane M. and Shelly Errington (eds), *Power and difference. Gender in island South-East Asia.* Stanford, Cal.: Stanford University Press, 1990.

Bulatao S.J., Jaime C., Hiya. *Philippine Studies* 12 (1964).

Chai-anan Samudavanija and Suchit Bunbongkarn, Thailand. Z. Haji Ahmad and H. Crouch (eds), *Military-civilian relations in Southeast Asia.* Singapore: Oxford University Press, 1985.

Chai-anan Samudavanija, State-identity creation, state-building and civil society. Craig J. Reynolds (ed), *National identity and its defenders. Thailand, 1939-1989.* Clayton, Vic.: Monash Papers on Southeast Asia No. 25, 1991.

Corpuz, O.D., *The roots of the Filipino nation.* I, II. Quezon City: Aklahi Foundation, Inc., 1989.

David, Randolph S., Poverty in the Philippines: its social roots. Bernhard Dahm (ed), *Economy and politics in the Philippines under Corazon Aquino*. Hamburg: Institut für Asienkunde, 1991.

Djiwandono, J.S. and Yong Mun Cheong (eds), *Soldiers and stability in Southeast Asia*. Singapore: Institute of South-East Asian Studies, 1988.

Doronila, M.L.C., The nature, organization, and sources of students' national identity orientations. Education Forum (ed), *Towards relevant education*. Quezon City: Association of Major Religious Superiors in the Philippines, 1986.

Enriquez, Virgilio G., *Indigenous psychology and national consciousness*. Tokyo: Institute for the Study of Languages and Cultures of Asia and Africa, 1989.

Evers, Hans-Dieter (ed), *Loosely structured social systems: Thailand in comparative perspective*. New Haven: Yale University, 1969.

Geertz, Clifford, *The religion of Java*. New York: The Free Press of Glencoe, 1960.

Geertz, Hildred, *The Javanese family*. New York: The Free Press of Glencoe, 1961.

Haas, Mary R., *Thai-English dictionary*. London: Oxford University Press, 1964.

Ingram, J.C., *Economic change in Thailand, 1850-1970*. Stanford: Stanford University Press, 1971.

Jackson, P.A., *Buddhadasa: a Buddhist thinker for the modern world*. Bangkok: The Siam Society, 1988.

Kerkvliet, B.J., *The Huk rebellion. A study of peasant revolt in the Philippines*. Berkeley, etc.: University of California Press, 1977.

Koentjaraningrat, The Javanese of South Central Java. G.P. Murdock (ed), *Social structure in Southeast Asia*. Chicago: Quadrangle Books, 1960.

Koentjaraningrat, *Javanese culture*. Singapore, etc.: Oxford University Press, 1985.

Lapuz, Lourdes V., *Filipino marriages in crisis*. Quezon City: New Day Publishers, 1977.

Lapuz, Lourdes V., *A study of psychopathology*. Quezon City: New Day Publishers, 1978.

Lynch, Frank, Social acceptance reconsidered (1973). A.A. Yengoyan and P.Q. Makil (eds), *Philippine society and the individual*. Ann Arbor: University of Michigan, 1984.

Mulder, Niels, *Mysticism and everyday life in contemporary Java*. Singapore: Singapore University Press, 1980 (2nd rev. ed.).

Mulder, Niels, *Individual and society in Java. A cultural analysis*. Yogyakarta: Gadjah Mada University Press, 1992 (2nd rev. ed.).

Mulder, Niels, *Inside Thai society: interpretations of everyday life*. Amsterdam: The Pepin Press, 1995,a (5th rev. ed.).

Mulder, Niels, *Inside Indonesian society: cultural change in Java*. Amsterdam: The Pepin Press, 1995,b.

Mulder, Niels, *Everyday life in the Philippines: a Southeast Asian interpretation of Filipino culture*. Quezon City: New Day Publishers, 1996,a.

Mulder, Niels, *Filipino images: the cultural construction of the public world*. Quezon City: Ateneo de Manila University Press, 1996,b.

Nakamura, Mitsuo, *The crescent arises over the banyan tree; a study of the Muhammadiyah movement in a Central Javanese town*. Yogyakarta: Gadjah Mada University Press, l983.

Porio, E. et al., *The Filipino family, community and nation*. Quezon City: Institute of Philippine Culture, 1981.

Prizzia, R., King Chulalongkorn and the reorganization of Thailand's provincial administration. R.D. Renard (ed), *Anuson Walter Vella*. Honolulu: University of Hawaii, 1986.

Reid, Anthony, *Southeast Asia in the age of commerce, 1450-1680*. New Haven, etc.: Yale University Press, 1988.

Reynolds, Craig J., Jit Poumisak in Thai history. *Thai radical discourse*. Ithaca: Cornell University, Southeast Asia Program, 1987.

Riggs, Fred W., *Thailand: the modernization of a bureaucratic polity*. Honolulu: East-West Center Press, 1966.

Robison, Richard, *Indonesia: the rise of capital*. Sydney: Allen and Unwin, 1986.

Sairin, Sjafri, *Javanese trah: kin-based social organization*. Yogyakarta: Gadjah Mada University Press, 1982.

Suntaree Komin, *Psychology of the Thai people: values and behavioral patterns*. Bangkok: NIDA Research Center, 1990.

Sutherland, Heather, *The making of a bureaucratic elite: the colonial transformation of the Javanese priyayi*. Singapore: Heinemann Educational Books, 1979.

Terwiel, Barend J., *Monks and magic: an analysis of religious ceremonies in Central Thailand*. Lund: Studentlitteratur, 1975.

Thak Chaloemtiarana, *Thailand: the politics of despotic paternalism*. Bangkok: Thai Khadi Institute, 1979.

Tønnesson, Stein and Hans Antlöv (eds), *Asian forms of the nation*. Richmond, Surrey: Curzon Press, 1996.

Van Niel, Robert, *The emergence of the modern Indonesian elite*. The Hague, etc.: W. van Hoeve Ltd., 1960.

Wolters, O.W., *History, culture, and religion in Southeast Asian perspectives.*
Singapore: Institute of South-East Asian Studies, 1982.

Wurfel, David, *Filipino politics. Development and decay.* Ithaca: Cornell
University Press, 1988.

Index of names

Subject index